BOB REID'S RAILWAY REVOLUTION

BOB REID'S RAILWAY REVOLUTION

Sir Robert Reid, how he transformed
Britain's railways to be the best in Europe

GEORGE MUIR

UNICORN

First published by Unicorn
an imprint of the Unicorn Publishing Group LLP, 2021
5 Newburgh Street
London W1F 7RG

www.unicornpublishing.org

10 9 8 7 6 5 4 3 2 1

ISBN 978-1-913491-79-6

Cover design Unicorn Publishing Group
Typeset by Vivian@Bookscribe

Printed in Malta by Gutenberg Press Ltd

CONTENTS

FOREWORD

Sir John Armitt, CBE, FREng, FICE.

This book is not simply the story of a famous British Rail Chairman but a history of Britain's railway through the 20th century. A history of the country's core public transport system, its peaks and its troughs. It reflects the constant search for the right governance and structures, the battles between innovation and bureaucracy. Debates which still resound today.

Sir Robert Reid or Bob Reid One as he became affectionately known joined the railway as an apprentice in 1947 and thirty-six years later became Chairman following Margaret Thatcher's 1983 election victory. By that time the railway had lost 50 per cent of its passenger business to the motor car and Freight revenues were in continuous decline.

Bob Reid gave it a new and different leadership and impetus, disciplined attention to detail and a focus on delivery. For the thousands of dedicated railwaymen and women a boost to their pride in a railway regarded by many outside of the UK as one of the best in the world.

George Muir's book tracks the rise, fall and recovery of an industry which today is still critical to the economy and well-being of our nation. At the same time, it provides a clear picture of the life of a remarkable man.

For five years I had the privilege of being the CEO of Network Rail and in more recent years the Chairman of National Express. This gave me exposure to most of the issues which Bob Reid had to deal with whilst the railway's many strengths will have originated from the railway he established.

This fascinating book will be as interesting to those who like to reminisce in the story of British Railways as it is to aspiring leaders.

John Armitt

INTRODUCTION

Who is the best manager who has ever run the railway? Stephenson, Brunel, Sir Richard Moon of the LNWR? I don't know. But ask anyone now living and with a long memory of their time in the railway and one name always comes back: Bob Reid. Not his successor, also called Bob Reid, but the first one: Bob Reid One. He ran the railway for ten years, throughout the 1980s.

The war left a vast, creaking, worn-out enterprise employing, it is hard to believe, 650,000 people and using a million freight wagons. It had achieved prodigious feats of logistics. Half the freight traffic of the country was carried by rail. What else delivered the troops and fighting material to the Dorset and Hampshire coasts before being shipped across the sea to the D-Day beaches?

But when war ended, almost every piece of equipment – rolling stock, signalling, track – had to be renewed and modernised. Almost every assumption about how best to manage and operate the railway had, most reluctantly, to be abandoned and be replaced by new ideas.

And all around was change. Motor cars became affordable, roads were improved, and motorways built. People loved them, and so did the freight companies. Business drifted away from the railway. Much was done to develop faster, better services, but passenger numbers remained low and rail-freight halved.

Talented people were appointed to chair the railway and each in his own way worked to make it better: Brian Robertson, Richard Beeching, Stanley Raymond, Henry Johnson, Dick Marsh and Peter Parker. Many good things were done.

But after thirty years, a solid base from which the railway could grow again had not been found, the future was bleak and the government most unhappy.

Then, in the last, turbulent months of 1979, with no solution in sight, this slightly awkward person, someone you could almost have described as an outsider within the railway community, emerged as the new chief executive.

Bob Reid thoughtfully, methodically, utterly determinedly forced through the changes he had long known were needed. He called it a business-led railway. A new generation of managers, with a new remit, were put in charge. They revelled in the clarity and responsibility they were given.

InterCity, Regional Railways, and most famously Network SouthEast under Chris Green were transformed. Passengers returned. They liked the railway, and revenue for the first time for 30 years began to grow.

Bob Reid's railway was a revelation. The American, Lou Thompson, Railway Adviser at the World Bank writes that 'Sir Bob was, I believe, a seminal figure in breaking the shell around the traditional monolith that operated the railway'.

In later years, EU surveys of passenger satisfaction consistently showed BR to be among the best in Europe.

Bob Reid died in 1993. In a fine obituary, Peter Parker wrote, 'I can think of no railwayman who did more to modernise the railways – its assets and its attitudes – than this remarkable man.'

Peter Lazarus, permanent secretary at the Department for Transport, wrote, 'I have known all those who have led the railways since nationalisation of the industry in 1948. I am in no doubt that, amongst many men of talent and ability, Bob was in very many ways the best.'

This then is Bob Reid's story: where he came from, what he believed in, what he did. Within this story is another, the story of the railway. The book seeks to describe what earlier chairmen sought to do and why. It is a railway story and a Bob Reid story.

PEOPLE WHO HAVE HELPED

In researching this book, many people have shared their knowledge with me. As their words are often vivid, with colour and insight, they are used to tell the story wherever possible. Paragraphs beginning with a colon are what they have said, with minor editing to make the words easier to read.

I have been most particularly helped by Janet Reid, Bob Reid's daughter. I would like to thank her most deeply; without her help, this book would never have started. And I thank the many others who have helped me with stories and insights, most especially the long serving originals, Frank Patterson, Gordon Pettitt and Cyril Bleasdale who have seen it all and knew Bob Reid in his younger days in the railway, John Nelson and Jim Collins who served their time as his PA and went on to manage large parts of the railway, Chris Green who brought to life Bob's vision in Network SouthEast, Lou Thompson of the US Federal Railway Administration and Railway Adviser at the World Bank who could see the significance of Bob Reid's reforms, David Clough the railway historian, Theo Steel, and Bob's travelling companion and friend, Anton Buckoke. I would particularly thank my friends Chris Stokes and Richard Goldson who read the draft in a very raw state and had much to correct. But of course, remaining errors are entirely mine.

Many have most generously allowed me to use their copyright material: Cyril Bleasdale, managing director of the lively, informative *Railnews*, Robert Griffiths author of the excellent *History of ASLEF*, Crécy Publishing for use of Gerard Fiennes's *I Tried to Run a Railway*, a classic for perception and brevity, and Murray Hughes for the *Railway Gazette International* extract. Other copyright permissions have been acquired as necessary. If any have not been acquired, we apologise and will seek to rectify.

HOW THE BOOK IS ORGANISED

The book is in four parts:

Part One covers Bob Reid's early life and his career in the railway up until 1974, together with the railway story up until 1960.

Part Two covers events in the railway from 1960 to 1980 without mention of Bob Reid. Chapter 10 has a fair amount of railway detail which some readers might be happy to skip.

Part Three takes up Bob Reid's story from 1974 together with the railway story from 1980.

Part Four is a postscript discussing how Britain's railways have come to be amongst the best in Europe.

Bob Reid's story is therefore in Parts One and Three.

THE FOUR PARTS TO THE BOOK

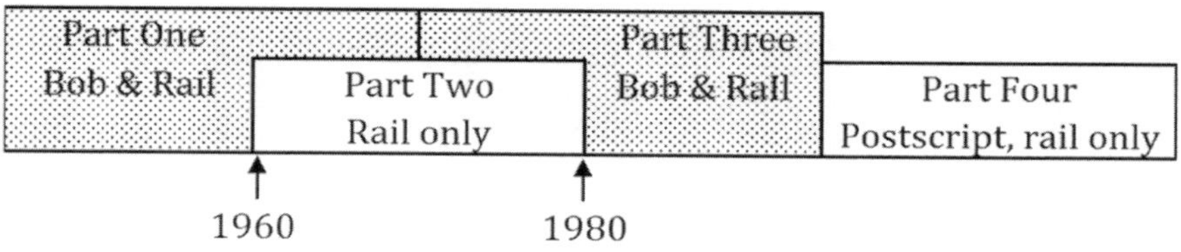

ABOUT THE AUTHOR

Writing this story has been a daunting experience. So many people have far greater knowledge of the railway than I and knew him personally. But I have not wilted, for I have some knowledge. Before joining the railway I worked as an engineer and later, after some twists and turns, as a banker with Morgan Grenfell, advising companies on their financial affairs, seeing in that work all kinds of successes and failures. I joined the railway late in my career at the time of privatisation in 1996, becoming the first managing director of the train operating company, Connex South Eastern. It was something for which I was quite unqualified in comparison with the most able people who had grown up in British Rail and had kept trains running through thick and thin, for years and years. When that job came to an end, I was appointed head of the Association of Train Operating Companies, for which I was qualified. These were turbulent times, far more so than now. For ten years I participated in and observed every kind of success and failure you can imagine. In quiet moments I puzzled over the underlying causes.

Intrigued by the whole subject, I therefore seized the opportunity when I retired to study and write a book about the most renowned railway manager of recent times.

David Bowick, CEO
1971–78

Ian Campbell, CEO
1978–March 80

Geoffrey Myers, COO
1986–87

David Kirby, COO
1987–89

John Welsby, CEO
1990–1994

John Edmonds,
Railtrack CEO, 1994.
(Here introducing the
Anglia region in 1988.)

Ray Buckton, ASLEF

Sydney Weighell, NUR

Tom Jenkins, TSSA

Jimmy Knapp, NUR

Gerry Fiennes, joined
1928

Prue Leith, Board
Member from 1977

Sir Bob Reid,
Chairman 1990–94

PART ONE

BOB'S EARLY LIFE
and the
POST-WAR RAILWAY

BOB'S FATHER

Reid was a railwayman through and through; he started out, after all, as a young man, a traffic apprentice, carrying luggage and checking parcels onto freight wagons at a small station in the Scottish countryside. But his parents' life was very different.

When he was born in Sevenoaks on 7 February 1921, his father was far, far away in Rajshahi, a place just north of the Ganges on the vast, hot Indian plain, hundreds of miles from Calcutta and the sea. For leisure, his father had duck and snipe shooting in the winter and pig-sticking in the summer. 'The finest sport in the world,' his father wrote, 'whenever the ground was dry. The wild boar is the bravest brute God made. He goes like smoke for a short burst when first beaten out in the open, then will turn and charge, with a 'woof-woof' all he ever says.'

He was a District Magistrate in the Indian civil service, a high-flyer, destined years later to become Governor of Assam and Bengal. One would not have foreseen that his son would become a railwayman.

Bob was born shortly after one of his father's periods of long leave. The youngest of four, with two brothers and a sister, he was brought up and looked after when his mother was in India by his aunt, Aunt Magdalene, in a fine Nash house overlooking Regent's Park. As he and his father are both called Robert, the father shall be called Robert and the son Bob.

There is a good record of Robert's life in India in his book *Years of Change in Bengal and Assam*. It shows someone who is clever, reliable, intent on the well-being of the people, but conventional in his views. The book's title is apt, it was a period of time which spanned huge changes.

His first proper posting in 1908 was to Muzaffarpur on the Ganges plain, to help deal with a local famine. There was no electricity, no telephones, no water closets. Motor cars were so rare they would seldom be seen. A weekly leg of mutton would arrive, a risky meal in hot weather after a slow, ten-mile journey on a porter's head. He would never have seen an aeroplane, but the railway, a harbinger of change, had arrived and was spreading out across the country.

Though a lonely place, it was there, in November 1909, that he met

Simplified Family Tree

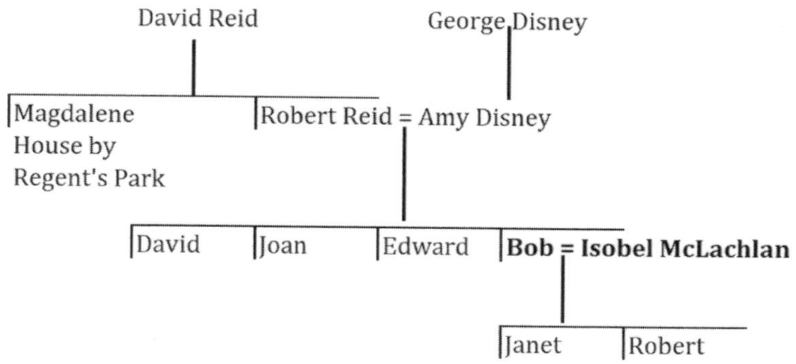

Robert living when not in India: –
When first married, in Sevenoaks
Later, in the 20s bought The Warren in Thorpeness on the Suffolk coast
After the war, sold The Warren and bought Holbrook Lodge, Holbrook
And later Heath Lodge, near Woodbridge – all in Suffolk
Bob living: –
As a young boy, Sevenoaks
Then, growing up, with Magdalene or at The Warren
When in the railway, various, then from 1974 in Purley
And from 1991, moved to East Bergholt, Suffolk
while keeping a place in London

and married his wife, Amy Helen Disney, whom he very much loved. Amy was 'English but with a bit of Northern Irish'. She was full of energy and ideas and kept her husband going when things got tough; it was a good marriage. Their son Bob got his energy from her, explains Janet, Bob's daughter.

They had three children, two boys and a girl, before Bob was born. Though he never joined his father in India, the periods of leave were long and the letters regular. Bob was close to his father and he would have grown up hearing stories of life in that hot, faraway country.

There was a long period of leave in 1923 when Bob was 2½ years old. It would be the first time Robert had seen his son. There was another when Bob was 7½, lasting a full year until December 1929. By then, they had sold their home in Sevenoaks and moved to The Warren, right on the coast at Thorpeness in Suffolk. It was a happy place where the children could stay when their mother was home from India. During this period, Bob, as was the custom of the time, started school life in a boarding prep school.

A further period of leave began three years later, in April 1933, when Bob would have been 12 and about to go off to public school. There was another in 1936, when Bob would have been 15, and another in the summer of 1939, when Bob was 18. Five in all.

With the reform of government in India, falling short of independence, but providing that Britain step back from control of local administration, a new type of State Governor was required, a constitutional Governor, someone who would work with and promote Indian political life. Robert, though not an aristocrat, had an aristocratic bearing, was affable and understood what was required and how to make it work. In 1936, he was appointed Governor of Assam – which he loved. On two occasions in the following years he served also as Governor of Bengal and therefore of the great city of Calcutta.

But it was Assam he loved. As Governor he was responsible for the outlying areas and toured them all, often on foot, for days on end.

There are lyrical passages in his book describing the countryside: 'There is nothing to beat the climate in spring: the bright sun, cloudless blue sky, and perhaps a glimpse of a big river in the background or, most mornings, very far off, the glorious glistening snows of Kanchenjunga.'

That he loved the work is evident from the number of tours of the frontier and his visits with the peoples living in these remote areas. The hardship, he seemed to relish. They had a day in Cherrapunji, reputedly the rainiest place in the world. He met the Dafla, the Aka, and the Miri, primitive tribes. He met the Abors, short people with powerful legs, well adapted to steep hillsides. He met the Khasi and the Lushais, 'at first unfriendly for they, too, were raiders of the plains', and he met the Nagas, 'warlike and only recently weaned off human sacrifice, but proud to welcome the Governor with a vast parade of marching and dancing'.

News from distant Europe became increasingly dark. In 1938, Hitler marched into Austria and threatened Czechoslovakia. The Munich Agreement was signed. It suggested peace but the prospect of war was very real.

When it came, it seemed far distant from Assam. But all changed when Japan entered the war. Days after bombing Pearl Harbor they began their sweep down through Malaysia to capture Singapore and threaten India.

It was then, on 15 December 1941, eight days after the bombing of Pearl Harbor, that Robert and Amy got news that their son Bob, then enlisted in a tank regiment in North Africa, was missing – but heard no more. Fearful for their son, and fearful for their home in Assam, it was a terrible time. Only later did they hear he was not dead but had been captured.

Assam is a finger of flat land and low hills pushed up towards China and into the eastern end of the Himalayas. It is not a door into India, for it is surrounded on the north and east by high mountains, but airfields in Assam were the closest to China. A massive airlift, thousands of sorties, from the very northern tip of Assam flew 'over the hump', the eastern Himalayas, to support Chiang Kai-shek in China in his fight against the Japanese.

By then, the army was dominant in his province, and Robert's term as Governor came to an end. His last sight of his beloved home in Shillong, the capital of Assam, was in May 1942. He left, depressed and uneasy, to become the China liaison officer in Calcutta. It was a nebulous role with the objective of 'keeping China in the war', a task to which a liaison officer could contribute nothing. Robert returned to England in June 1943. But his son Bob was not there; he was a prisoner of war in Italy.

Robert spent the rest of the war heading Post and Telegraph Censorship at the Ministry of Information. He settled in Suffolk, where he lived for twenty years, prominent in local affairs. He died in 1964 aged 81.

There is, however, this postscript which speaks for itself.

After capturing Singapore, the Japanese invaded Burma and sought to invade India. Their forces aimed to cross the mountains from Burma into Assam, the land Robert Reid loved so much, and reach an important railhead by the Brahmaputra river. There was fighting all the way, in the jungles of Burma where the Chindits, the long-range penetration group, made their reputation, and in the mountainous lands of the hill peoples on the border with Assam.

The high pass, which the Japanese reached and through which they had to pass, was in Assam at a place called Kohima. There, a great battle was fought, the turning point of the defence of India. Lord Mountbatten described it as probably one of the greatest battles in history: 'in effect the battle of Burma.... naked unparalleled heroism.... the British/Indian Thermopylae.'

Three years previously, while Robert was still Governor, an Assam Regiment had been formed. Its strength came from the hillman, the Nagas, the Khasis, the Cacharis, the Kukis, and the Lushais.

This from the book *Defeat into Victory*, by Field Marshal Slim. He was the 'soldier's soldier', the commander of the Burma Corps:

> The main might of the enemy advance fell on this regiment in the first battle of its career. Fighting in its own country, it put up a magnificent resistance, held doggedly one position after another against overwhelming odds, and in spite of heavy casualties, its companies never separated, never lost cohesion. The delay the Assam Regiment imposed on the 31st Japanese Division at this stage was invaluable.

And this:

> The gallant Naga's loyalty, even in the most depressing times of the invasion, never faltered. Despite floggings, torture, execution, and the burning of their villages, they refused to aid the Japanese in any way or to betray our troops..... They guided our columns, collected information, ambushed enemy patrols, carried our supplies, and brought in our wounded under the heaviest fire..... Many a British and Indian soldier owes his life to the naked, head-hunting Naga, and no soldier of the 14th Army who met them would ever think of them but with admiration and affection.

These are the people around whom Robert conducted his tours as Governor and for whom he had such great affection. They were fighting for their own lands, but it was a terrible war.

2 BOB'S EARLY LIFE

As he grew up, it was evident that Bob, though able, was not academic like his father and elder brothers. While his brothers went to Winchester, Bob was a late developer, more sporty than academic, and required coaching in Latin. He went instead to his father's old school, Malvern College.

This he did not like. It is not clear why, but it is not surprising. These were still hard places and, if you were not clever or did not fit in, life was difficult. Unlike his father, his school record is sparse, showing only History VI, school prefect, Shooting VIII (Captain) and White Medal, awarded to the best shot at Malvern. He was a good shot.

He left at the end of the school year in July 1939, aged eighteen, and spent some time with his parents that summer, who were briefly in England. As talk of war had been everywhere he had joined the Westminster Dragoons, a reserve unit. At the beginning of the war, this Territorial Army cavalry unit became an Officer Cadet Training Unit.

War started in September. It was at first the 'Phoney War', nothing happened, so in October Bob went to Brasenose College, Oxford for the first academic year, and joined the regular army in 1940.

The Westminster Dragoons had a direct link with the Royal Tank Regiment so, when Bob joined the regular army, it was to be the 8th Royal Tank Regiment, where he became a captain.

He spent time in Thorpeness, on the Suffolk coast, in the summer of that year, waiting to be called up. There he met Bobby. She was much taken with him, and he with her, but it was not to be. The call-up papers came, and he was away.

WAR AND CAPTIVITY

The 8th Royal Tank Regiment left the UK in April 1941, travelling by ship, the long way around the Cape, to disembark at Suez in June. Arriving at Suez shortly after was a certain Brigadier Brian Robertson, who was appointed as Assistant Quartermaster General to the 8th Army, then taking shape in Egypt.

Bob's regiment was assigned to the New Zealand Tank Division, part of the 8th Army. Its task was to attack a German and Italian force under Rommel which had surrounded Tobruk. Tobruk, a fine port on the North African coast, was being heroically defended by an Australian garrison. Rommel had to capture it if he was to have any chance of attacking the British in Egypt and taking possession of the Suez Canal.[1]

Bob's regiment was equipped with Valentine tanks, heavily armoured, but vulnerable to attack by German tanks whose guns had a far longer range than the 'piddling little two-pounder pop-gun' of the Valentine.

Bob Reid's son, also Bob, explains that his father missed the first engagement for he had come down with jaundice, but fought in the second, the battle of Sidi Rezegh: furious fighting involving many armoured units and hundreds of tanks manoeuvring across the desert. There were heavy losses. General Auchinleck issued his orders: 'there is only one order, Attack and Pursue'. Two days later, on 27 November, the New Zealanders, the unit in which Bob Reid was fighting, reached the Tobruk garrison and relieved the siege. Rommel fought on for some days until, on 7 December, he ordered withdrawal from the Tobruk area. The Allied offence had achieved its aim.

At some point during this battle, Bob Reid's tank was hit and burst into flames, but he got out, with some burns and was taken prisoner.

Janet, tells the story:

> Janet: He was captured very early on. 'I will take your field glasses,' said the German officer taking him captive. And that was that.
>
> : As a prisoner, Dad was taken back across the Mediterranean to Bari in the south of Italy. He never talked much about it, but I think it was pretty grim. He was then sent to a prisoner-of-war camp at Padula, which is south of Naples. We went there once as a family. It was a former Carthusian monastery. I think in a way… I am not saying he liked it, but it was okay. He did not mind the Italians because they were so different. The war was not what they wanted.
>
> : It was tolerable at Padula and of course, as he was an officer,

he was not allowed to work, but Dad was a good bridge player and that is what they did. They had to have something to pass the time. At some point they were moved up to another POW camp, which again we visited later as a family, at Fontanellato, which is very near Parma in the north of Italy. It was a large brick building intended to be an orphanage but used instead as a POW camp for officers.

: There was an active convent next door where they could get their washing done. When they got it back there were little notes from the nuns saying, 'We are praying for you' or 'We are thinking about you'. He liked the Italians. The prisoners would sometimes be taken out for exercise, and of course the Italians were much shorter than the POWs. Dad was six foot one. So they could walk really fast and make the Italians run. A stupid thing, but it keeps your spirits up.

: But then came the Armistice. And one day, Dad said, the guards simply disappeared. They opened the doors and, no guards.

The Italians were reluctant partners of Hitler's Germany and the war was going badly. The Allies had landed in Sicily in July 1943 and were about to move with great force on to the Italian mainland. The King, Victor Emmanuel III, hoping to end the war, ordered the arrest of Mussolini, and on 3 September signed an Armistice treaty surrendering Italy to the Allies. It was this that led to the guards abandoning the prisoner-of-war camps. The Germans, however, reinforced their troops in Italy, got hold of Mussolini and established him as head of a puppet government supporting the Germans.

It was a dangerous, horrible time for any Italian to the north, on the German side of the front line, which was moving, battle by battle, up the peninsula. The final 18 months was in effect a rumbling civil war between those Italians – a small, dangerous minority – who supported the German puppet government and the great majority who did not.

It was particularly dangerous for those wishing to help and hide Allied prisoners of war who were on the run.

Janet: Eric Newby, a writer, was in the same camp as Dad and has written a book about these events, *Love and War in the Apennines*. Newby had sprained his ankle so, although both walked out of the camp together, they got separated. Dad and two companions did not go very far; they got to a farmhouse near Parma, where the landscape is very flat. It had these great big granaries. The farmer, despite the fact he had one young child and another one on the way, hid them. If these three British soldiers hiding in his hay loft had been found, he would have been shot. But he hid them for about three months. They used to come down only at night so Dad said he never saw the countryside during the day, it was not safe.

: They owed the farmer a huge debt but after a time felt it was not fair on him, it was just too dangerous for him and the family, so they made their way out and got as far as the Milan railway station. It is enormous. A great big memorial to Mussolini. There the Germans found him. Dad said they were made to put their hands up and face the wall with the soldiers behind them and he thought, 'Well, that's it.' But it was not. They were put in a truck and, perhaps going through Czechoslovakia, ended up in Germany and spent the rest of the war in a prison camp, Oflag 79, on the outskirts of Brunswick, near Hanover.

: It was an old army barracks converted into a prison camp. Dad never really talked about it. I think it was much grimmer and of course the climate was colder and there was almost no food. It was not nice and I think he lived on turnip. So, as a family, we never had turnip. But my mother had an aunt, Auntie Kate, who was an excellent cook and he would at least eat her turnips because she could cook them so beautifully, but otherwise he never would.

The camp was notable for one particular thing. The officers in the camp, to do something extra for life when they returned to England, resolved to found a boys' club. They, Bob Reid amongst them, promised money to get it started. IOUs and promissory notes were written out on bits of paper. All were honoured and the club, the Brunswick Club, was set up in Fulham, London, where it still is.

Janet: The camp was liberated by the Americans in April 1945 and Dad returned home. He had been a POW for three and half years which, I think, was a hugely formative experience for him. Well, it would have been because Dad had had a very privileged childhood, all the rest of it, quite conventional: school, university and then, all of a sudden, a prisoner with nothing. 'When you have nothing,' he said, 'you feel very free.'

: I think Dad was immensely mentally strong, apart from being physically strong, and I am sure it was partly that wartime experience, because he came home having had a ghastly war. People talked about having a 'good war'. Well, Dad did not have a good war, did he? You are not supposed to get captured.

: There was not much rehabilitation for the prisoners when they got back, though they were made to do a lot of PT. I think he was very, very thin. It was not like the Far East, but still very thin. Dad was six foot one. I cannot remember his normal weight, perhaps 12 stone or something, but I think it was down to eight. My grandmother took him way up to the north of Scotland, I mean literally to the very north because you could get food there after the war and she fed him up. Also, because he had not been used to a normal life for so long, he was not his normal self. He could not have been. Granny was very good. Very practical.

: He went back to the army, I am not sure how long, and then back to Oxford and did a wartime degree which was just a year. He had to decide what to do next. He thought of staying in the army because his brother was in the army, but decided it was not for him and, at some point, he would have to leave it and he would be competing with people who had had a 'good war' and been decorated. He thought of the diplomatic service but that was not really for him either.

: It was one of his tutors at Oxford who said, 'Why don't you try a big organisation like the railways because I think that would suit you?' And that is what he did, in 1947.

The Oxford tutor who gave him this advice was himself the son of a Great Western storekeeper.

(National Railway Museum/Science & Society Picture Library)

3 BOB JOINS THE RAILWAY

BOB CHOOSES LNER, 1947

After his year at Brasenose, having fun one would like to think, Bob joined one of the Big Four railway companies in September 1947, shortly before nationalisation. These were Southern Railway, Great Western Railway, London Midland and Scottish Railway (LMS) and London and North Eastern Railway (LNER). He chose LNER because he hoped to be posted locally, near his home in Suffolk, but LNER's business stretched the length of the country, from London to Aberdeen, with numerous small branch lines, and he was instead sent as far away as could be, to be under the District Traffic Superintendent in Aberdeen for his initial training.

His first appointment was to Banchory, a station sixteen miles from Aberdeen and deep in the countryside. It was on the Deeside Line, a branch line running up a wide valley into the Grampian Hills to Ballater, the local station for Balmoral Castle. It had a passing loop, and therefore a signal box, and probably a small goods yard. He got to know other parts of the railway; he spent time, for instance, at Huntly, on the main Aberdeen–Inverness line.

The railway Bob joined no longer exists, neither in its routes nor in the way it worked. What Bob joined was the Indian summer of the great pre-war railway, the railway of the Big Four.

Half of Scotland was served by another of the Big Four, LMS, but a dense grouping of lines in the far north-east – Moray, Banff and Aberdeenshire – was run by LNER. It was the old Great North of Scotland Railway. It served a rich farming and fishing area, sending south seed potatoes and trays of eggs, and fish from the ports of Peterhead, Fraserburgh, Banff and Buckie.

Frank Paterson (we will hear more about him later) was a clerk in Fraserburgh in 1950, around the same time as Bob was in Banchory: 'Every day', he said, 'a fish train was sent from Fraserburgh to Billingsgate. It was the 11:22 a.m. I remember it well for every day I

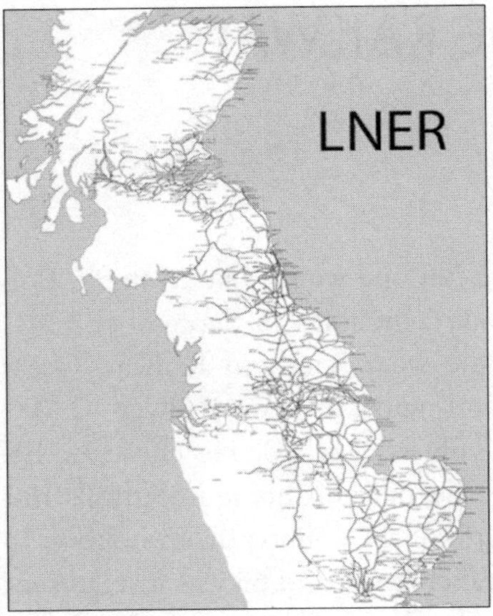

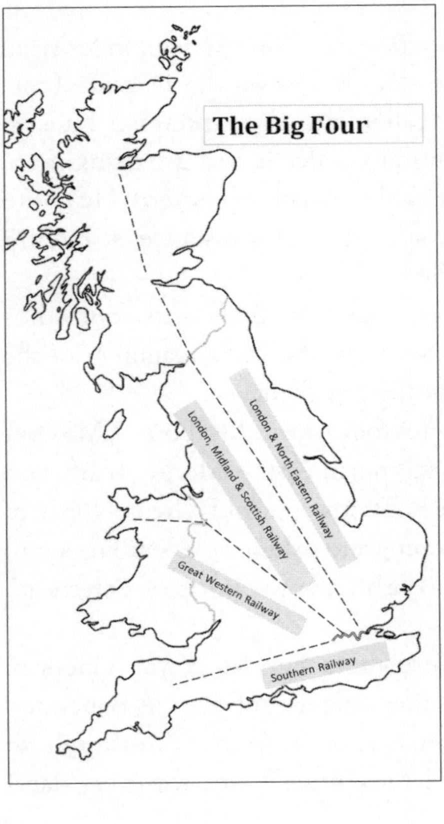

had to wire through the 'consist', what was in each wagon, which fish merchant it was to go to.'[2]

The fish had been auctioned on the dockside that day and were to be in Billingsgate for sale the next morning. It was packed with ice or Drikold (frozen blocks of carbon dioxide) in wooden crates with the names of the fish merchants it was to go to and loaded on to insulated vans.

On a good day there could have been ten or twelve vans loaded with fish. The train went first to Aberdeen, where it picked up a load, plus one from Peterhead. About thirty wagons then set off for Billingsgate. They went at a fair speed – 70mph – for it was a 'fitted train' (that is, one with continuous brakes, a brake on every wagon, controlled by the driver), and it was one of the early freight wagons to have roller bearings. It would be given priority at junctions and would arrive at Billingsgate early the next morning. Fish trains from Grimsby and Immingham would arrive too, and there were meat trains and probably vegetable trains pouring south to feed London. They do not run any more. A Dr. Beeching economist decided they were unprofitable, which they probably were, and the fish and meat and vegetables now go by road.

So much has changed since then. Of the railway in the north-east of Scotland, which used to have fifty stations and serve all the towns, only one line remains, the main line from Aberdeen to Inverness, with just nine stations.

THE BIG FOUR (1923–48)

There is much good that can be said about the pre-war period: well-made, simple equipment was designed and operated with remarkable expertise. Indeed, as the country entered the war, the assets of the Big Four were, as Mr T.R. Gourvish writes, agreed to have been in 'relatively good shape'.[3]

Mr Gourvish was commissioned by the British Rail Board to write the official history. He had access to all the necessary material and, over time, produced three volumes, with 1,800 pages in all. It is a good source of reliable information.

At their best, the Big Four pushed the art of running a railway to awe-inspiring levels. It was massively labour-intensive, but the labour force, whether on stations, on the track or in huge clerical offices, was organised and managed with discipline and great attention to detail.

Consider the business of handling locomotives at terminal stations. Mainline steam locomotives, such as the *Flying Scotsman*, had to face forwards, so required to be turned around at the end of their journey on vast turntables. Most large terminal station had one.

The Roundhouse, now a hall for events and music, is where the Euston locomotives were turned around in the early days of the railway before the locomotives became too long to fit inside it.

Smaller tank locomotives could be driven forwards or backwards but, either way, at a terminal station they had to be decoupled from the front of the train on arrival and moved to the other end to take another train out.

The Jazz Service is an example of how efficiently this manoeuvre could be done. The Great Eastern Railway had extended its lines east from Liverpool Street out to Enfield, Chingford and Palace Gates. To accommodate the vast crowds coming from these new suburbs – some trains were carrying 1,200 to 1,400 passengers – it developed a most remarkable train service which came to be called the Jazz Service. It got its name from the coloured boards indicating 1st, 2nd or 3rd class carriage or the destination of the trains. These reminded some journalist of the colour and gaiety of the craze for jazz sweeping the country in the roaring twenties. The intensity of this Jazz Service has seldom, if ever, been exceeded, even today.

Trains would arrive in Liverpool Street at one of four platforms. They had no corridors – that would be a waste of space! Each carriage had six or eight compartments, each with its own door and each with perhaps fifteen people sitting or standing crammed into it. As the train slowed coming into the station, whoever was nearest the door would slide the window down, stick their head out and as soon as they dared squeeze down the handle, let the door swing open and leap on to the platform, legs running so as not to trip.

Sixty doors would open nearly simultaneously. People poured on to the platform, many before the train had stopped. The platform would clear; the locomotive taking the train in would be decoupled and another coupled up at the other end ready to take it out again; new passengers would board and the train set off out of the station. It would be at rest for just four minutes. As the train left the platform, the locomotive which had taken it in would follow it out and turn off on to a spur ready to be coupled up to the front of the next train, having taken on water and coal.

Each step in the process is simple enough. The achievement is the carrying out of it reliably, hour after hour. At peak times, trains would leave each of the four platforms every ten minutes, sending twenty-four trains up the line every hour: one every two and a half minutes. That too is remarkable, as it is well beyond the eighteen trains an hour which would now be regarded as the height of intensive working on a two-track railway, without computer control.

As Locojoe, who worked the service, wrote in the online LNER Encyclopaedia:

> The Liverpool Street–Enfield service was very tightly timed but the N7 0-6-2Ts were good, powerful little engines with good

> acceleration. Being fitted with Westinghouse air brakes also helped as they worked much quicker than vacuum brakes. Braking was left until the last possible moment, so this meant running into the stations very fast; you had to be careful not to overshoot the end of the platform..... Our normal day's work would be three round trips, that's 60 miles with more than 80 station stops. As well as all that we had to prepare and dispose of the engine. Some people think local work was easy, but there was nothing easy working the Jazz.

On the busier lines, the movement of trains was controlled and collisions prevented using 'track circuits': simple electrical equipment able to detect the presence of a train on the track and accordingly causing the signals behind to be red or green. They are still in use today. On rural lines, the 'switches and crossings' where two tracks join or cross, and the semaphore signals were connected by wires and levers to the signal box and controlled manually. The signalman, by pulling one lever or another, could set the points so a train would proceed in one direction or another. A maximum of 350 yards was allowed for the control of points by hand levers, so signal boxes had to be dotted along the line in great numbers.

To prevent errors by signalmen – a train being sent mistakenly into the path of another – underneath the floor where the signalmen worked was a complicated contraption of moving rods. These moved when the levers were pulled in such a way as to prevent errors. It was called interlocking.

On busier lines, electric motors under the control of the signal box were used to operate the switches and crossings and the semaphore signals where these had not been converted to colour light signals.

At the heart of most of the larger signal boxes were electromechanical relays, simple pieces of equipment, each carrying out basic logical functions – replacing, for example, the moving rods of the interlocking system – and used in huge quantities.

Signal boxes with the best equipment could control moderately wide areas, but even so, quite a number were needed. There was one at Waterloo and others at Wimbledon and Woking, for example. But on rural lines without electronics there remained thousands of small, manual signal boxes checking trains leaving or entering the stretches of track between them.

Fog was a problem, drivers could not see the signals, so fog men would be sent out to huts placed along the line. 'When there's fog or falling snow – to the bothy we must go'. They carried detonators – tiny explosive devices – to lay on the track if the signal, which the fog man was close enough to see, showed stop. The detonator would explode when a train passed over it and warn it to stop.

Great Western, in 1905, was the first railway to put into wide use an automatic system to warn drivers of red signals and had an excellent safety record. The system was developed and came to be called AWS – automatic warning system – and adopted rather late by the whole railway after the Harrow and Wealdstone accident in 1952.

Design was one thing, money something else. The company responsible for the current line from Waterloo to Woking had the funds to build flyovers at junctions. Trains can turn off over the flyover on to branch lines without crossing the path of oncoming trains on the adjacent line. But the company responsible for the lines from London Bridge out to Kent did not. They could afford only simple 'flat junctions', which meant crossing trains would block the line for a train coming in the opposite direction. Flyovers increase the capacity of a line while flat junctions diminish it.

To allocate revenue between them, the Big Four had an accounting system, the Railway Clearing House. It employed hundreds of clerks. As journeys might cross a boundary between the Big Four, the Clearing House was required to allocate revenue to each of the Big Four in proportion to the length of the journey on its track. The system was far from perfect, but there was at least an attempt to allocate revenue to the company which had the costs, thus allowing accounts to be prepared showing a more or less realistic profit or loss.

This is the railway of the Big Four: vast in scope, simple equipment operated with great skill by huge numbers of people, ancient manual equipment on lightly used lines and newly designed electrical equipment carrying out complex tasks on busy lines. Some parts were better managed than others, but there was a wealth of experience in operating the kind of railway it then was.

THE WAR (1939–45)

Every day for five years, thousands of trains ran between the coal mines, steel mills, munitions factories, military camps and docks, keeping the machinery of war supplied.

All possible means were employed to conserve stocks of coal. Speed was limited to 60mph and trains were made to carry huge loads. It was not uncommon for a long-distance passenger train to be doubled up: twelve carriages filling with passengers at one platform at King's Cross and twelve at another. One of the twelve would be pulled forward and then backed up to be coupled to the other before setting off: a 24-carriage train. At stations where it stopped en route, it might draw up three times, for no platform was long enough for the whole train.

What the people operating these trains were thinking would become important for the railway in later years.

At a key moment, General Montgomery called on the three railway trade unions – ASLEF for the drivers, NUR for guards and others, and TSSA for clerical staff – to urge for their continued assistance. He needed it for the great throw of the dice, the gathering of an army, an air force and a navy on this side of the Channel to be launched again on to the continent of Europe.

The imminence of that step was apparent when the Ministry of War Transport issued an order to the Railway Executive Committee to immediately enrol 4,000 extra locomotive staff, half from the armed forces and half from other industries. It was a sign which lit hopes in the minds of those in the know that an invasion of Europe was approaching.

Much use in this story has been made of the excellent *History of ASLEF, Driven by Ideals,* by Robert Griffiths, the source of the description of union affairs.

While nothing like the lot of a soldier, the wartime life for civilians was grim – but eventually victorious. That experience reinforced in people's minds strong feelings for how the country should be run after the war. The old ways were not to return. It was they, the workers and the soldiers, who had won the war, and it was they who should run the country when it ended.

People dreamed and talked of what kind of society they wanted. It was not market forces which had organised the supply lines that kept troops in the field; it was the government. It was not market forces which had preserved civilian life, it was ration books and the government.

With their experience of the war and bitter memories of unemployment and poverty in the 1920s and 30s, many people joined trade unions. Socialism and a planned economy, Clause 4 of the Labour Party constitution, 'the common ownership of the means of production, distribution and exchange', became widely accepted as the way to build a better country.

Trade unions had by no means disappeared; far from it, they had nearly doubled their membership. The need for war might have been accepted, but not the fairness of how it was organised. In one year, there were 2,000 separate strikes.

Five weeks after the war ended, the wartime coalition came to an end, Parliament was dissolved, and an election called to be held three weeks later. The Labour landslide, 393 seats to 197, was a shock given the heroic status of Winston Churchill, but it reflected the voters' belief that the Labour Party, not the Conservatives, would be better able to rebuild the country.

I remember, somewhat after the event, being told by my parents – my father was a lawyer in Edinburgh – about this great upset; but my nanny, when we were out walking and far from my parents' ears, very tactfully explained that she too had voted Labour and hoped for better things.

The Labour Party's manifesto included:

> Public ownership of inland transport. The coordination of transport services by rail, road, air and canal cannot be achieved without unification. And unification without public ownership means a steady struggle with sectional interests or the enthronement of a private monopoly, which would be a menace to the rest of industry.

This, exactly as promised, came about with the passing of the 1947 Transport Act. Railways, buses, road freight, canals and docks were all placed under the British Transport Commission, which was given a duty to coordinate their activities. The Big Four would be no more. They were grouped together under a Railway Executive which reported up to the new British Transport Commission.

Worker representatives were given a place on various boards, but control continued to lie with the managerial class – graduates of Oxford, Cambridge and Sandhurst – which did not at all reflect the aspirations of the unions. The view of ASLEF was clear: unions should have had joint control. Such a view, or versions of it, was fundamental to the union movement.

Unions did not see their job as simply the promotion of the material interests of their members – their pay, hours of work, safety and such things. There was more to it than that. There was a deep, almost subterranean belief that issues, however small, were but skirmishes in a bigger battle, the enduring conflict between workers and capitalists.

The book referred to, *History of ASLEF, Driven by Ideals*, was published in 2005, sixty years after the period we are talking about and some years after the 1996 privatisation, yet it ends with these two paragraphs:

> Privatisation of the railways represented a historic defeat for the people of Britain, for the labour movement and for the railway unions including ASLEF. In an era of management power, technological change and union mergers, what future could there be for one small union in such circumstances? The Associated Society of Locomotive Engineers and Firemen had become an anachronism.
>
> Yet it would soon write another chapter in its extraordinary history. Under privatisation, the drive for capitalist profit contained within it contradictions which could be exploited by a combination of political intelligence and industrial muscle. What John Bromley had called the 'glorious fighting days' would return.

Some of the most bitter disputes in later years, often over matters with very little effect on pay or hours of work, can only be understood in this light. It was a thinking which, for forty years, would bedevil or enlighten – depending on your point of view – industry generally and the railway in particular. Confronting it, when Bob Reid became chief executive, was his first and most difficult task.

On the bright side, it should be noted that while acrimonious disputes on the railway were a yearly occurrence, actual stoppages were rare. Union leaders did still want trains to run; people depended on them.

> Gourvish writes: In retrospect the railway companies were extremely proud of their achievement during the war in carrying greatly expanded traffics under exceptionally difficult operating conditions. In 1944, the ton-mileage of freight carried was 50% higher than in 1938 and the passenger-mileage was up by no less than 67%, and all this without significant increasing basic equipment.[4]

With the war over and the lights back on, a massive surge in civilian use of the railway was seen. People streamed across the country looking for relatives, possibly looking for their children, visiting friends, even going on holiday. The railway could indeed be proud of what it did, but it had reached a plateau. Almost everything about it had to change. It was on a plateau quite unsuited to the transport landscape that would soon unfold.

BACK TO BOB, HIMSELF

Let us return to Bob Reid.

Arriving at Banchory, therefore, in 1947, was this tall, reserved young man, son of a Governor of Assam, public school-educated, just down from Oxford, with his cut-crystal English accent: you can hear it in a recording made some years later in the BBC archive. He was mixing with people from very different backgrounds, with soft Scottish accents or possibly the hard-to-understand Doric of Aberdeen. He stood out, and it would not have been easy.

His appointment was as a traffic apprentice. It was a management [illegible] job. He would not have fetched the tea, probably, but he [illegible] have carried suitcases and done every other tedious job which apprentices are wont to be given. He was to learn how the railway worked. One of his tasks was to keep the meticulous records, of freight and passengers and of expenditure and income, all written by hand in large ledger books.

One incident he remembered later. 'A group of directors arrived one morning in their saloon for a station visit. We were working in the office on our high stools – quill pens had just about disappeared by then – and they were greeted by the stationmaster. They walked straight through the station, looked at some ghastly shrubs outside, turned around and saying everything looked all right went off again without acknowledging our presence. A classic example of how senior managers should not behave.' [*Railnews*, March 1990]

Frank Paterson, whom I have already mentioned, joined the railway in the year before Bob as a junior clerk at a neighbouring station, Culter, on the same line. (This was a year or two before he went to Fraserburgh.) Frank's grandfather had worked on the railway and his father had been a train lighting examiner, a working railwayman, not a supervisor, and was in the wages grade, not in the salaries grade.

Though not academic, Frank was clever and went to a grammar school, Robert Gordon's College in Aberdeen, and afterwards joined the railway.

At Culter station, Frank got friendly, chatting on the single-needle telegraph with a lady clerk named Ethel Lamb working up the line at Banchory, the same station as Bob Reid. Tapping out in Morse code – the use of the telephone was forbidden, being too expensive – she told Frank about the new arrival, this traffic apprentice called Bob who had turned up at her station. It seems that she had accused him one day of 'being very bright, maybe, but you can't balance the books'. Bob had responded with a jocular comment in her autograph book. There must have been some edge to it for, years later, married and working in the Southern Region, this same Ethel Lamb, then Ethel Bryce, felt a nervous shiver when she again met the former traffic apprentice, her new general manager.

Bob liked Banchory and met his future wife in Aberdeen through mutual Indian civil service friends. She was Isobel Jean McLachlan, a hospital almoner – a job named after the word alms. She was, in effect, a social worker in a hospital. She had wanted to be a doctor, but as her mother had died before the war and her father during the war, there was no money and so no possibility of her training as a doctor. A hospital almoner was second best, but she accepted it.

Bob stayed two years in the area before moving to Edinburgh in 1950. He and Isobel married in 1951. Janet, their first child, was born two years later, in June 1953.

In Edinburgh, he seems at some point to have been the Assistant Yardmaster in Portobello, but in 1950 he was appointed to a post in the operating superintendent's office where, after special training, he carried out a series of jobs on the freight traffic evaluation squad to streamline the Scottish Region following the amalgamation in Scotland of the LNER with the LMS.

But it was soon time for another move, this time to York, in 1953, with Janet, a three-month-old baby.

YORK (1953–60)

York was a good posting. The family was there for seven years, from 1953 to 1960, and it was where Janet's brother, also called Robert, was born.

Bob moved up through the ranks – there is no suggestion that it was particularly fast. He was first posted to the general manager's office. Four years later, in 1957, he was made head of the development section (the Rates and Freight Development Section) in the District Goods Manager's office at Leeds, to which he commuted. Then, in March 1958, he had his first serious job: Goods Agent at York.

Bob's office was in the building where the National Railway Museum is now located. Janet visited him there as a little girl. He was responsible for the handling of freight arriving at or leaving York. In the Railway Museum, the Station Hall is a wonderful place to visit and was where Bob did much of his work. Frank Paterson explained what this involved.

Frank: Goods arriving as 'trainload' would have gone to private
rs, the biggest being at Rowntree's or possibly British Sugar.
as 'wagonload' and had not been sent directly to someone's

private sidings, it would be shunted into one of the sidings in the yard and be unloaded by the recipients or by railway staff. Any coal that arrived would have its own place to be unloaded.

But if a wagon was carrying sundries – something less than wagonload but larger than a parcel – it would be shunted into the Station Hall. There, Bob had a staff of two or three hundred men. It was filled with activity. Men would unload the wagons, sort the goods and carry them to the drays – flat-bedded carts without sides – pulled in the past by dray horses. Grain sacks were a particular challenge. Weighing two hundredweight, that is 224lbs or 16 stone, men struggled carrying them from the wagon to the drays on their backs. The drays, pulled by live or more likely mechanical horses, would then be trundled around the town delivering goods to the consignees.

The same procedure happened in reverse for goods leaving York. Bob's job was to oversee all these processes and make sure the customers were well looked after.

For Bob, it would soon be time to move again. From a local newspaper cutting:

> Mr Robert B. Reid has been in York as British Railways Goods Agent only two years, but that has been long enough for a good many people to appreciate his qualities and, while congratulating him on his promotion, there will be genuine regret that he is leaving the city. Mr Reid recently became a member of the York Rotary Club.

Bob had been promoted to a job in Glasgow. He would go there at the beginning of 1960, soon after his 39th birthday.

Bob's time in York, from 1953 until 1959, besides being good for the family, had been an exciting time for the railway. Change was in the air, and there was confidence in the future. A Modernisation Plan had been accepted by government, and there was money to invest. The plan was being directed by General Sir Brian Robertson, and his work will be discussed in the next chapter.

Major Brian Robertson, aged 38: everything you could wish for (source unknown)

4 ROBERTSON'S MODERNISATION PLAN

THE BRITISH TRANSPORT COMMISSION

Cyril Hurcomb was the first chairman of the British Transport Commission. He had been permanent secretary, or the equivalent, in the Department for Transport for the previous twenty years. Besides the railway, he had to gather under the Commission the buses and the underground network of London, dozens of bus companies elsewhere, 2,000 miles of canal, 32 ports, and long-distance road haulage. In a word, everything but air.

His was a vast, sprawling empire which the Commission had a statutory duty to 'coordinate' – a fatuous and impossible mission, what the Tories referred to as 'socialist planning'. Each mode was put under its own executive board. The largest and most troublesome, of course, was the Railway Executive. It was headed first by Sir Eustace Missenden and then by Sir John Elliot, both railwaymen from Southern Railway.

On the Executive sat- poor chap - as the part-time deputy chairman, the soldier's soldier, General Slim – needs must, army pensions! – a truly great man. Happily for him, he was rescued within a year to return to the army as Chief of the Imperial General Staff and later to be Governor-General of Australia.

From four regions, the railway was divided into six. Scotland was separated out to become its own region and in England, LNER was divided into Eastern and North Eastern. The six regions therefore were Scotland, North Eastern, Eastern, London Midland, Southern and Western, each under a general manager who, with the departmental heads, reigned supreme, so far as they were able.

The departmental heads were key people. They had already set about making good the backlog in track maintenance and the losses in locomotives and rolling stock, and did so in their own way, as they thought best, so far as they could. There was some central direction to contend with, but it was erratic in nature. The regions could be

The Six Regions: Southern, Western, London Midland, Eastern, North Eastern and Scottish
BRITISH RAILWAYS
SCALE OF MILES
Key to BR regions
Western
London Midland
Southern
North Eastern
Eastern
Scottish

quite different in the technical choices they made, and the differences continued for a long time.

In the matter of locomotives, an immediate decision arose: whether to stick with steam or adopt diesel. The chief mechanical engineer on the Railway Executive decided to order steam engines on a large scale. Sir John Elliot, in his book, *On and Off the Rails*, explains that though seemingly mistaken, there was some reason for his decision. The initial cost was a quarter of the cost of a comparable diesel locomotive which, as Britain had no pre-war experience of diesel, were then unreliable. And, for fuel, Britain had coal but no oil. The advantages of diesel, its greater power and greater simplicity in operation compared with coal – getting coal from a mine into a firebox is an elaborate business – would not be seen on the railway for many years.

Interestingly, Germany saw the fuel question differently and moved to electrify. It too had coal and planned to use it to generate electricity for the railway. In Britain, as Elliot explains, though electrification was in the mind of the Railway Executive, there was no prospect of the great investment required being available.

GENERAL BRIAN ROBERTSON (1953–61)

Five years went by under Hurcomb, 1948–53, with very little achieved save the administrative task of pulling everything together and catching up with maintenance.

Eventually it became clear that a plan for the modernisation of the railway was needed, which the government indicated it was prepared to fund. It would be the task of the next chairman, General Sir Brian Robertson, who took up his position at the end of 1953, to prepare and implement such a plan.

The accepted view is that Robertson fluffed the task, and that the Modernisation Plan was a 'lost opportunity'. Regrettably, whichever way you look at it, this is a fair judgement. That it should be so is tragic, for Robertson should have been the perfect chairman to lead the railway. He was a most remarkable person, and his father even more so.

Great endeavours, the running of a railway, call on more than a package of 'competencies' which you might acquire from a trainir course. Who you are, where you come from, what hinterland you have, your 'bottom' as it was called, matters. What instincts do you bring to bear? In this, fathers very often matter: their lives and careers generate the stories you grow up with and paint the worldview you are comfortable with.

Brian Robertson's father, William Robertson, was born in 1860, the son of a village tailor. On leaving school – he had a good education at a church school – he worked first as a garden boy, then, still young, as a footman – silver-buckled, wigged and powdered – in the household of the Earl and Countess of Cardigan. 'Boy, I was a damn bad footman', he said later.

Cardigan had been the hero of the Charge of the Light Brigade – 'into the valley of death rode the six hundred' – and had filled the house with memorabilia from that battle and heroic pictures of himself. Robertson, a boy of seventeen, seeking wider horizons, took the obvious step. He joined the cavalry, the 16th Lancers, as a trooper. It was much against his mother's wishes. She wrote to him that the army 'is a refuge for Idle people.... I shall name it to no one for I am ashamed to think of it .... I would rather Bury you than see you in a red coat.....'[5]

From there, the lowest possible rank, William rose steadily, year by year, making a name for himself in India, where he learnt soldiering and five of the local languages. He secured that rare thing for someone with his lowly background, a commission, and rose to become, years later, Chief of the Imperial General Staff, the head of the entire British Army; and all of this in class-ridden Victorian and Edwardian society. He is the only person, it is said, to have held every rank in the army. He headed it, briefly, under Kitchener, in the last years of World War I, and was friends with Churchill and the King. 'Wully' Robertson he was called.

His son Brian was exposed to all these momentous matters. His father arranged for him to be an aide in the headquarters of General Haig during the Battle of the Somme. They were dreadful times.

Many years later when, in 1953, Brian Robertson came to the [illegible]mission he would bring every element of experience you could [illegible] he even knew railways. He had not become a fighting soldier [illegible]ermaster, an expert in logistics.

General Montgomery described him as an 'ironmonger of genius' – ironmonger being the nickname for a quartermaster – while another described him as the Prince of Administrators. It was he, based with the 8th Army in the North African desert, who organised the supply of food, fuel, ammunition, ordnance – everything an army needs – the movement of troops and prisoners of war and the placing of supply dumps in advanced locations and of reserves behind the lines.[6] It was he who ensured supplies to the tank regiments, where Bob was fighting in the desert, in the battle of Sidi Rezegh. It was he who made possible Montgomery's victory over Rommel, and the army's thousand-mile sweep across the desert from El Alamein to Tripoli. It was he who supplied part at least of the armies landing in Italy and their threat to the German position in Italy which triggered Victor Emanuel's Armistice, the disappearance of the guards from Bob Reid's prisoner-of-war camp, and his freedom to walk out into the countryside.

On the ending of the war, General Robertson was appointed military governor of the British sector of Germany, one quarter of the country, covering the great industrial centre of the Ruhr. Acting with the heads of the American and French sectors, he oversaw Germany's transformation from a military machine to a peaceful society.

Institutions of civil society were re-established, factories focused on armaments destroyed and those with a civil purpose enabled. The German railway ceased to serve military purposes and was channelled towards civilian ends. Trade unions re-emerged and were allowed their normal activities, including the calling of strikes. A new constitution was prepared, the Basic Law, and normal politics resumed.

Brian Robertson was determined to avoid punitive measures against

Robertson, standing straight, addressing the National Union of Railwaymen conference, 'Your Union has pledged itself to co-operate with the Commission on British Railways Productivity' – he hopes. (NRM)

Germany, for he knew they would sow resentment: 'dragon's teeth' he called them. West Germany should become a bulwark against the Soviet bloc. To this end, America agreed to the Marshall Plan and with the Europeans formed NATO.

The fourth quadrant, the Russian controlled quarter of Germany, was the problem. In Churchill's words, 'an Iron Curtain had descended across the continent'.

A dramatic consequence was the Berlin airlift. The city was divided between the four Allied powers but sat within the Russian zone, who blockaded all road and rail access to the city. Its population, after some weeks, began to run out of food. Some on the American side argued that force should be used to gain access, spearheaded by tanks, but Robertson, for the British, proposed instead that an airlift was a wiser plan. The first planes carrying food flew in June 1948 and continued to do so, on a massive scale, in the tensest possible atmosphere between East and West, for nearly a year until the Soviets relented.

At a farewell dinner in June 1950, on his leaving Germany, with the French and American military governors present, the French military governor gave a warm tribute:

> In the Trinity which we constitute – one in three, three in one – I would not decide who, Mr McCloy or myself, is the Son or the Holy Ghost. But you undoubtedly were the Father. If we had to elect a permanent chairman, you would have been our choice..... You were informed of every precedent, of every text and never has your memory, your learning, your knowledge of the problem been at fault.[7]

This was the remarkable and most experienced person, son of an equally remarkable father, who, in 1953, was appointed chair of the British Transport Commission.

He had been told by Churchill – the Conservatives had won the 51 election – to 'give British Railways leadership' and leadership hat he was trained for. He was of an imposing personality, ere, a man of integrity; not without humour, it is said, but know and, above all, demanding of loyalty and respect.

He was determined to lead from the top. He was not a figurehead. He was the chief executive, as he said himself. Photographs of him with other railwaymen, addressing for instance the NUR, show this tall man standing erect, not stiff, erect, shoulders back – in the manner civilians cannot match. He was in charge.[8]

The Conservative government, dissatisfied with Hurcomb's achievements, had decided to put its faith in decentralisation and had legislated in the 1953 Transport Act to abolish the Railway Executive, a body structured, as required by Hurcomb, to suck authority from the regional managers up into the centre.

As Sir John Elliot, chairman of the Executive, explains in his book, 'from the start, relations between the Executive and its regions were prejudiced by the unfamiliar 'functional' chain of command, under which direct managerial contact between members of the Executive and the departmental officers in the regions went clean over the heads of the chief regional officers'[9] who hated the arrangement. 'General Management as such virtually disappeared.'[10]

It was no better for the Executive's chairman. 'I quickly found', wrote Sir John, 'that I was not a manager at all, but merely 'primus inter pares', with all the members co-equal, each with their own portfolio, rolling stock, operations, staff, and each responsible only to himself – a collection of prima donnas, in fact, with no conductor.'[11]

In these two paragraphs are contained the two central organisational problems the railway would face for 30 years: (i) central control or local control and (ii) engineer-led or general manager-led.

To take the first: what had to be decided at the centre and what left to the regions. It is far from a trivial matter.

Alfred Sloan, the great architect of General Motors, set down in a paper in 1920 two conflicting principles:

> 1. The responsibility attached to the chief executive of each operation shall in no way be limited. Each such organisation headed by chief executive shall be complete in every necessary function and enabled to exercise its full initiative and logical development.

2. Certain central organisation functions are absolutely essential to the logical development and proper control of the corporation's activities.

Sloan wrote years later in his book, *My Years with General Motors*, 'I am amused to see that the language is contradictory, and that it's very contradiction is the crux of the matter..... I still stand by the fundamentals.'[12]

John Egan, the great architect of Jaguar Cars, writing about Sloan's book said, 'it chronicles G. M.'s approach to the great dilemma of corporate life – the balance between centralised and divisional management in large companies..... In Britain we have seen too many examples of the damage that can result from fudging this issue.' That, in a nutshell, was the problem the railway would face.

The second issue is found in the railway more intensely than elsewhere: the dominance of the professions, what Elliot referred to as the 'functions', the rolling stock professionals, the civil engineers, the operators, the personnel managers. Each, within their departments, set about doing what they thought was right, and sought to give instructions that would flow down the line, bypassing the chief regional officers, until they reached the staff on the ground who did the work.

THE 'CLASSIC' RAILWAY ORGANISATION

The following description is taken from the *Manual of Railway Operation* by T. Bernard Hare, written in 1927, at the time of the Big Four. Things do not seem to have changed much by the time of the Modernisation Plan.

Each of the Big Four, from the top to the bottom, was divided into four departments: passenger, goods, civil engineering (dealing with the permanent way) and mechanical engineering (dealing with rolling stock). The heads of these departments sat on the Board and reported to the chairman.

The local unit of the railway was the district. At that level, the functions of the local heads of the departments were as follows.

First, the Passenger Superintendent – responsible for all things concerning passengers at a station and for the running of trains, whether passenger or freight.

Second, the Goods Agent – responsible for the handling of freight from its arrival at a station to when it leaves, including its collection or distribution by road around the locality where that was offered. In practice, the responsibilities of the Goods Agent and Passenger Superintendent were adjusted in various ways to avoid conflict and overlap.

Third, the civil engineer – responsible for the permanent way. Later, signalling and telegraph (S&T) became a separate department.

Fourth, the mechanical engineer – dealing with rolling stock.

Each of these reported not to a local head, but up the line to the department heads at head office. Put crudely, it was a silo organisation. In practice, though the details are not clear, there was some local coordination under a local manager, and 'traffic managers' are also referred to.

The manual describes this as a 'departmental structure', which was different from that in the United States. There, due to its great size, the structure adopted was 'divisional', whereby the local departmental heads in each division reported to a local general manager.

When the Big Four were nationalised, the departmental structure (silos) was retained by the regions and recreated at a national level in the Railway Executive. Within the regions, heads of the departments reported to the regional general manager and also to functional heads at the head office. This dual responsibility, though unavoidable, became a major source of tension and conflict.

Of course, there was a degree of coordination, but it was a struggle. It was a profession-led railway. Profession-led railways generate silos, and silos limit efficiency. At the time of the Big Four, the smaller, focused Southern Railway with a strong chief executive could handle the matter, while the larger, more diverse London Midland and Scottish could not.

This problem was capable of resolution, but not for 30 years; it was Bob Reid who forced through the change from a profession-led railway to a business-led railway – something for a later chapter – which enabled a rational allocation of responsibilities between the centre and local managers.

Having abolished the Executive and seeking to ensure the autonomy of the regions, the government required that Area Boards be established over each region with policy-forming and supervisory roles.[13]

This truly was an absurd arrangement, a gross example of the fudging of an issue, for the rebuilding of a shattered railway and the delivery of a modernisation plan required central direction. Little decentralisation therefore took place and substantially all the functions of the Railway Executive moved up to the Commission.[14] It had as a consequence a mountainous task, and moved from 55 Broadway to more spacious premises at 222 Marylebone Road, where Robertson joined it as chairman in November 1953.

To the task Robertson brought a clear mind and a great capacity for detail. He might conduct a discussion, taking notes the while on the writing pad he carried, and say at the end, 'Let me read out a summary of what we have agreed' and would do so, reading out clear, lucid prose.

It was evident that he had scant regard for railway officers. He, who had swept Rommel from the sands of Africa, was not likely to be comfortable with people who managed freight wagons in Yorkshire. He was bad, it is said, at choosing people, at knowing who amongst railwaymen to trust and who not, so he trusted none and brought in those he did, other generals.

With a such a task ahead of him, Robertson did what he did best and built an administrative system, vast in scope, to oversee and direct the business. Famously, at the highest level, he established a group – a most resented group – called the General Staff and recruited to it army officers he knew.

The meeting room where one might meet, or at least see, the chairman was laid out like a High Court; board members arrayed on one side of a long, high table facing rows of seats where supplicants and witnesses and what not – senior railway executives – waited their turn to speak.

The headquarters remained unpopular with the regions. Decisions would bounce from committee to committee. Even quite small investment matters had to be referred up for approval. So torturous was the process that, far from securing central control, strong-minded and determined general managers could often ignore whatever was happening and go their own way.

Neither Robertson nor the General Staff were the originators of the confusion – army officers are not given to indecision. The fault lay with government and its conflicting objectives: that the regions should be autonomous and, at the same time, that the Commission should oversee the modernisation of the railway. Robertson was prevented from establishing a single body within the commission, let alone a single individual, to oversee the railway lest, in the government's view, the Railway Executive be re-established by stealth.[15] Robertson undoubtedly knew what should have been done; perhaps he should have stood his ground, but he did not. To oversee the railway without offending government, he was led, against his wishes, to create a network of committees and a Commission later described as a 'creaking dinosaur'.[16]

The entire business was described by the Comptroller of the Commission as 'a first-class English mess'.[17] Though cumbersome in other respects, the work to produce the Modernisation Plan was carried out with great speed. In its third paragraph, the document proclaimed that 'the technical details are the result of six months' intensive work by a planning committee'.

It was a committee chaired, as you might expect, by a former general, General Daril Watson. Watson was a remarkable and certainly a most experienced person. He had been Assistant Chief of the Imperial General Staff and later Quartermaster General to the Forces, the most senior logistics appointment in the army. He knew how to move stuff around. Both he and Brian Robertson were familiar with the plans being implemented by German railways – which must in some ways have seemed a blueprint.

When he got to work the financial position was precarious. The railway was supposed to be profitable, and according to Gourvish very nearly was at that time. Indeed, for a few years freight revenue had increased – it took time for road hauliers to get things together – but from 1955 freight on the railway would fall away and the financial prospects became bleak.

So many adjustments can be made to railway accounts – depreciation of one kind or another, exceptional items, interest, government support, how fixed costs are allocated – that a consistent statement is impossible. Even in Gourvish, it is sometimes hard to reconcile one table with another.

With that proviso, the following chart shows the profit margin from 1948 to 1969: small losses until 1954, then steepening losses until 1961 as freight disappeared from the railway. From then on, fairly consistently, the railway costs would exceed revenue by between 20 and 25 per cent. The improvement in the last year of the chart reflects the receipt of government support, accounted for as revenue, under the 1968 Act.

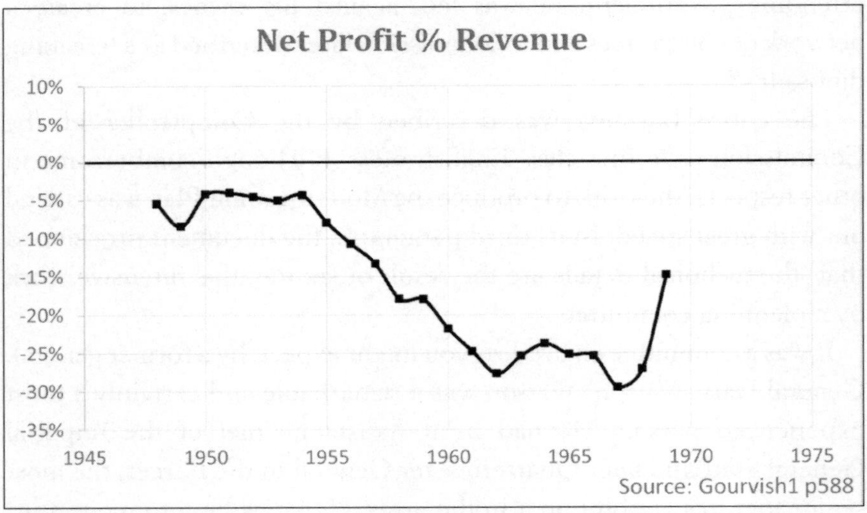

What Watson saw was a heavily loss-making passenger sector and a freight business with a mix of profit-making and loss-making activities. There are no details for the year Watson got to work, but the position two years later, in 1956, is shown in the table.

Sources of Revenue and Profit in 1956

1956, £m	Revenue	Profit	Comment
PASSENGER			
Fast/semi-fast	81	1	Breakeven
Stopping	21	-50	Very heavy losses
Suburban	29	-27	Heavy losses
Total passenger	131	-76	
% of TOTAL	27%		
FREIGHT			
Parcels	48	8	Good profits
General merchandise			
- Wagonload	72	-27	Heavy losses
- Smalls (under one ton)	46	-17	Heavy losses
Trainload			
- Minerals	53	6	Good profits
- Coal	129	34	Excellent profits
Total freight	349	4	
% of TOTAL	73%		
TOTAL	480	-72	

Source: Gourvish1 p192 and p195

The outstanding feature is the small share that the passenger business has within the total: revenue of just £131 million, 27 per cent out of a total of £480 million. It was largely a freight railway.

The main passenger lines were those we know today. Fast and semi-fast services on the long-distance routes broke even, but suburban commuter services lost money. The scale of these commuter losses is surprising, but it is business with very high morning and evening peaks, but little used at other times. Business on these lines, whether profitable or not, was holding up quite well, though not growing.

Elsewhere, branch lines meandered across the country, with hundreds of stations just a few miles apart served by slow, unreliable stopping trains. Once upon a time these may have been profitable, but buses and cars offered a better service and passenger numbers had fallen away. When General Watson got to work, these lines were deeply loss-making.

Parcels, mail and newspapers were all carried on the railway. They are lumped together under the heading 'Parcels' in the table. They were distinct from the rest of freight in that they were carried not in freight wagons, but in coaching stock attached to passenger trains.

The business of accepting parcels for carriage in the guard's van of passenger trains was small and was accounted for within the passenger business.

With the growth of mail order, the Parcels business grew and a specialised business evolved with parcel trains and a system for collection and delivery: either collection at the station by the customer or delivery to the customer's premises.

Mail was a complex business, organised with the Post Office and loaded and unloaded by their own staff. The famous film, *Night Mail*, shows it being sorted on the train from London to Glasgow in the 1930s with Auden's words and Benjamin Britten's music. Newspapers were carried on special, fast overnight services.

Taken as a whole, the Parcels businesses was profitable, although the collection and delivery element almost certainly was not.

By far the biggest part of British Rail was freight in freight wagons. Trainload freight, loads large enough to fill a train, such as the fish from Fraserburgh or more significantly coal or minerals, was profitable. The problem was general merchandise.

An extraordinary range of goods was carried and services offered. It carried pigeons for pigeon racing – arrangements could be made for the birds to be released to begin their race back home. It carried coal in tiny quantities to almost every station in the land – homes were heated by coal in those days. It carried the sundries which Bob Reid's team sorted in the Station Hall in York. It carried livestock. It carried entire circuses – including the elephants. It had delivery services so that items arriving at stations could be sent on to their final destination. And it carried loads large enough to fill a wagon. Many manufacturers had private sidings and loaded and unloaded the wagons themselves.

But the most attractive of these loads were increasingly being sent by road, and the business was under threat. Indeed, the whole market was moving against the railway. Sixty per cent of costs were wages, which had been unrealistically low. Unions and official inquiries were therefore forcing through above-inflation wage increases. Road transport was changing. British Road Services continued to be owned by the Commission, but the same Act of Parliament which had abolished the Railway Executive had opened the way for private operators to compete with the railway in the long-distance freight market. Roads were being improved, there were more cars and, though there were not more lorries, they were much larger and were travelling further. No longer would they be used just to take goods to the nearest railhead and to deliver them at the other end. Increasingly, they would travel the length of the country and deliver goods to their final destination.

To keep the business, the railway had to price very carefully.

Against this background – major loss-makers and a market moving away from rail – General Watson proclaims in the first paragraph of the Modernisation Plan:

> The British Transport Commission are convinced that an efficient and modernised railway system is essential to the economy of the country, and that it should be able to attract and retain sufficient traffic to make it economically self-supporting for many years to come. For reasons which are too well known to require repetition here, British Railways today are not working at full efficiency, mainly owing to their past inability to attract enough capital investment to keep their physical equipment fully up-to-date.

And there you have it. The problem is capital. Give us enough money and all will be well. It would be a message repeated, like a gramophone stuck in a groove, by every chairman for the next thirty years. There was no recognition that the shape of the railway, the particular combination of services it provided, was fundamentally out of keeping with the requirements of its customers.

On reading the Plan which, it was claimed, would turn things around, the virtues and failings of army generals emerge in bright colours.

The virtue is clarity. The document is just thirty-six pages long. It covers the salient points, has a clear summary, is devoid of jargon and contains a programme which cannot be misunderstood. It was to be read by all ranks. Troops under General Watson's command would never set off to assault the wrong hill.

The summary in the report, signed off in December 1954, is as follows.

First, the track and signalling must be improved to make higher speeds possible over trunk routes, and to provide for better utilisation of the physical assets; there will be an extended use of colour light signalling, track circuits and automatic train control, the further introduction of power-operated signal boxes, and the installation of centralised traffic control where conditions are suitable; and the extended use of modern telecommunication services ... £210 million.

Secondly, steam must be replaced as a form of motive power, electric or diesel traction being rapidly introduced as may be most suitable in the light of the development of the Plan over the years; this will involve the electrification of large mileages of route, and the introduction of several thousand electric or diesel locomotives ... £345 million.

Thirdly, much of the existing steam-drawn passenger rolling stock must be replaced, largely by multiple-unit electric or diesel trains; the remaining passenger rolling stock, which will be drawn by locomotives (whether electric, diesel or steam), must be modernised; the principal passenger stations and parcels depots will also require considerable expenditure ... £285 million.

Fourthly, the freight services must be drastically remodelled. Continuous brakes will be fitted to all freight wagons, which will lead to faster and smoother operation of freight traffic; marshalling yards and goods terminal facilities will be re-sited and modernised, and in particular the number of marshalling yards will be greatly reduced. Larger wagons will be introduced, particularly for mineral traffic, and loading and unloading appliances will require extensive modernisation in consequence ... £365 million.

Fifthly, expenditure will be required on sundry other items, including improvements at the packet ports, staff welfare, office mechanisms, etc.; and a sum of at least £10 million for development and research work will be associated with the Plan, making a total of ... £35 million

TOTAL . . . £1,240 million

The plan points, correctly, towards electric and diesel engines, multiple units, resignalling and electrification. The building of steam trains is to stop; diesel and electric propulsion is the future.

The major loss-maker, general merchandise, was to be saved by greater efficiency in the handling of wagons, with fewer but larger modern marshalling yards, and fewer, larger and faster wagons.

The other loss-maker, passenger stopping trains, was mentioned only briefly: 'The substitution of diesel power will greatly reduce the operating costs of those slow and stopping train services which are retained to rail, and it will enable faster and more frequent services to attract new traffic.' Some new traffic did return, but in tiny quantities: two farthings make a ha'penny. Underused branch lines had to be closed, and some were, but never enough to make a difference.

With casual naïveté, the document asserts:

> The total economic effect of the plan.... is an improvement of the order of £85 million a year. This is made up of an improvement assessed at £35 million on the passenger services and £60 million on the freight services, less about £10 million for increased expenses, mostly upon those items which are common to both.

An £85 million swing would have led to a profitable railway, but in fact losses grew. The expectation that the plan would deliver an £85 million 'betterment' was always pie in the sky.

Many insights into events at this time can be found in the brief, charmingly written book *I Tried to Run a Railway* by Gerard Fiennes. Almost every opinion expressed was borne out by events. His book has been used a great deal for the next few pages. He describes the plan as 'little more than a change from steam traction plus a host of mouldering schemes which the British Transport Commission and the regions had found after a hurried search in their pigeonholes. We had made the basic error of buying up the tools before doing our homework on defining the job.'

In this, he is right, for in the entire thirty-six pages there are not thirty-six words about the competition the railway would face from road transport. Instead, there is this laconic phrase, 'despite the growth of alternative forms of transport, it is clear that the country must continue to look to the railways to carry the main flows of traffic, both passenger and goods, for many years to come.'

These 'alternative means of transport' would eat deeply into the business of the railway. Drivers loved the new roads being built and traffic on them, both passenger vehicles and freight lorries, soared.

The following twelve pages, until the heading Poor Management at the Top, contain details of the issues faced at the time.

FREIGHT

The change in how freight moved around the country stands out. In 1950, road and rail carried about the same quantity. But after a few years, road hauliers learnt how to take advantage of what was available – with motorways and larger lorries, most types of freight can be carried by road – and their business soared till the late 1990s. Notwithstanding the increase in freight carried, road hauliers did not need more lorries; there are now no more than there were in Robertson's day, but they are bigger and they travel further in a day. The tonne-km per year for the average lorry has risen five-fold, from 72,000 to 374,000.

On the railway, there was a long steady fall in freight carried, from 37 billion tonne-kilometres per year in 1950 down to 13 billion tonne-

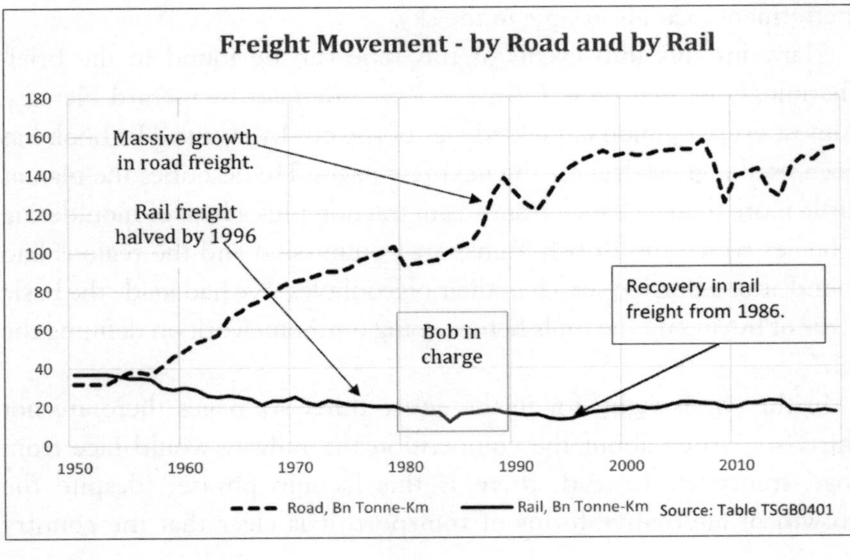

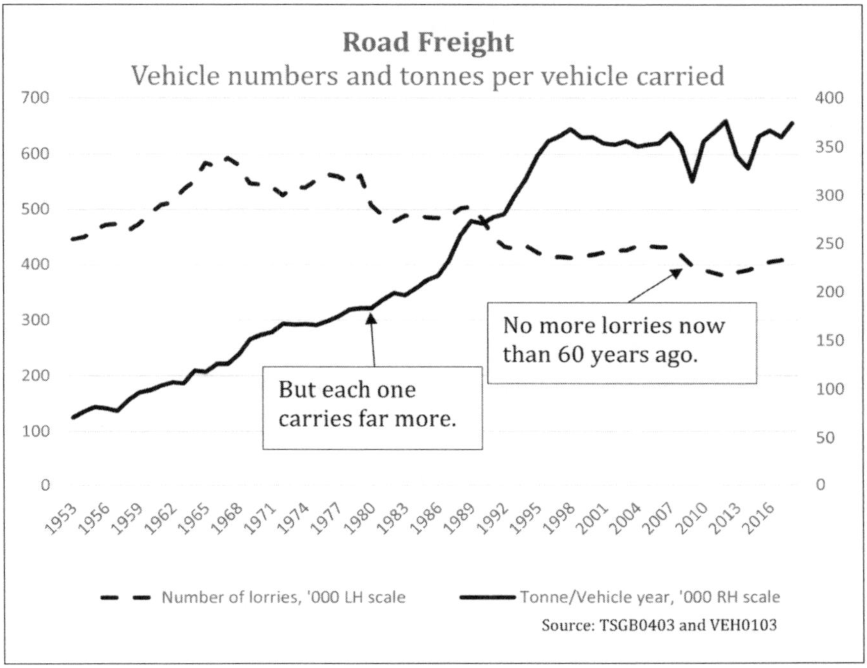

kilometres per year in the mid-90s. (The dip seen for 1984 is the effect of the miners' strike.) Since then, private rail freight companies have managed to increase the business, which rose to 22 billion tonne-kilometres per year before retreating slightly when power stations ceased burning coal.

PASSENGERS

In 1950 cars and rail carried about the same number of people. Since then, road use rose dramatically, ten times.

On the railway, passenger numbers remained fairly flat for many years; there is a lot of travel which really is best done on a train. After a small early decline, numbers stabilised at about 30 billion passenger-kilometres per year until 1996. That year, the year of privatisation, saw the start of a very strong growth in passenger numbers on the railway, rising to their present level of 68 billion passenger-kilometres per year (2019).

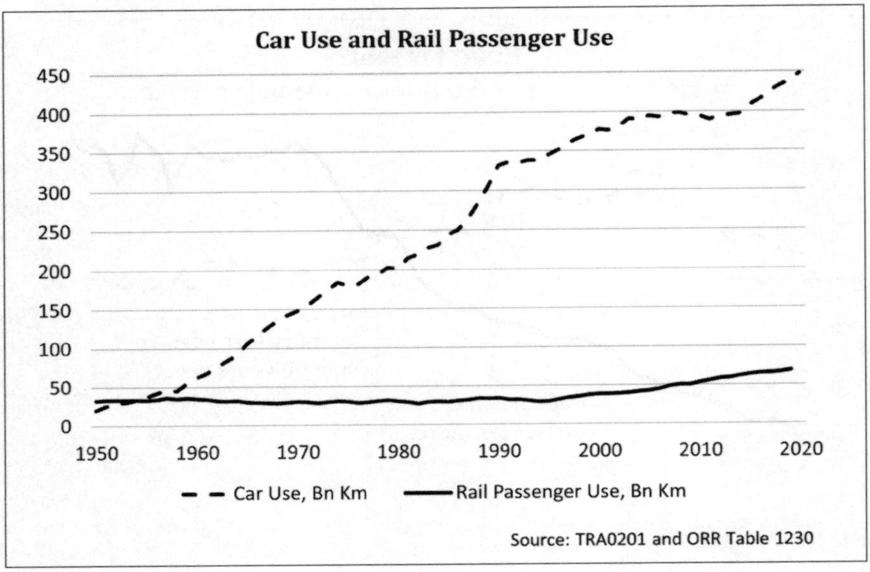

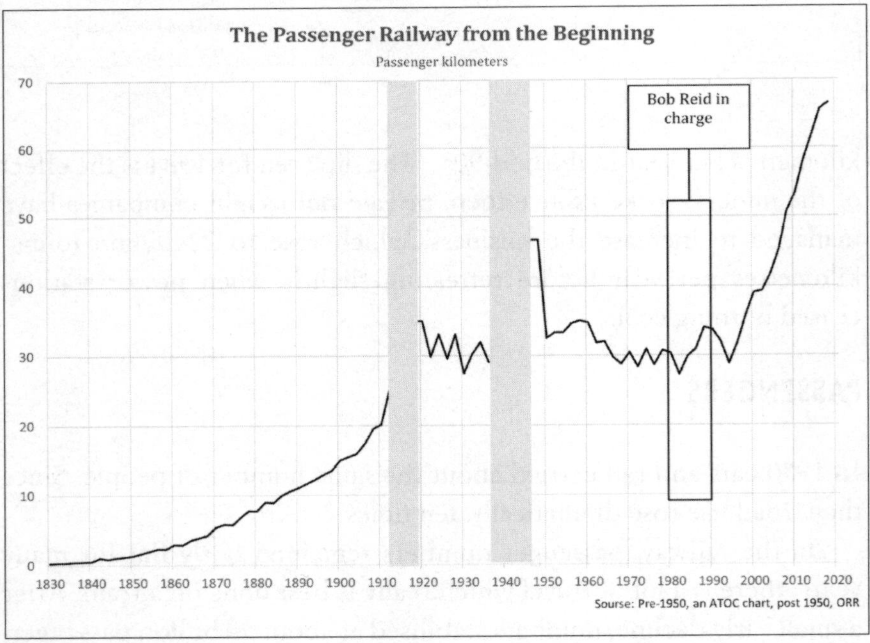

Passengers on the railway: massive growth in the 19th Century till 1914 (few roads), then essentially flat till 1996 (the age of the car), and then, with roads full, a doubling on the railway

THE PLAN

The Modernisation Plan, and the thirty years that followed are really the story of how the railway would adjust to these changes. With the change in passenger and freight numbers, where the railway had to look for its revenue switched. Freight stopped being the largest source of revenue. In Robertson's day, freight contributed three quarters of revenue. Now it is under 10 per cent. From being a freight railway, it would become a passenger railway.

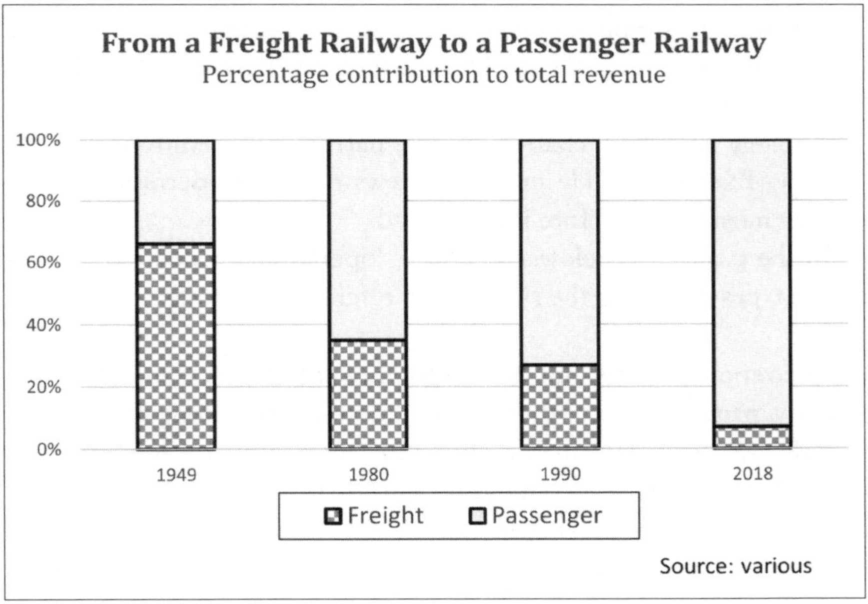

The scale, even direction, of change from rail to road was entirely unforeseen by the Transport Commission. The lack of foresight is extraordinary. Generals who had seen the Sopwith Camel turn into the Spitfire and a handful of tiny biplanes over a battlefield become wave after wave of bombers blackening the sky over Germany, gave the most cursory consideration to how road transport would be transformed over the next twenty years.

Signs of change were all around. Even while the plan was being put together, the government was approving money for the first motorways. Technology was moving. The first commercial computer was on show in 1953. The first commercial jet airliner went into service the year before. Television had become available, and 25 million watched Queen Elizabeth's Coronation in June 1953.

Railwaymen had, for the most part, been no more perceptive than the generals. The outline of the plan had in fact been drawn up by Sir John Elliot before Robertson arrived.

There were two exceptions: Gerard Fiennes and a part-time member of the commission, H.P. Barker. His name should be celebrated. He was the managing director of Parkinson Cowan, a Midlands manufacturer of kitchen equipment, gas stoves and the like. The company had turned its attention to supplying the aircraft industry during the war and had a wider horizon than one might have thought. Barker is described as having a 'restless, enquiring mind and a deep involvement in modern technology and had chaffed at the narrow conservativism of the Railway Executive.'[18] He made his views on the Modernisation Plan known most firmly, before it was issued.

In the paragraph below, the phrase 'operational conception' refers to the types of service the railway was offering. He wrote:

> The report seems to me to accept implicitly a proposal, which I deny, namely that the present operational conceptions of British Railways are viable in the long run, given modern equipment. Evidence is now forthcoming and will be forthcoming in increasing in quantity in the next two years to show that a solid proportion of our movement operations, as carried out today, are grossly uneconomical, and by inference that no amount of improvement in equipment would make them viable in the conditions of 1970.[19]

He was entirely right. But the Plan was not all wrong; it was right about a raft of detailed matters. Dozens of projects got under way, from the electrification of lines to the fitting of continuous brakes on freight wagons. How the commission managed these had somewhat mixed results.

THE DETAILS

There follow below brief comments on some of the projects set out in The Plan. These comments set the scene for the work of later railwaymen and chairmen.

CONTINUOUS BRAKES

Prompted by an accident in 1876, all passenger trains had been fitted with continuous brakes: a brake on every carriage, allowing the train to be stopped more quickly. They were controlled by the driver and did away with the need for a guard or 'brakeman', winding a handle to put on a brake in the brake-van.

Some freight trains were also fitted. Frank Paterson's fish trains had continuous brakes, so were allowed to travel faster. The powerful little engines running the Jazz Service had continuous brakes – in their case they were Westinghouse air brakes ('you could leave braking to the last moment'). Air brakes respond faster than vacuum, the two types available.

The Modernisation Plan determined that continuous brakes be fitted to all freight wagons. There followed however confusion as to what type of brake should be fitted and many years of difficulty in marshalling yards in making up trains with the different types of braking system, or no braking system, on the wagons. H.P. Barker described a fully fitted fleet as a 'pipe dream'. The plan was always going to be difficult.

ELECTRIFICATION

The advantages of electrification had been well understood for many years. London Underground had expanded into the suburbs and Southern Railway had rolled out a similar system, a 750DC third rail, into Kent, Sussex, Surrey and Hampshire. The Modernisation Plan provided for the rest of the region to be filled in.

Based on favourable French experience, the Commission decided on 25kV AC for routes elsewhere. It was the right choice. Lines from Liverpool Street and Fenchurch Street out into Essex and some Glasgow suburban lines were electrified.

Two mainline routes were proposed for electrification: the East

Coast Main Line, a project which had to be shelved for lack of money; and the West Coast Main Line. Work on the latter was carried out in two stages: the first, from Liverpool, Manchester and Birmingham to London, from 1959 to 1967 (begun under Brian Robertson), and the second, north to Glasgow, from 1970 to 1974 (begun under Henry Johnson).

DIESEL

Amusingly, Gerard Fiennes blames the famous chief engineer of LNER, the designer of the *Flying Scotsman* and the *Mallard*, for the slow introduction of diesel.

> In the teeth of those who will not hear a word against Sir Nigel Gresley I assert that few men have done a greater disservice to British Railways than when he proved to the board of LNER that they should continue with the policy of steam traction. If ever Bill Hoole, driver and apostle of steam, reads these words he will take a day off to throw the book at me. Nevertheless, Gresley condemned us to around 2,000 hp when we needed over 3,000 for twenty unnecessary years.

With no experience to build on – diesel locomotives had not been built in Britain before the war – the switch to diesel was always going to be difficult. It started sensibly enough. A selection of different designs was procured and a three-year period set aside to test and evaluate them. But within two years, Robertson, facing a worsening financial position – none of his financial forecasts were anything other than wildly incorrect – and believing that diesel would help turn it round, required the testing to be curtailed and orders placed.

In his words, in 1957:

> 'The need for diesel locomotives was immediate in order that the commitments contained in the White Paper of 1956, a promise to break even by 1961/2, might be fulfilled. If the purchase were delayed until full experience was available, many of them would be redundant before their life was expired.'[20]

It was a dreadful decision displaying lamentable business naïveté. The works were not ready, nor the maintenance depots, and 'the railways were left with a diesel fleet containing 41 different designs, many of them defective in operation'.[21] Even if everything had been ready, how could the use of diesel locomotives produce so much extra profit that the looming losses would have been covered? Any grasp on reality Robertson might once have had had vanished.

Reliable diesel locomotives did exist in America; diesel had been in use there for twenty years. There was one made by General Motors which Robertson saw when he went to America and considered buying. There were some financial and commercial difficulties to overcome but he faced a campaign against the very idea. O.S. Nock, a proud historian of British locomotives, fulminated in an editorial in *The Engineer* that it would be 'a slap in the face to British industry'.[22] Orders were instead placed with the North British Locomotive Co. of Glasgow for locomotives which were, when delivered, 'expensive, technically deficient and late'. About this episode, Gourvish dryly observes that 'a great opportunity to obtain a fleet of reliable, standard design had been lost'.[23]

DELTIC

Within this dismal picture, some bright spots did emerge. In one case rather more than a spot: the Deltic diesel. It was an ingenious design using a type of powerful, high-revolution, lightweight diesel engine which had been developed for motor torpedo boats during the war. Two such engines were incorporated in each locomotive, with diesel-electric power transmission. The prototype was available in 1955, and ran well, but there was scepticism and foot-dragging and it was not until 1959 that orders were placed. Just twenty-two were built between 1961 and 1962. That was enough. They transformed the service on the East Coast Main Line until 1978 when their successor, the High Speed Train, became available. (Nock pages 62 and 70.)

Fiennes writes (and you will note the dig at London Midland):

> I never hear the high full-throated thrum of the Deltic without returning thanks: thanks to the people in English Electric who

> thought of putting an engine off a motor gunboat into a locomotive; thanks to their board who built at their cost a prototype; thanks to the London Midland who after extensive trials did not want it; thanks to our own people who over-rode the opinion of the experts that high-revolution engines were out; thanks to English Electric who took on the task of maintaining them; thanks to the Deltics themselves for proving the experts wrong and for keeping the East Coast service going from strength to strength in speed, frequency, punctuality and popularity. We began to plan a new timetable round the Deltic based on an average speed around 65–70 mph.

Gordon Pettitt, a management trainee at the time, explains.

> Gordon: The Deltic was the first big engine, the others had not been designed for mainline use. It came about because Gerry Fiennes had been totally unimpressed with the power available – 2,000hp, and this one was 3,300hp. The engines were just outstanding.

> : I was on the first run of the prototype, from Haringey goods yard out on to the mainline and away. Fifteen coaches, speed restrictions everywhere, some down to 20mph, for we were still getting rid of the backlog of the war years, but enough clear track to see what it could do. It was a real surprise. These engines were just outstanding.
> : The Germans never built a better diesel. They were going for electric.

FREIGHT

WAGONLOAD AND MARSHALLING YARDS

Gerard Fiennes, like Barker, had a 'restless, enquiring mind'. His chief complaint about the Modernisation Plan concerned the freight strategy. Indeed, years later the economist Sir Christopher Foster wrote about the Modernisation Plan: 'It was full of mistakes but the absolutely key mistake was that they believed the future of the railway was freight, so enormous money was poured into it'.[24]

The picture was certainly extraordinary.

There was an astronomical number of wagons. There were over a million. Where on earth do you put a million freight wagons? They must have been clogging up and littering railway sidings all over the country. As a seven-year-old boy, I played on some of them in the wagon yard at North Berwick. I remember the warm smell of the oil-soaked wooden wagon floors.

What proportion were used for more than a few days a year? The plan envisaged a reduction from the 1,141,500 wagons to a still enormous number, 752,000, by 1974, twenty years later.

The wagon renewal programme was equally extraordinary. In one year, the engineering workshops were to deliver 60,000 new wagons. They may have been simple pieces of equipment, but that is still a huge number.

Such a quantity of wagons is only required for wagonload freight, loads big enough to fill a wagon but not a train. This was the particular subject of Gerard Fiennes's complaint. Sending a single wagon from any depot in the country to any other is an extremely complicated business. Besides the freight depots at either end, it requires marshalling yards where wagons arrive, are sorted, and are sent on to their way to different destinations and a system to return empty ones to where they are next needed.

To make the system more efficient, the Commission planned to construct fifty-five large, new marshalling yards and close 150 of the small, badly sited ones which it had inherited. Gerard Fiennes, when in the Eastern Region in about 1955, threw himself into the task of designing an improved layout for these new yards.

> Naturally I had my bath downstairs gossiping through the partition to Norrie while she cooked. One day I yelled at her to bring a pencil and an old envelope. I started to draw a double direction marshalling yard, an outline which has become virtually standard in Britain. Ripple Lane, Temple Mills, Tinsley, Thornton, Margam – and would have been applied to Swanbourne, Walcot

> and Brookthorpe if later in life I hadn't succeeded in putting a stop to building marshalling yards on green fields.
>
> I took the envelope to Harold Robinson who was Chief Freight Trains Clerk in the Eastern Section. I believe in committees of two, one of whom has the ballast. We started to work out a philosophy about marshalling yards; where they should be, how many separations they would have to shunt, what effect would peaks of arrivals have on them. We very quickly arrived at a conclusion where they should be, namely in the principal areas of production and consumption. Therefore London, Sheffield, Manchester, Liverpool, West Riding, Teesside, Tyneside, Glasgow would be right. Whitemoor, York, Edinburgh, Carlisle would be wrong.

But Carlisle did get built. It was one of the first to be finished. Photographs show an enormous site with about forty tracks in parallel, 56 miles in total. It was busy for a while but not for long, and was partially closed ten years later and fully closed in 1981.

Later, when Fiennes was chief operating officer for the railway under Beeching, he got the marshalling yard programme halted.

LINER TRAINS AND FREIGHTLINER

Gerard Fiennes claims that what was wrong about marshalling yards was obvious. He tells of the Freight Manager at Liverpool Street 'arguing in about 1950 that the future lay in full train loads for everything; and that any sorting should be done not with the wagons but with the body, that is to say by crane in what we now call Liner Train Depots.' In other words, if a customer wants to send less than a trainload of freight, the freight must, at the very beginning of its journey, be sorted and loaded on to a train along with other freight going to the same destination – thus avoiding marshalling yards. If no such liner train is available, then the freight must go by road. The idea was not new but putting it into practice was difficult.

Later, Beeching adopted the idea, and a network of container-carrying trains, a development of the idea, operating between dedicated terminals, was introduced under the name Freightliner, the first running in 1965.

MERRY-GO-ROUND

In the early 1960s, when Gerard Fiennes was chief operating officer under Beeching, he developed the concept of the Merry-Go-Round. It arose when a proposal came from Scotland to buy a large number of wagons to run between a colliery near Edinburgh and the new power station at Cockenzie. Fiennes seized on this proposal as he had been puzzling over the economics of delivering coal to power stations. What he had in mind was to use the largest wagons possible, travelling in a continuous loop between the coal mine and the power station, and being loaded and unloaded at each end without stopping.

Fiennes reworked the Scottish proposal and changed it from 550 x 24-ton wagons, as first proposed, to 44 x 32-ton wagons – a great saving in rolling stock. Merry-Go-Round it was called, a most efficient and profitable system widely installed for power stations and other uses.

GENERAL MERCHANDISE

Freightliner is a good business, Merry-Go-Round is a good business, but what of wagonload? Ingrained in the minds of railwaymen is the belief that it is possible, somehow, using every ounce of skill and experience, to put together a profitable wagonload service. For twenty years, immense expertise was dedicated to the task, and it seemed that it might come off under the name Speedlink, a service based on fast, airbrake-fitted trains, all the best equipment, running on selected, high-volume routes, and promising next-day delivery. But, inescapably, it was wagonload and required marshalling yards in some form. A pilot service was launched in 1972 and rolled out with more services in 1977.

Chris Stokes was Freight Officer in the Nottingham Division in 1981/2 at the height of the drive to establish Speedlink.

> Stokes: Many of the Speedlink services were extraordinarily uneconomic. For example, steel from South Wales was delivered to the Metal Box factory at Sutton in Ashfield from Toton marshalling yard by a daily train with just a couple of wagons. Quite reasonably, the Area Manager cut the service to three days a week – and Metal Box switched the traffic to road.

Nonetheless, the Board persevered and success seemed eventually to be in sight, with 150 services a day, carrying 8 million tonnes a year – but that is small for the railway. Losses grew and it came to an end in 1991.

Speedlink, Freightliner and Merry-Go-Round were all in the future. Brian Robertson had conventional wagonload to deal with. Despite its losses, he and his staff did everything they could to hold on to it. It was his view, in 1958, that 'British Railways could not survive without retaining much of the general merchandise traffic including consignments in less than wagon loads, which they were carrying today..... The policy should be to retain as much of this traffic as possible by proper charging and good service'.[25]

It was Barker's view, and he said so quite clearly at the time, that this was a mistake, that the railway should accept the inevitable, do what it could do profitably and focus on trainload freight and let the rest move, over time, on to road.

FREIGHT – SUMMARY

1. Parcels carried in the parcel vans of passenger trains – part of the passenger business, laterally called Red Star, profitable and growing in scale during the 80s until eventually it succumbed to DHL and was lost at privatisation.
2. Large-scale parcels, collection or delivery – almost certainly unprofitable. Continued until 1981.
3. Trainload coal – became Merry-Go-Round. Very profitable but now finished following the closure of coal-fired power stations.
4. Other trainload freight –reasonable business, but some commodities, (e.g. steel, petroleum) in structural decline. Aggregates growing.
5. General merchandise – various attempts to make profitable.

- Sundries, less than wagonload, given to National Freight Corporation in 1968 and transferred to road.

- Wagonload. Various attempts to make profitable. In the 1970s branded Speedlink (fast overnight freight trains with limited use of marshalling yards), which had some success in the amount carried but became heavily loss-making and closed in 1991.
- Freightliner (containers on liner trains) – 51 per cent transferred to National Freight Corporation in 1968 but returned in the 1980s. Profitable to and from container ports but mostly not competitive with road for inland traffic.

POOR MANAGEMENT AT THE TOP

Poor management was a feature of the Commission. Fiennes talks disparagingly of his many bosses at the Marylebone Road headquarters. They did not understand how to delegate, what should be left to the regions to decide, what required central direction, indeed what directions to give, how to make the balance work.

In truth, poor management or not, the railway was in a bind. It felt its responsibility as a common carrier and it feared that it could not simply close down general merchandise, for its costs would remain and be thrown on to the other services, which were themselves only profitable in part.

Barker's recommendation that it should have focused on what it could do profitably and allow the rest to move over time on to road would have been tough to put into practice for there were problems on all sides. So much was missing: business acumen at the top, experience in new technology, access to external, including foreign suppliers, a government accepting responsibility for the railway, and trade unions sympathetic to any plan for change.

The most serious was the failure of government. It was, or should have been, its job, not the Commission's, to decide the size and type of railway the country should have. It had strategic plans for other parts of the economy, most notably for the redirection of industry to the deprived parts of Britain, demonstrating a warm heart but a casual disregard for economic reality. But for the railway, it had no

Vicky sums it up rather well (Mirrorpix/Reach Licensing)

plan. It hankered after a profitable railway and toyed repeatedly and unrealistically with the idea of cutting it in half – as if that was the answer.

A railway leader of great astuteness might have found a way through these problems, but that was not Brian Robertson. He was shrewd – the Berlin airlift, the most respected of the military governors – but he was not shrewd in the ways of the railway. There is a wonderful Thoreau saying, 'Beware of all enterprises that require new clothes'. For the railway, Robertson required new clothes.

All this may seem overly critical, but Gourvish, the authority on these matters, writes that the Commission was regarded as failing on pretty much every level: 'a large, cumbersome body which failed to react quickly enough to the competitive challenge of the road transport and the difficulties thrown up by the need to modernise the railways.'

In a telling comment made towards the end of his time, Robertson gave as an excuse for the slow pace of change that the Modernisation Plan had been presented 'at a time when the idea of contracting the system was entirely strange thinking in the country generally'.[26] Despite his many talents, he built on and reinforced pretty much exactly what he found when he arrived. Like many talented people brought into the railway from the outside he failed to understand what was required or how to bring it about.

The new Transport Secretary, Reginald Marples, owner of a business building motorways, could see the issues in a much clearer light, as will be discussed in a later chapter. It did not take him long to wind up the Commission and to put in its place a Railway Board with a very different person to be in charge, the doctor, Dr Richard Beeching.

5 THE GERMAN RAILWAY

SPEED RECORDS

In the 1950s and 60s, Germany proceeded to modernise its railway very much more smoothly and assuredly than Britain. The reasons shed light on the difficulties faced by Robertson when he became chairman of the British Transport Commission. A good way into the matter is to consider a *Times* newspaper heading from much later, 7 June 1973:

High-speed train sets up record 131 mph

This, of course, refered to the speed achieved by Britain's high-speed diesel train, the HST. It is truly one of the finest diesel trains ever made. On board the train, the papers said, was Mr R.B. Reid, our Bob Reid, then Deputy General Manager of the Eastern Region – lucky chap.

It was good fun, and most satisfactory. No longer could steam enthusiasts taunt the railway that the speed record was held by a steam engine, the *Mallard* with its 126mph run in 1938. True, the top speed of the Japanese Shinkansen was much more, being raised from 130mph to 160mph, and the French had run a train at 205mph, but these were electric and the French run was a 'freak trip', as it was pointed out, designed only to achieve a record. The HST was a genuine prototype for a train intended to run in service. It ran very well.

'It handled as easily as an expensive motorcar', said the driver.[27]

But, back to the point of the story. *The Times* article began: 'A British Rail speed record of 131 mph was set today.' Good. Success. But why was this a British Rail record and not a world record? Nowhere was it explained that thirty-four years previously, in the year before the war, a German diesel train, the SVT 137 – the *Hamburg Flyer* – travelled faster. It was a German train which still held the diesel world record of 133.6mph, a speed which the HST on that run did not quite match. Germany had experience, very extensive experience, of diesel trains long before Britain started to make the switch from steam.

Nonetheless, British Rail had produced a better train. A week after the 131mph run, the driver, now allowed to go a little faster. He swept past the German record to a speed of 141mph.

'It was a great feeling,' said the driver. 'I had no idea I was going so fast. The train went so smoothly, I could have rolled a cigarette or written a letter. It would have gone to 150 mph if they had let me.'[28]

Consider another incident. While Frank Paterson on the Deeside Line was gossiping with Ethel Lamb, tapping out gossip in Morse code on a single-needle telegraph, Gordon Pettitt, who was then doing national service in Germany, but on railway business, was speaking to Ursula, a young lady he was getting to know, on a perfectly normal telephone. This is how it came about, as Gordon explains.

> Gordon: My father was a train driver. He drove steam trains on the branch lines around Hatfield. If I knew it was him, I would wave to him on the line running across the field in front of our house. His father too had been a train driver. That involved – my, it was a long time ago – white gloves. He wore white gloves, his train was kept so clean.
>
> : I never wanted to be a train driver, but I did want to join the railway. I passed the exams to become a clerk in 1950, but soon had to do national service. It was either Korea or Germany. I wanted Korea but Germany it was, and I was sent to work in the traffic office of the Royal Engineers in Bad Oeynhausen near Hanover.
>
> : My job was to monitor troop trains; one was the night train to Berlin which it was my duty to log when it crossed the border into East Germany. What was remarkable was that I was able to dial any station or railway depot or signal box on the railway. I did not need to be connected by an operator; it was an entirely automatic telephone network, and had been built pre-war.
>
> : True, if I had to telephone someone outside the railway I had to be put through by an operator. I was required to do this quite often and began to recognise someone's voice. It was the voice of Ursula, the English-speaking telephone operator; and that is how we met. We have been together over sixty years.

: When I was lucky enough to get a footplate pass, I would travel around the railway and watch what was going on.
: You have to understand what that railway was like before the war. I will give you an example of how advanced it was. I decided to go on a stopping train, pulled by a Prussian 4-6-0 steam locomotive built goodness knows when – their performance, wonderful – from Bad Oeynhausen to Hanover. It began to go round a curve at Porta where there was a permanent speed restriction of 80kph. All of a sudden, bang, the train stopped. That tells you quite a bit. The driver had exceeded the permitted speed and speed detection equipment installed before the war had stopped the train. Here we are, in 1953; I am on a train which gets stopped because it has exceeded a speed restriction, automatically. It was a pre-war system installed on all the main lines, probably suspended during the war, but the first time this could have happened in the UK would be on Eurostar, forty years later.
: I used to go out regularly and sit on a platform, watching. Freight train after freight train thundered through, one after another, Class 52, big steam locomotives built during the war to haul a thousand tons at 80 kph on level track, all fully braked – there were no unbraked freight trains anywhere, it was totally unknown – and look at the size of the wagons. Take Volkswagen; coal for Wolfsburg came from the Ruhr in hundred-ton wagons, with automatic discharge.
: It was totally amazing to me.

In Britain, by contrast, as the Modernisation Plan says, 'the Commission have recently introduced the largest coal wagon that can run on two axles on British Railways, with a capacity of 22½ tons'.

Gordon: Germany gradually electrified. But even the steam trains were advanced. A German steam locomotive had electric lights in the cab, electric lights all along the running board so the driver could see when he went to oil in the dark, and electric headlights.
: Forget the *Coronation Scot* and the *Silver Jubilee*; Germany had a network of high-speed trains before the war aimed at the business

market. A hundred mph was the norm.

These high-speed trains were diesel multiple units and ran between Berlin and a dozen German cities. The first in 1933 from Berlin to Hamburg was named the *Flying Hamburger*. It had a high top speed, though in practice the average over a long journey, even on the Berlin–Hamburg 'racetrack', was not above 76mph.

Sir Nigel Gresley, the LNER chief engineer, had visited Germany, seen the *Flying Hamburger*, considered buying it even, but the steam-powered Class A4 could pull a heavier train, carry more passengers and was a better commercial proposition.

There are good reasons for the advanced state of German railways which Gordon had seen in 1953. One of the reasons, he says, was that long before, in the 1920s, while the railways in Britain were amalgamated into four private companies, in Germany they were unified and put under direct federal government control – with many advantages.

BACKGROUND TO GERMAN RAILWAYS

Looking back over German history helps understand that country's railways. It is a theme of this book that the characteristics of a nation – its geography, its culture and the mission it sees for itself – are reflected in its railway.

For Britain, it was the navy which protected the homeland. There is Admiral Lord St Vincent's wonderful remark, referring to the threat from Napoleon, 'I do not say that the French will not come. I say only that they shall not come by sea.' But for Germany it was the army: educated citizens, superior technology, and railroads.

The historian Cornelius Torp, talking about Prussia in the nineteenth century, writes:

> Beyond doubt, railroads constituted the most dynamic and thus the most important part of the German industrial core complex, displaying all the decisive characteristics of a 'leading sector'. The German railroad sector expanded at a breath-taking speed,

> far above the average as compared with the rest of the national economy.
>
> In the long run, however, the success of Germany's heavy industry rested on the combination of a set of structural factors: a high degree of vertical integration, strong cartels and tariffs reinforcing each other [Adam Smith it was not], and the realisation of economies of scale that could only be achieved via large export quantities.

We see the result today: Siemens, BASF, Bayer, BMW, Daimler, Merck, Volkswagen, ThyssenKrupp.

German railways were in fact nationalised much earlier than Gordon suggests. At first, the railways developed rather slowly, and indeed it is said that the first train driver was an Englishman, William Wilson, who commanded an enormous salary, and the trains were imported. There was no unified German state, only regional states, so the first railways were tiny, isolated, one-track lines serving the large cities. But attitudes changed, railways came to be seen as contributing to the unification of Germany, and they were soon built out across the land, as both private and state companies. Their importance was so great that after 1871, when the German Reich was established, the three largest states – Prussia, Bavaria and Saxony – nationalised the railways in their territories.

From then on, the system was directed by government. A central supervisory authority was established in 1873, a uniform standard of signals in 1875, a uniform classification of goods in 1877 and a series of operating regulations to apply to all German railways in 1893.[29]

Cornelius Torp continues.

> The nationalisation of the railroads in Prussia from the late 1870s onwards enabled the Prussian government to open up peripheral regions and thus to pursue classical infrastructure policy. Important parts of the educational system were geared toward the requirements of the private sector..... These discrete components fit together tightly and allowed for Germany's tremendous economic success before the First World War.

In Germany, Torp goes on to say, a new and stable production regime developed which could be called 'organised capitalism', a 'coordinated market economy' or 'corporatism', in contrast to the Anglo-Saxon 'liberal market economy'. Fundamentally, so the thinking went, society is something which should be managed. It was a market economy, but a coordinated one. In Germany, sustained, methodical support by the state for the railway was natural; in Britain it was the opposite, a reluctant necessity and neither sustained nor methodical.

Relations with the workforce were different too. In 1946, when Germany had to choose socialism – not impossible, as a quarter of Germany was communist – or free-market capitalism, what emerged was a great compromise. It emerged not easily and not at once but over time the system called, roughly speaking, *Mitbestimmung* ('co-determination' or 'joint decision-making') was established in law. It was underpinned by a dense network of rules and regulations setting out what was or was not permitted.

The depth of the commitment to *Mitbestimmung* is remarkable and quite profound. At the top of industry, by a law passed shortly after Brian Robertson had left Germany, but certainly in preparation while he was there, worker representatives were to make up half the members of supervisory boards in certain sectors.

At the bottom, by the Works Constitution Act, companies were required to establish factory councils. These had far-reaching rights concerning personnel matters such as hiring, lay-offs, retirement, overtime, part-time workers, vacation, etc., and had access to information about the company's finances and plans – to an extent which seems strange to us. In exchange, factory councils were barred from calling strikes or organising demonstrations.

The unions themselves were organised by industry and not by craft as in Britain – ASLEF being a craft union. Vast industry-based unions, controlled from the top, allowed and were intended to allow very little room for dissent by the rank and file.

For unions, and indeed management, their country, the Federal Republic, was something precious. They had seen the horrors of disorder, dictatorship and war and wished to take no chances. A railway union leader stated at his union's Congress in 1961: 'This state here, this West German Federal Republic, dear friends, is our state..... What is important to me is to defend freedom against all ultras, be they right or left.'[30] What a wonderful remark that is.

Unions became committed to growing the economy. The kind of turf wars seen in Britain over almost any change in working conditions did not happen in Germany, or at least happened far less. On the contrary, business became the national mission.

Some elements of the system of consultation can be seen in Britain, particularly on the railway, but in a much weaker form and voluntary, not governed by law. British Rail was highly unionised and had 'factory councils' at every level. Union leaders knew what was happening in Germany and wanted the same, but without the obligations that came with it. What emerged therefore was a pale copy. At the top was the Rail Staff National Tribunal, the RSNT, whose decisions were supposedly binding but not backed by law. Fundamentally, unions did not accept that business was the national mission, so a 'great compromise' was never likely to emerge.

Peter Parker, much later, tried to engage unions as partners in the planning of British Rail; in the document *Challenge of the Eighties*, he laid out facts and figures and plans for the unions to study and hoped they would embrace the measures needed, but to no effect.

If all this is put together, the German talent for organising and running large, forceful, heavy industry, its talent, genius even, for the application of technology, and a workforce proud of business success, you can see circumstances highly favourable to the operation of a railway.

The shine has faded somewhat, but in the 1960s and 70s Deutsche Bundesbahn achieved formidable levels of punctuality and service. A friend who knew Germany well remembers relying without hesitation when making a change of trains on the three minutes timetabled between the arrival of one and the departure of the other.

How exactly that was achieved is beyond this book, and beyond this author, except to say that Germany very soon had the financial means to invest in its railway, much of the credit due to one man, who must be mentioned, Ludwig Erhard.

Erhard was the German Minister for Economic Affairs from 1948. He swept away wartime controls on business and opened the economy to competition. It was a courageous step: 'The sense of the economy flows from the all-embracing life of a people, with its ultimate roots in values which cannot be rationally grasped'. And was matched to a moral sense. It was 'rooted in a particular kind of spiritual attitude'.[31]

Mitbestimmung had two parts: support for workers and freedom for businesses. He drove the latter, which had moral value just as had the former. The measures he put in place created the conditions for the 'German miracle'. After removing controls on business within Germany he cut down the tariffs and quotas which obstructed international trade. It was a hard, hard message, born of desperation. He knew it would give foreign suppliers access to the German market. But, he wrote:

> The ruined German economy could not offer a living to the German people if it did not succeed within the shortest possible period in catching up with the level of output of the most progressive countries of the world.
>
> We have to face the alternatives without pity or prejudice. If the German economy and the Germans still have sufficient power and energy to permit the experiment of a return to the world market through competition, then the path before German reconstruction was open. In particular there was then a chance to give the millions of refugees a decent occupation and open the way to a standard of living for the German people commensurate with Western civilisation. Insofar as this energy was lacking, successful reconstruction would have been unthinkable.[32]

As it happened, Erhard's dismantling of internal controls over industry in 1949 was in direct conflict with the views of Brian Robertson, the military governor at the time, who had argued for the opposite. 'Everything of consequence,' wrote Robertson, 'is, or should be, controlled by the government..... During this period of scarcity which will inevitably continue for several years this situation will prevail.' Fortunately for Germany, Robertson was not able to prevent the dismantling and it was Erhard's policies which ended the 'period of scarcity', not Robertson's.[33]

German industry recovered, exports grew and the balance of payments, having been hugely negative, moved extraordinarily quickly to large surpluses. From a deficit in 1950, it moved to a large and growing surplus from 1952. It was the German economic miracle.

West Germany

Balance of payments, (exports over imports)

(1956 DMm, monthly average)

1950	-25
1952	+203
1956	+389

Source: Erhard p242

The rebuilding of the railway was part of the German miracle. Germany could afford to do so, and all went well for thirty years, till 1980. The years since then have been much more difficult.

Deutsche Bundesbahn, the name of the railway in the West before unification, was able to electrify the main lines – a map of 1968 shows a mass of such lines, a complete network – develop diesel for other lines, continue with steam for some years – there was no cliff edge between steam and diesel – and make a huge investment in freight, for which, given the geography of Germany, the railway retained natural advantages. There are massive flows from the northern ports down through Germany to Switzerland and even into Italy. Wagonload freight is still carried, something not seen in Britain for twenty years.

It is not clear that there were any distinctive features of the organisation of the railway in Germany to bring this about, other than the active involvement of the state in its planning. The railway was not a normal company but, in fact, an agency of government. Drivers and many others in the railway were therefore government officials and as such were prohibited from going on strike. But they were well paid, drivers in particular.

Being an agency of government, an ancient law set out the precise form in which their accounts had to be kept. It was not a form which made management accounting easy. Certainly, there was no accurate revenue allocation between the ten divisions.

In some respects, changes were made slowly. '*Langsam und stetig*' ('slow and steady') is a virtue. The railway was slow to close country stations and rural lines. Every instance was political, with political trade-offs. Besides, an official plan, the Leber Plan of 1967, aimed to put heavy freight back on to the railway. It never happened, but it was a reason not to close lines.

SINCE 1980

Things changed in the 1980s. By then, the cost of Deutsche Bundesbahn was becoming more than the government was prepared to tolerate. It was an engineer-led railway; such railways can be good, but they cannot be efficient. This is taken from *Railway Gazette International* of June 1983.

> No sooner does a new government take over in Bonn than a report on what to do about the German Federal Railway's deficit arrives on the transport minister's desk.
>
> What is surprising is the failure of DB's new management team to come up with no more constructive proposals for dealing with the railways perennial financial haemorrhage than.... the latest 'hard option' that entails cutting the network from 28,000 to 15,000 route kilometres and shedding 100,000 jobs.
>
> The last time widespread closure proposals were was thrown into West Germany's political arena there was uproar.... This time both Bonn and Frankfurt have been extolling the virtues of the Bahnbus which does not translate as railbus but as a bus operated by the railway.
>
> Management find this a softer option than tackling such problems as locomotive manning (trains running at more than 140km/h (87mph) still require two men in the cab) or one-man operation of railcars (the prototypes delivered in 1981 have only now started trials, but with two men on board), let alone asking

questions about over-specification of rolling stock and over-lavish provision of track and structures.

This sounds very similar to Barbara Castle's perception ten years earlier that railway chairman had no real idea how to cut losses and instead just reached for the easiest but politically most difficult solution, closing stations.

In Germany, the cost problem got worse and came to a head in 1989. It was a magnificent railway but production-led and very expensive. The Chancellor, Helmut Schmidt, remarked, 'We can afford either the railway or the armed forces, but not both.'

From another book, talking about 1989:

> There were no less than 16 previous reform attempts, but they had all failed. In the light of the Bundesbahn's disastrous financial situation, the Minister of Transport created the 17th government commission in the summer of 1989. The commission's assignment was to draw up a reform proposal which would free the government from the budgetary risk posed by the railway and to create a viable railway system able to operate on a commercial basis.[34]

The commission's work was overtaken by the fall of the Berlin Wall and the merger of East and West, with the necessity of merging their railways, so creating Deutsche Bahn. The financial reform eventually implemented was to require that InterCity to profitable – so they hoped – and that local railways be paid for by the Länder. It was the latter reform which would most change the face of German railways.

In Britain, by the time Helmut Schmidt made his despairing remark, Bob Reid had shown how the cost problem could be addressed. He, as will be described in Part Three, was not a 'cost cutter'; what he did was force through the change from an engineer-led railway to a business-led one. With costs coming under control, the Secretary of State for Transport, Paul Channon – unlike Schmidt – was able to compliment the railway on its 1987 financial performance – 'all your staff deserve the warmest congratulations' – and approve new investment.

In Germany, similar business-led thinking, so far as one can see, did not emerge. Indeed, since 1980, the two railways have followed quite different paths. Deutsche Bahn fought off attempts for it to be split up and privatised. It pursued business growth – logistics of all kinds – like any other major corporation. It is now a vast worldwide enterprise with the passenger railway contributing only 43 per cent of revenue, the rest being logistics: rail, road, shipping, air. Nearly half its revenue is outside Germany.

In contrast, the lean, value-for-money railway which Bob Reid created was split and privatised. The move was certainly controversial and much disapproved of on the continent, but the results, in many respects, have been impressive – as discussed in the Postscript.

Ludwig Erhardt in about 1952, a great man for courage and judgement.

6 BOB: GLASGOW, DONCASTER AND YORK

GLASGOW (1960–68)

So far, we have covered Bob's railway years in Banchory, his move to Edinburgh and marriage to Isobel, his move to York and his promotion there to Goods Agent, supervising all things in the Station Hall.

His next move, in 1960, when Bob would have been 39 years old, was to Glasgow, as Janet describes.

> Janet: Then he got promoted to a job in Glasgow. My mother, though she had come from Glasgow, was not keen on the move, but in the railway, needs must, and it was fine. We all enjoyed Glasgow. It was a very friendly place.
>
> : We were in Glasgow from 1960 to 1968 and Dad had a number of jobs there. He was the District Goods Manager then something like the District Passenger Manager. His last job was Planning Manager for the Scottish Region. I do remember that. I remember Dad saying, 'Oh, I am not sure about this Planning Manager job.' I think he was worried that he was being shunted off to one side and that he was getting off the track, but he said afterwards that it was one of the most interesting jobs he had had and it was excellent experience for him later on. One of the things he did was work on the redevelopment of Queen Street station.

From various newspaper articles, the sequence appears to be as follows.

March 1960–June 1961. (1 year) Assistant District Goods Manager.

June 1961–December 1963. (2½ years) District Passenger Manager, Glasgow and South-West. From an article: 'He was one of the key men involved in the introduction of blue trains on the Cathcart Circle in Glasgow and the Green diesel train service to Lanarkshire.' The

Cathcart Circle is a circular, or at least pear-shaped, railway line, electrified in 1962, leading from the Central Station south across the Clyde to Cathcart in the Glasgow suburbs.

December 1963–67. (3½ years) Divisional Commercial Manager. A headline: 'Ex-Banchory railman gets top job'. From the article: 'He will concentrate on developing the freight business of the railways in his division as well as looking after passenger traffic.' And from a later CV: 'He was closely concerned with developing the carriage of strip steel by rail and the introduction of trainload conveyance of new cars to and from the Rootes factories at Linwood and Coventry.'

Things were not easy on the passenger side. The Provost of Largs on the Ayrshire coast described the service as 'quite shocking', and a long article from 1967 describes Bob's meeting with the Hamilton town councillors to discuss the matter. They too had problems with their service, which Bob had to explain: the stations would not have their gas lighting replaced by electricity for a year; train delays were the knock-on consequences of engineering work required for the electrification of another line; there had been an unusual rise in breakdowns in diesel multiple units because all the spare sets were in use; the absence of a seat and the need to stand for a short distance was inevitable; and there was no hope of extra trains or coaches as 'this service is a severe loss-maker and there is no case I can put forward to justify the injection of fresh capital to provide additional rolling stock'. Played with a straight bat. And evidencing his understanding that the railway is a business.

MR ROBERT B. REID, district passenger manager for the Glasgow and South - West Division of British Railways, who yesterday became commercial officer with responsibility for developing passenger and freight traffic in the division.

(Glasgow Herald)

As he was moving, though slowly, up through the ranks he was sent to the Staff College at Woking for three months in 1963. Mixing with a group of thirty or so people, he studied finance, balance sheets, statistics, management skills, leadership skills, that sort of thing. There were outside speakers and an overseas visit, in his case to Poland which at that time was 'pretty grim'.

There were two people Bob got to know in Scotland with whom he would have many dealings in later years. The first was James Urquhart who was the Divisional Manager from 1964 to 1967, and therefore Bob's boss, and the second Ian Campbell, an older person, who was Chief Civil Engineer in the Scottish Region from 1965 to 1968. Bob had little time for either. Later, he would be working for Ian Campbell as his deputy in York and later still the three would be on the Board together: the McMafia.

1967–1968 (1 year) Regional Planning Manager, a job he greatly liked, as Janet said.

CYRIL BLEASDALE

One of the people whom Bob met when he was in Glasgow was Cyril Bleasdale. Cyril went on many years later to be one of the first sector directors. He tells the story of how he first encountered Bob:

> Cyril: I was on a course at Derby as a junior manager. Two of us had been given an exercise to do, looking at to-be-collected parcels traffic. Parcels were carried on the railway and you could either collect them yourself at the station or have them delivered. We charged the same for both. The question was: should to-be-collected be cheaper?
>
> : We went to Glasgow. I think part of the exercise was just to travel around. We met the commercial manager there, a man called Bob Reid. Awfully nice man. He came across as a little stern, but a thoughtful person and I was quite impressed. I said to him, 'I am thinking of reporting back and saying that it is a popular service; nobody else can give you same-day service and it is not cost free. You save the cost of delivery, but you have to separate the traffic,

store it, staff the counters where people come in to sign for their parcel. It is very much in demand and my idea is that it should carry a surcharge.'
: So, Bob said, 'Hmmm, well, if you think that, you should say so.'
: When we got back to Derby, I proposed this. There was a commercial man from the Manchester division or somewhere and he said, 'What a stupid idea! You don't not do something and charge more!' But I stuck to my guns. I said to the chap who was with me, 'Let us keep up with this, even if everybody is saying it's stupid.' I think I did this because Bob had given me confidence. And, you know, in a way that underlines Bob's tenure. He gave confidence to people to carry out their jobs. If you asked me what would be the trait you would associate with Bob Reid, it was to give you confidence. If you fail, do not expect a great deal of mercy. This was his underlying quality. He put his trust in people and he stood back, but he was sensitive if people let him down; that hurt him.

A word about the training Cyril had in the railway – Cyril was an operator – for it contrasts with Bob's.

Cyril, like Frank Paterson and Gordon Pettitt, joined the railway around the same time as Bob, a few years either side of 1950. Cyril joined when he was sixteen. His first job was as a pay clerk in the Edgehill marshalling yard, a big one. On Fridays he had to go round reading meters, gas meters and water meters. There were no electricity meters; all the signal boxes used paraffin or gas lamps. It took him into a new world, which he loved, jumping on and off freight trains to take him around to check the meters. He would call up to the signalman, 'Keep it on for me' – referring to the signal – and he would leap on to the engine as it came slowly through.

Cyril: It was fun but he was told if he wanted to get on he needed to do the 'block'. That was the name for the railway rules for signalling. He took the course and in three years passed out with the qualification to be a stationmaster – signal boxes came under the stationmaster – and got his first job as such at the young age of 21.

He was clever and enthusiastic about the job, but one of the train drivers would not have it, saying 'We're not having bloody young boys as stationmasters' and refused to move his train on Cyril's instructions. The driver got out of his cab and stalked off to see the signalman. Eventually he returned, but in a grump, and only very slowly moved his train. Cyril had stood his ground and things worked out.

Cyril did various jobs as stationmaster and went through the LMR management training scheme. He became involved with the electrification of the West Coast Main Line in 1960. His job was to work on the track layout. He walked all the way from London to the outskirts of Rugby over various days, deciding where the masts for the overhead wires would go. You cannot risk them blocking sight of the signals. Cyril, as he said, 'always did track layouts'.

Cyril, as this description shows, was an operator. By contrast, Bob was not. He had never done track layouts or given instructions to drivers or signalmen. His experience was commercial: how the railway's product – freight or passenger traffic – served the market.

DONCASTER AND YORK (1968–74)

Thus far Bob had moved slowly up through the ranks. After twenty years he had reached the level of Planning Manager for Scotland, a respectable position – and he had been to the staff College at Woking – but that could have been as far as he got. Indeed, as Janet explained, he thought he was being shunted sideways.

There was, however, something special about him. Cyril Bleasdale noticed it. And so, most happily, did Charles Haygreen. He was the management development director and, so the story goes, it was Charles Haygreen who 'prised Bob out of Scotland'. From then on, things moved more rapidly.

Janet tells the story of the next move.

> Janet: Planning Manager was the last job Dad had in Glasgow; then he got promotion and ended up in Doncaster as the Divisional Manager. We had a lovely house. The best thing about Donny was the house. It was hard for the family being moved around, I have to

say, because although in those days in something like the army there was a lot of support, schools and welfare officers and all that, in the railway there was not much help.

: So we went from a big metropolitan city where my brother and I liked our schools and all was fine. Then we went to Doncaster, which in those days was a big mining and railway town. I was fifteen, which is absolutely the wrong age to change schools as you are doing your O levels at 16. Looking back, it was all rather traumatic. But we managed. You have to. Both my brother and I went away to boarding schools. Maybe our parents thought that if Dad had to move again our education would not have to be disrupted.

: We were in Doncaster from '68 to '74. Dad was Divisional Manager for the first four years.

The regions, the Eastern for example, were divided first into Divisions (seven in Eastern) and below that into Areas (about forty in Eastern). The old Districts were disappearing, being merged into the larger Areas. As a divisional manager, Bob got the experience he lacked. Divisional managers were responsible for train drivers, signallers, the safe operation of the railway and much else on top of the commercial affairs of the division. It was a rounded management job, on a small, or not-so-small, scale. He had a staff of 5,500. It was a job you had to do before you could progress higher in the ranks.

Bob was welcomed by the newspapers when he arrived in May 1968 and gave a long interview to the *Doncaster Evening Post* the following year. As a public figure, it mattered what sort of person he was. The article opens by describing Mr Robert Reid as one who often travelled on the footplate of locomotives so he could chat to the railwaymen. 'I do not believe you can run a railway and inspect it by dashing around in a car.'

We then hear in that interview, for the first time, Bob talking about the railway as he saw it. It was a time of change, with Barbara Castle's 1968 Transport Act.

'We are now business oriented by applying real business principles to the running of the railway. It is a great stimulus to myself and other managers to get away from the idea of feather-bedding just to run a service where the cost of the operation does not matter too much.'

He does not complain about the financial settlement, far from it. Under the Transport Act of 1968, a lot of debt was written off and there was to be an explicit subsidy for loss-making local services. Other services were to pay their own way. 'Mr Reid', the article says, 'does not think the railways have done too badly.'

He is optimistic that the railway can break even. 'The future lies with the haulage of raw materials for industry.' For his division this meant oil haulage out of Immingham, the movement of raw materials and finished product for British Steel at Scunthorpe and the movement of coal from the Yorkshire coalfields to the railhead at Immingham. For passenger traffic, congestion on the roads promised growth.

This sums up the attitudes and beliefs he would carry with him for the rest of his career: a marked dislike of feather-bedding, an enthusiasm for a railway run on business principles, and an acceptance without complaint of the government's financial settlement.

Later, talking to the Hull Chamber of Commerce about their service, he put it most bluntly, 'We are in it for the money, not for love..... Everything depends on the volume of business we get from Hull.'[35] He stresses the efforts he will make to develop that business but: not enough business, no railway. It is just as he told the Hamilton town councillors and year before: if losing money, no more rolling stock.

Interestingly, he is described as a Scotsman and it is stated that his parents came from Fife, which is strange as neither did. But perhaps a Scotsman was how he saw himself. He had spent a lot of time there. And his hobbies: 'rambling, shooting and fishing', which he had always enjoyed. He had liked mountain walking and climbing and sailing in his youth. He was very practical. Woodwork and joinery was an abiding interest when he had time.

RICHARD GOLDSON

At that time there was a management trainee in the Eastern Region called Richard Goldson. Richard remembers Bob Reid very well and tells this story. Incidentally, Richard went on, twenty years later, to project manage the implementation of the final form of the reforms Bob Reid would introduce in 1990 (called OfQ, pronounced Oh-fur-Q).

Bob, then a Divisional Manager, was chairman of the regional training committee. One of his tasks, which he carried out most assiduously, as he did everything else, said Richard, was to interview the traffic management trainees. Richard was one of these.

The interviews, held in the old boardroom in York, were terrifying experiences. Bob was not a man who aimed to set you at ease; he was stern in manner and appearance and quite formal in his mode of speech. 'My goodness, he put you through the hoops.'

On one occasion Richard forgot to attend his interview. A memorandum was soon received upbraiding him for this lapse and setting a new date. The rescheduled interview went well. Richard had a wonderful job. He was setting up and running one of the first merry-go-round systems of coal delivery. His trains ran in a continuous loop carrying coal from the Selby coalfield to the new power stations of Ferrybridge, Eggborough and Drax. Richard had a complete train set to get his arms around and was able to describe his job with enthusiasm.

'You seem to be enjoying yourself. Carry on,' said Bob. 'You may now go.' Richard turned to retire, but halfway back across the vast carpet he heard most clearly, 'Do not ever forget a training interview again.'

This was followed somewhat later by another, most strange interview. It was not with Bob. He had been made Deputy General Manager for the region, but he continued to conduct the interviews with the management trainees. A memorandum was received by Richard (everything was by memorandum in those days), summoning him to attend the office of a senior manager, a cold and distant person, junior to Bob Reid but far up the hierarchy above Richard. The purpose of the meeting had not been specified but it soon became clear.

'Now,' said this person, 'you are soon to meet Mr Reid for your training interview, are you not?'

'Yes indeed,' said Richard.

'When you see Mr Reid, if Mr Reid asks you how the Parcels business in the Leeds division is going, you could tell him.... this and that..... If Mr Reid asks you about the guards at Leeds City what you could say is.... this and that...'

It was a conversation, remembers Richard, which indicated the power and influence, the fear even, and the aura around Bob even then. Richard says his presence 'stalked the region' so that even such a senior person as this manager had to find ways to have his story put in a good light.

Bob had been promoted to Deputy General Manager of the region in January 1972. Ian Campbell was the General Manager. The two did not see eye to eye.

Talking about this time, Bob later said [*Railnews*, March 1990]: –

> 'Beeching had shown us the way, in managing as well as in analysing. He was an inspiration to many of us. I saw that giving people real responsibility, communicating with them at all levels, being absolutely clear about what I wanted and what I expected them to do seemed to work wonders. Why couldn't this be done on a grand scale?'

But Bob found that kicking against the culture was far from easy. Doncaster was a hive of activity and industrial expansion yet the railway was suffering from severe operational problems and there was no organisation to 'sell' the railway and look after the customer.

> 'The operators were sacrosanct, they were running the railway but they didn't think about the customer. There were even attempts to unseat me.'

Undeterred he attacked wastage and sought to cut costs.

After 3½ years at Doncaster and having stepped up to Deputy General Manager of the Eastern Region, he should have had the ideal opportunity to take his marketing ideas further, but to no avail.

> 'No one wanted to know. I was by-passed by the chief officers.

> Deputy General Manager was a grand title, conjuring visions of a great command, but it carried with it little real power. I was continually defeated.'

CYRIL BLEASDALE

Cyril Bleasdale, who had met Bob some years before in Glasgow, had been appointed to take over from him as the Divisional Manager in Doncaster. They talked together of course.

At that time, in the early 70s, the chairman of the railway was Richard Marsh and the managing director David Bowick. They knew the railway was not being managed well and brought in McKinsey, who came up with what was called the Field Organisation.

> Cyril: They said to McKinsey something like this: 'Look, we, British Rail, think the regions are too difficult to manage. We are under these barons, the general managers. Please come up with a new organisation.' But McKinsey got it totally wrong. They looked around and thought the answer was smaller regions. They came up with eight, which were going to be called Territories. It was crazy. They must have spent a long time at it, deciding the size of these Territories, but was there anything in common in them which you could focus on, to make them worthwhile? No, and of course there was no bottom line. How can you calculate a bottom line when so much of your traffic goes straight through your area?
> : Bob thought it was awful. He said to me, 'I'm due to go to Manchester as the new territory manager there.' He must have been about 52. He said, 'Well, I will do three or four or five years and that will be it. I will sit my time out.' These were more or less the words he used. He was quite despondent about the whole thing.

The problem which McKinsey failed to see was beginning to dawn on some people, Cyril in particular.

Cyril: We had a major conference with David Bowick. He was

getting worried by all the negative opinion coming up from the roots challenging the new organisation. I stood up amongst these people and argued that there was a missed opportunity, that the great difficulty with being a divisional manager was that we had no profit-and-loss account. You could not work one out. There was no business element to being a divisional manager and this Field Organisation would not not have one either.
: I remember the answer: 'Oh look, we have been through all that, Cyril, we have been through that debate and this is the best way forward.'

But it was not the best way forward and it was abandoned. Things carried on as they were and Bob did not have to go to Manchester. He stayed in York, but not for long. In January 1974, he was made General Manager of the Southern Region, a big, big job.

The family was on the move again. This time to London, to be continued in Part Three.

Bob Reid's postings, since he joined the railway, are summarised in this chart.

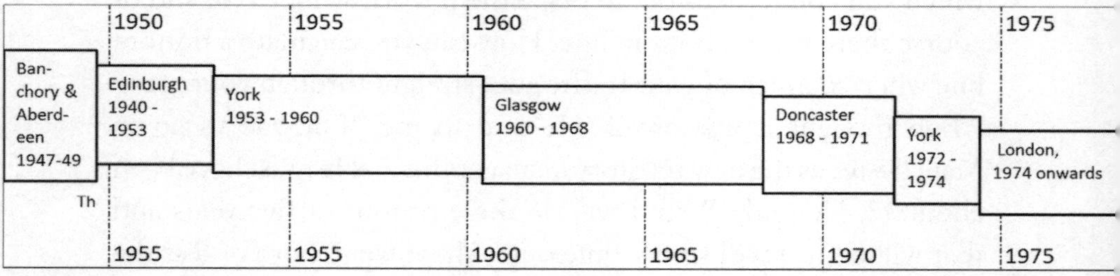

PART TWO

THE RAILWAY 1960–80

Dr Beeching, a big man: 'opened more things, including minds to ideas, than he closed', said Gerard Fiennes (gettyimages)

7 THE BEECHING PERIOD

Bob Reid served in the railway for 45 years, under nine chairmen, including himself. That time can be divided into five periods named below for those who most obviously set their stamp on the character of the railway in their day:

- **Robertson Period (~1950s).** The Modernisation Plan, a conventional re-build.
- **Beeching Period (~1960s).** Station closures and opening minds.
- **The Castle Transition (~1968).** The new realism.
- **Johnson/Bowick Period (~1970s).** 'Modern management', things got built but stalled.
- **Reid/Parker Period (~1980s).** A revolution in thinking.

Neither Hurcomb, Raymond, Marsh nor Parker (on his own, 1976–79), though fine people, had such effect.

While Bob Reid was moving slowly up through the ranks, much else was changing in the country and across the world. Compared with the staid 1950s, the 1960s promised change. Macmillan gave his famous 'winds of change blowing through the continent' speech. There

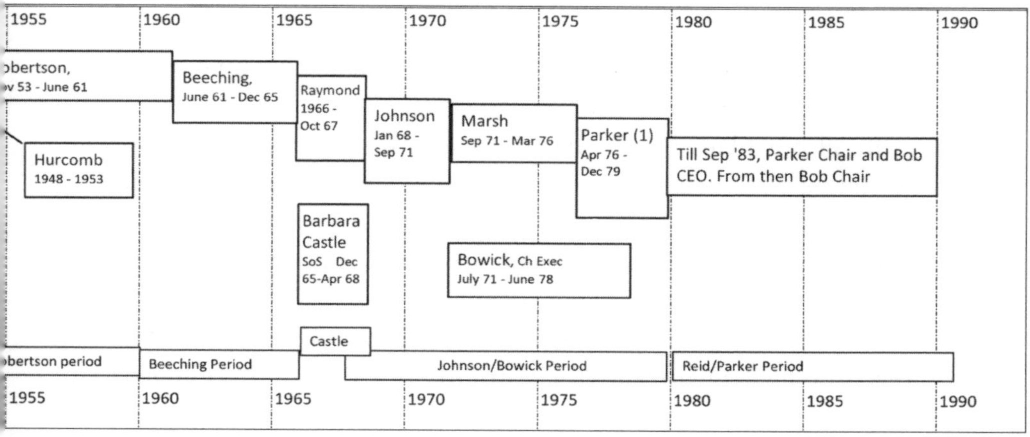

were the Beatles, Lady Chatterley's Lover, though not in WHSmith, Beyond the Fringe, Flower Power and CND. The 60s were fun. 'If you remember it..........'

And the world woke up to technology. You can put a date on it. It was 12 April 1961, the day Yuri Gagarin circled the Earth in a Russian-built spacecraft. He was ejected from the craft miles above the Earth's surface and drifted down under a parachute to land with a bump in a field somewhere in southern Russia. There he met a farmer and his daughter. 'When they saw me in my spacesuit with the parachute dragging along as I walked, they started to back away in fear. I told them, don't be afraid, I am a Soviet like you, who has descended from space, and I must find a telephone to call Moscow!' The daughter, years later, asked about the occasion said simply, 'He had such a nice smile'.

With America in shock at the Soviet triumph, President Kennedy made the famous commitment: 'We choose to go to the moon in this decade, and do the other things, not because they are easy, but because they are hard.'

These were stirring times. At least some were stirred, but the response in Britain was muted. It was the Swinging Sixties: pop music, Mary Quant, things Britain had a talent for. Technology mattered but there were so many more interesting things to do.

Harold Wilson, in opposition, tried to make his party face up to what was happening with his famous 'white heat of technology' speech to the Labour Party conference in October 1963. He proclaimed:

> The next 15 years will embrace a period of technical change, particularly in industrial methods, greater than the whole of the industrial revolution of the last 250 years.
>
> In all our plans for the future, we are re-defining and we are re-stating our Socialism in terms of the scientific revolution. But that revolution cannot become a reality unless we are prepared to make far-reaching changes in economic and social attitudes which permeate our whole system of society.
>
> The Britain that is going to be forged in the white heat of this revolution will be no place for restrictive practices or for outdated methods on either side of industry.

All of which was evident in the railway.

THE DOCTOR

Just six years after the Modernisation Plan was published, the most famous name in railway history – better known even than Stephenson or Brunel – appeared on the scene: Dr Richard Beeching.

Harold Wilson was in opposition and Harold Macmillan Prime Minister. He had taken over when Anthony Eden resigned in 1957 over the fiasco of the Suez campaign. 'Quiet, calm deliberation disentangles every knot' was Macmillan's style. After winning the general election in 1959, he appointed Ernest Marples, a controversial figure – a scoundrel to some – but a businessman and a most effective minister for transport.

Marples and a friend, Reginald Ridgway, had got hold of a five-ton ex-army truck and a crane, and built up a substantial civil engineering company. The company, Marples Ridgway, prospered and won road-building contracts – the Hammersmith Flyover among them – even though Marples was by then a government minister.

Conflicts of interest there were, and much else besides – years later he would flee the country pursued by creditors and the taxman – but as a minister who had built roads, he had a clear-eyed understanding of transport, particularly of the unstoppable growth of road traffic. He was able therefore to move transport thinking forward. He introduced the MOT test, parking meters, the single and double yellow lines, and traffic wardens. While he did not initiate the motorway programme, he opened the first section of the M1 and saw a further twenty motorway sections opened.

It was the age of the car.

Most significantly for the railway, which was again under the spotlight – the promises in the Modernisation Plan having come to nothing – Marples arranged for Dr Beeching, then technical director of ICI, to join an advisory board in 1960. It was the Stedeford Advisory Group which was looking into the financial position of the railway, still chaired by Brian Robertson. The clear aim was to reduce its cost and, in Marples' mind, move resources from rail to roads.

Most agreed that the Commission, overseeing canals and ports and road freight and London transport and railways, was never going to be effective and that its component parts had to be established under separate boards. Beyond that, however, there was much disagreement.

Stedeford and others pursued organisational solutions: the correct composition of the top board, clear financial constraints and targets, strong central control or, alternatively, devolution of powers to area boards controlling semi-autonomous regions. Such organisational solutions, it was supposed, would lead naturally to better performance. For them, it was axiomatic that there was a profitable railway which could be discovered by a more cleverly constituted board or railway organisation.

Beeching disagreed and argued strenuously with Stedeford. He argued that recommendations about the organisation could not be made until there was 'a close understanding of the basic economics of railway operation in order to assess the future place of the railways in the country's transport system.'

Marples, rightly, sided with Beeching and moved decisively to put him in charge. Beeching took over the Commission in June 1961, replacing Brian Robertson, and became chairman of the new British Railways Board when it was established in January 1963.

Both Robertson and Beeching were remarkable and talented people, but as different as could be. Robertson brought a talent for administration, Beeching for the analysis and understanding of business. Robertson's mind seemed stuck in the world as it was at the time, while Beeching could envisage change. Robertson displayed a coldness to railway managers, Beeching the opposite.

They were, however, alike in being fallible. Both could be wrong. Beeching was right about what he is criticised for – closing branch lines – and wrong about something now forgotten – his freight strategy. Neither of them, neither Robertson nor Beeching, grasped in their minds what was happening on the roads.

One of Beeching's first moves was to bring Gerard Fiennes to the headquarters as chief operating officer. His job was to plan how railway operations could be improved. He writes:

> If there is one characteristic which I enjoy, it is the ability to get across my boss and 222 Marylebone Road was full of bosses, actual or would-be. The only exception to this was Dr Beeching. To cross whom I would never dare, nor want.
>
> To begin with, he oppressed me vastly with his intellectual gianthood. In his presence I was tense, tongue tied and often plumb stupid. He was as relaxed as they come. When I went to see him, I was the one person he wanted to see; the subject I wanted to talk about was the only one in which he was interested; and he had all the time of in the world..... Old Man Mauldin [Fiennes's boss from before the war] and he are the only two people for whom I would gladly go back to work.

Beeching, said Fiennes, 'opened a lot more things, including minds to ideas, than he closed'.

He had a determination to cut through the bureaucratic formalities which had encrusted the railway. At one meeting he shouted, 'throw the damn thing out of the window!'[36] referring to the Grey Book, the organisational manual, so carefully written at Brian Robertson's direction. 'Chaps know what they are supposed to be doing – we don't need to have it all written down in a book.'

He brought in new people and new ideas, he initiated the research department in Derby, bringing in Dr Sydney Jones, and he gave prominence to management training; work study, for example. These were key to his strategy for reshaping the railway. So too, given his enthusiasm and drive, was direction from the centre.

Control from the centre was reinforced, with the laudable aim of reducing costs. By then functional heads were responsible for national negotiations on pay and conditions, finance and investment, determination of the size of the network, commercial policy, the purchase of certain stores and equipment, senior staff appointments, the design, procurement and allocation of rolling stock and track, control of the main workshop, and research and development.[37]

Much of this is unavoidable in a railway, but it was not handled well. Planning, for all its supposed prominence, had no coordinating mechanism and, says Gourvish, was 'chaotic and confusing'.[38]

Beeching brought in Philip Shirley as finance head – an Australian accountant on secondment from Unilever – and gave him freedom to slice through dozens of committees left over from the Commission and seek cost savings wherever he could: 'a bloody good finance manager' but 'an absolute menace'.

> He would have an idea about every three months, the previous idea would not be anywhere near completed by then, but he'd take everybody off that, and put them on to the new one, so nothing got done at all..... A great catalyst, a swash-buckling, cost-cutting, knocker-down of sacred cows.... but naive as to the complexities of business.[39]

John Elliot had described the Railway Executive as 'a series of prima donnas with no conductor in sight'. Beeching's board was not much better. There was no conductor – Shirley was a roving finance man, not the same thing – and Beeching, Fiennes wrote, 'was rightly and sublimely unconscious of day-to-day operating work'. He spent his time on his reports.

He was not, in fact, quite as unconscious as Fiennes suggests. He intervened on two occasions in the conduct of union negotiations – redundancy terms for those affected by the closure of workshops and the settling of an outstanding pay claim – to make sure there was peace on with the unions as he had 'bigger fish to fry'.

Beeching produced two reports: the first, the 'Reshaping Report', in March 1963, which is the one for which he is famous, and a second arguing for investment but only on a small number of high-density routes. This second was largely ignored.

Even after much cutting back in the previous ten years, the railway still sprawled across the country, smaller than at its peak in the 1930s but still vast, and much of it hardly used at all. The central problem, explained in the Report, was this: 'One half of the total route mileage carries about 4 per cent of the total passenger miles. Similarly, one half of the mileage carries about 5 per cent of the total freight ton miles of British Railways.' The financial cost of such a situation is obvious.

There were at the time about 4,300 passenger stations and 5,000 freight terminals, mostly alongside the passenger stations. Beeching's conclusion, obviously, was that much of this had to go. The 'Reshaping Report' called for the closure of about half the passenger stations (2,363 stations out of a total of 4,300).[40] Most but not all of these were eventually closed and since then some new ones have been opened. There are now about 2,500. As for track, passenger services were to be withdrawn from around 5,000 route miles, about one third of the total, and 70,000 jobs were to be shed over three years.

There are good arguments that some of the stations should never have been closed. British Rail was not averse to manipulating numbers to suit its case. Andrew Adonis, when he was a schoolboy, helped save Kingham station in the Cotswolds when he showed that the official passenger count understated real use. Certainly, the closures have left a most uneven distribution of smaller stations. Exeter has a main station and five small ones; Norwich, a town with twice the population, has one main station and no small ones. Adonis has argued for the reopening, as a first step, of 92 stations and their associated track.

Richard Faulkner and Chris Austin, in their book *Holding the Line*, argue that very many should never have been closed. They point to ten 'gaps in the network' of particular concern because of demographic changes and the growth in population in the corridors concerned. They are, just giving their names: The Borders; East–West; Dunstable; Didcot, Newbury and Southampton; March–Spalding; Tavistock; Lewis-Uckfield; Skipton–Colne; Stratford–Honeybourne/Cheltenham; and Matlock–Buxton.[41]

Doubtless, Adonis, Faulkner and Austin are right – my friend Chris Stokes is sceptical – but even if they are, it doesn't mean Beeching was wrong. If he was wrong about 300 stations, that still leaves 2,000 rightly closed. In Gordon Pettitt's words (and he was there), 'It is still not an acceptance that this guy was the saviour of the railway, he really was. Without him, confidence in the railway would have been shattered and we wouldn't have what we have today.'

More difficult was freight. The majority of revenue, 65 per cent, still came from freight and Beeching was clear in his view: 'without freight the main railway network could not exist.' He was facing the same conundrum every chairman faced. Freight lost money, but without it the railway would not exist. The challenge was to find a way to make freight pay. Like chairmen before and after, Beeching persuaded himself that he had done so. He allowed his talent for analysis and creative thinking to become the solution.

His proposal was the building of a nationwide network of container-carrying liner trains. Studies were made of the actual movement of freight, road and rail. From these, Beeching proposed a massive nationwide network connecting fifty-five locations. There would be liner-train corridors up the east and west of the country, but extending also to Aberdeen, Swansea, Brighton even, and Norwich.

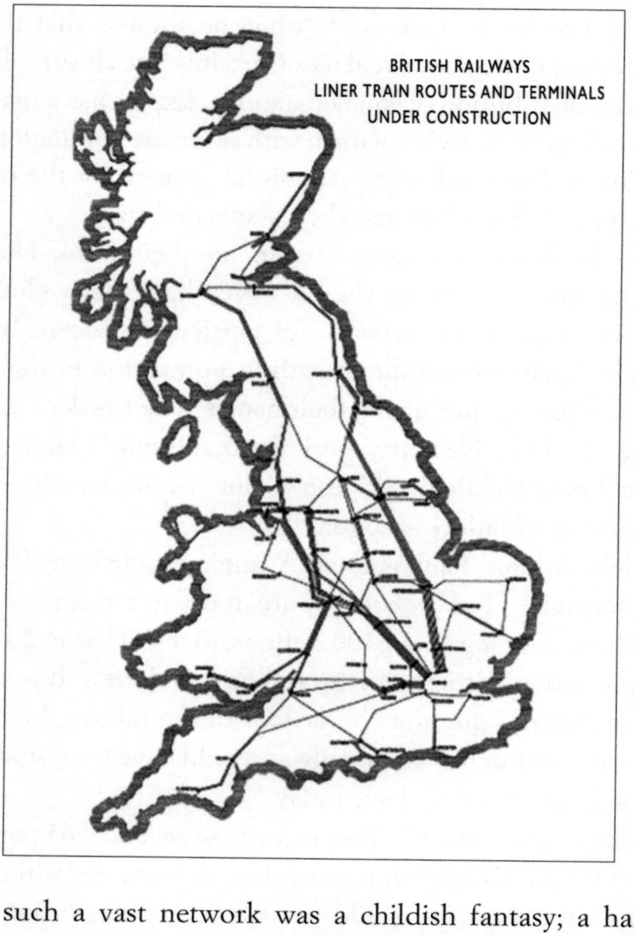

In truth, such a vast network was a childish fantasy; a harsh view perhaps, but it was never going to happen. There is a good business in container-carrying liner trains, but much more specialised than Beeching envisaged, carrying containers to and from ports. It is now called Freightliner. There is some business for inland containerised freight, but it is very small and the fifteen or so terminals once built were mostly closed. Beeching, however, believed in his plan. 'If the plan is implemented with vigour, much (though not necessarily all) of the railways deficit should be eliminated by 1970.'[42]

What is strange is that Beeching, for all his 'intellectual gianthood', gave no more consideration to the economics of road freight or to how it would develop than Robertson did. He studied the economics of rail freight but not of road freight.

The M1 had opened and other motorways were being built, but the word 'motorway' does not occur in either of his reports, nor was there any mention of the larger lorries which were appearing. In the early 60s, the maximum weight for an articulated vehicle was 24 tons, carrying a payload of about 15 tons. In 1964, while Beeching was working on his second report, the limit was raised to 32 tons, allowing a payload of about 20 tons. There would be further increases in permitted weight. It is now 44 tonnes, allowing an even greater payload.[43]

The clearest and most accurate explanation of the freight problem comes, as clarity so often did, from Gerard Fiennes.

> Between say 7 PM and 9 AM a lorry will run 250 miles with a load under constant supervision with ready communication with customers or employer, if anything goes wrong on the journey..... Between main centres for distances over 300 miles, liner trains are a clear winner; between 200 and 300 they have a significant advantage; below 150 miles road will continue to predominate.
>
> Except for distances upward of 300 miles – and in the UK, the land hauls over that distance are very few – road transport gives an entirely satisfactory service in safety, speed, reliability and convenience.

You might think that Fiennes would therefore be sceptical of Beeching's plans. On the contrary. 'Merry-go-round and liner trains were to be the two pillars positive and not negative on which the future of British Railways was to depend.'

Fiennes, for all his clarity of thought, was fundamentally mother-railway. Deep in his soul was the belief that mother-rail should be, had to be, a major carrier of freight. His job was to find ways to make this happen, which he was good at. He had no patience for the commercial side which was saying, 'the revolution in transport is so fast that plans must constantly change'.

But Freightliner terminals ran into two problems. They had to be as wide open for business as possible and had to allow access by private road hauliers. Jobs for railway delivery drivers were therefore at stake. The NUR dug in its toes and refused, for a time, to allow the terminals to operate – as Cyril Bleasdale will later describe.

More fundamentally, only customers with very special requirements had any interest in the service. In about 1966, Anton Buckoke, of whom we will hear more later, was sent to Plymouth as a sales representative for the freight business. This is what he remembers.

> Buckoke: Most of the time was spent saying, 'Well, this is the cost' and them saying, 'Well, thanks very much, I'll put it on a lorry.' The costs were ridiculous.
>
> : There was an attempt to make a new Freightliner service work, London to Plymouth, but it was never going to. We were trying to get freight off the road and into containers on the railway. But the goods would arrive in 40-foot lorries and we had 20-foot containers. There was a lot of two-way traffic on the road, from many different origins, very competitive. We couldn't compete.

Beeching's great network of liner trains never happened. What did were the specialised routes mainly to and from ports which became Freightliner. His plans for station closures did and were hugely controversial. Trade unions, the Labour opposition and the railway-using public all spoke up against them, but the facts were clear and it was in practice what happened.

The following two maps show the change, the first showing the network in 1963 and the second in 1984, twenty years later. There is a lot more white space in the latter.

THE ADVANCED PASSENGER TRAIN

Beeching brought in Dr Sydney Jones and he brought in Alan Wickens from the aircraft industry, a specialist in the stability of aeroplanes and missiles (as had been the Japanese technical genius behind the Shinkansen). Jones was successful in his first job at Derby research, solving the stability of two-axle freight wagons, which had been derailing with growing frequency. With that job done, he got bored.

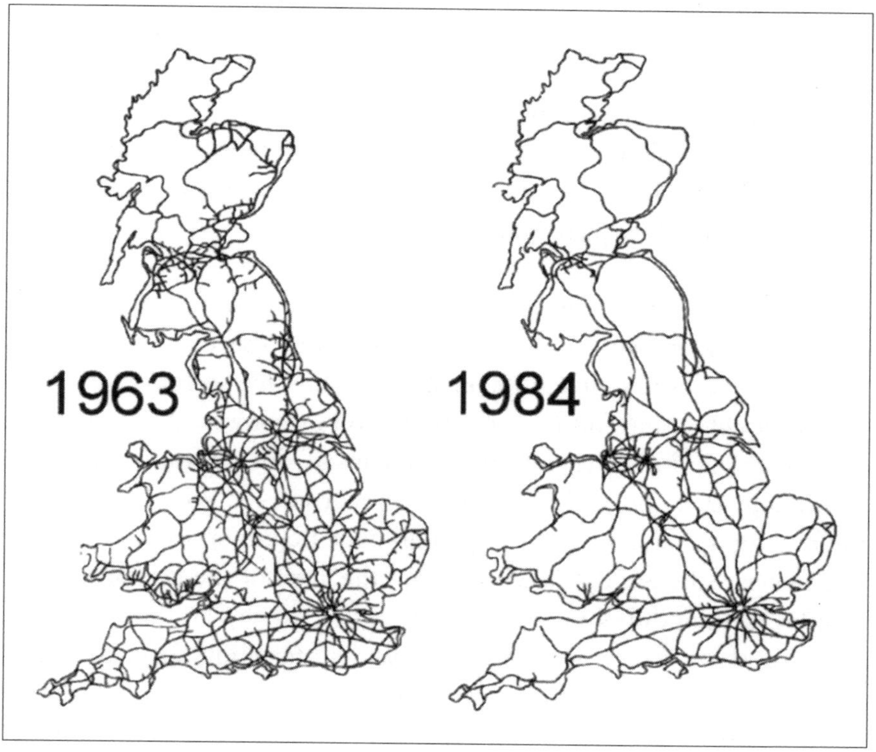

In his words, from a recorded interview some years ago:

In 1964, the first Shinkansen had opened and, also, the InterCity business was very forward-looking and had been increasing speeds and showing worthwhile improvements in revenue. There was a rule from that period that one mile an hour extra average

> speed is worth one percent more revenue. The introduction of the Deltics on the East Coast Main Line and the speeding up of services demonstrated this.
>
> So I said to Sydney Jones, 'I think we are flogging a dead horse looking at pallet vans and such like. We ought to be more adventurous and forward looking. I think we should be doing something on a high-speed passenger vehicle.'
>
> I think it was in November 1966 that I put forward a two-page proposal for a high-speed passenger research vehicle. It was to be a two-axle vehicle. It was going to be of light weight construction and was to have body tilt. It was soon pointed out that a single vehicle could not solve any of the interface problems; what was needed was a complete train.
>
> All this took time, but by 1969 Sydney Jones was able to persuade the Government to fund half of a programme to develop the Advance Passenger Train.[44]

So began the programme to develop a 140mph tilting train for British Railways. But almost everything about the plan was wrong, misconceived or undeliverable on any realistic time scale.

A complete train, running at 140mph, on existing track (Japan built new track) and able to tilt (the Shinkansen does not tilt) required technology to be pushed forward on every front, each one a challenge: the braking system, the in-cab signalling, the bogies (a two-axle vehicle was never realistic), the power system, the shell of the carriages. And besides, Britain did not need 140mph.

But perhaps its very wrong-ness was its attraction. It encouraged research in Derby on such a wide front that it became a leading centre in the world for rail technology, and made possible future developments of more conventionally conceived rolling stock.

FIENNES, BLEASDALE AND RAYMOND

Liner trains, Merry-Go-Round and much else had been keeping Fiennes away from what he liked most: running trains.

One day in October 1963, Fiennes was summoned by the Doctor

and given the job of his dreams, General Manager of the Great Western Region. He loved it; he was in his element. He got good people around him, he directed and encouraged; he knew where revenue could be generated and where costs could be saved. He welcomed the arrival of diesel trains and their extra speed taking businessmen to London, and he talked punctuality wherever he went. He fought to keep open lines threatened with closure and found ways to run them at lower cost.

Anton Buckoke again.

> Buckoke: Fiennes, he was a magnificent manager. No doubt about it. Respected by everybody from the top to the bottom. What did he look like? He was big, very straight, stood up straight. Strong features. He came from an old English family, the same family as the actor. I don't know how to describe him. He was a powerful person, he had a presence.

Fiennes was not at all blind to the finances of his region. Quite the opposite. Three regions of British Rail were in surplus and three making losses, one of them being the Western. He was determined to put that right. He writes:

> I have a simple philosophy about losses on railways. A railway which serves large cities lying between 50 and 300 miles apart; which has a coalfield; which has a large steel industry; which has no more than an average proportion of green fields; such a railway has no business to make a loss. If it does, then no one but the management is at fault.
>
> It remained for me to attack the tradition of the Great Western to employ three men where the LNER would have employed two, to use two parallel railways where one would do, and so on..... It became obvious that within a year or two we could carry with a staff of 40,000 the same traffic as had been carried a few years earlier with 92,000.

He presents a table in his book. It shows how cost and revenue stack up in each region. It shows costs as a percentage of revenue: low figures good, high figures bad. At that time the accounting system allowed regions to keep any revenue they collected; it was not allocated to any other region which might be required to carry the traffic, often the case with freight. Nonetheless, subject to that, general managers were well aware of costs and revenue and sought to reduce the former and increase the latter.

Operating ratio of each Region

(Costs as a percentage of revenue)

Region	1957	1966
North Eastern	89%	94%
London Midland	100%	134%
Eastern	101%	90%
Southern	108%	96%
Western	124%	108%
Scottish	126%	126%
Average	108%	108%

Source: Fiennes

Fiennes left the Western sooner than he had wanted, in 1966. He had improved the operating ratio from 124 per cent to 108 per cent, and it was heading towards break even. Break-even mattered to him. 'It is the greatest single disappointment in my life that I am not at Paddington to lead the greatest celebration of all time on the occasion when they restored the Great Western's tradition of earning an honest dividend.'

Good things were happening elsewhere. The first stage of the electrification of the West Coast Main Line, from London up to Manchester/Liverpool, was completed in April 1966. With its speed and comfort, the effect on passenger numbers was dramatic: 'the sparks effect'.

At the same time, the locomotive Gerard Fiennes had wanted, the Deltic, was transforming travel on the East Coast Main Line.

InterCity was born, the brand name for fast, comfortable trains on the main intercity routes.

While Gerard Fiennes was at Great Western, Cyril Bleasdale was not so far away, with a very different job; or; at least in the first instance, not a job at all. He had been designated to be the first manager of Freightliner in the country, at the new Freightliner terminal on York Way, near Camden. As he explains.

Cyril: Freightliner had a very slow start because of union opposition. The union wanted a guard on the train so, eventually, they created a caboose for this guard to travel in. But the guards, after a few trips getting thrown around in this thing, decided that it was the most uncomfortable journey you could possibly make. Sitting in the back cab of the loco was better.

: But the biggest problem was the open terminal. Private road hauliers were to have access to bring their container into the terminal. But the railway unions said, 'No, that's the work of the railway collection and delivery drivers.' It goes back to when we had horses and three-wheelers. This went on for a couple of years before it was resolved. Open terminals were permitted on condition that British Rail also offered collection and delivery with its own vehicles. In the meantime, I had nothing to do.

: Just down the road was Camden freight terminal and there was a vacancy there for the manager, but nobody wanted it: 'They're always going on strike, it's a nightmare.' The stories… people used to laugh at the stories. It was run by communists, a chap called Jack Nicholson, who was a big man in the London rent riots at that time, a Scot, and a very effective, articulate man. Committed communist, you wouldn't change his views. The job, a poisoned chalice. The other chap, the manager who retired, was so scared, he never left his office. Used to go off to meet customers at 11 o'clock and come back, well, having had a lot to drink at three.

: The Divisional Manager asked me to take the job. I wasn't sure. But he said, 'The General Manager is very concerned about Camden, because of Jack Nicholson. It's become *Evening Standard* stuff and political, and he wants to see you.' I went to see him. It was Henry Johnson, went on to become chairman. He asked why I didn't want the job. I said, 'I think, possibly, I'm not the right person.' 'Why?' 'Well, you know, the previous man always wore a bowler and I don't even wear a hat!' I was persuaded and off I went to Camden.

: When I arrived, the chief foreman came to see me – most of his time seemed be taken up with union meetings – and we walked around the depot together. There were so many people – 'What do they do, what do they do?' There was no mechanisation at all, everything was hand barrows. I was quite shocked. I hadn't realised that they were still barrowing big lumps of stuff, unloading the wagons, putting it on the bay and then loading the trucks. Of course, it was all about the bonus scheme. The bonus scheme was rife for disputes; it was one power the unions had. So I was faced with a lot of disputes, but I coped. I walked round, met the staff, got to know them. Had a good rapport with one union man, used to have a quiet drink together and he'd tell me what was going on.

: I had a girlfriend; if we'd been out somewhere, I'd take her home in the early hours of the morning – I was young, you don't think about it – and at 3 o'clock in the morning I'd go down to the depot and see how it was getting on.

: One day, they decided to go on strike. I had managed to avoid strikes for ages, but I wanted some big changes and they were going to strike. They demanded to have a meeting for both the night staff who would stay on and the day staff. I said 'You can have the meeting, and I will not deduct pay, but there is one condition, that I address the meeting.' 'Are you sure?' they said. 'The last manager who tried that got howled down and pushed off the platform.'

: I addressed the meeting. I do not know what I said, it is so long ago, but I remember how I finished. 'If you support this change, and it is a big change, you will not be worse off. And I will make you one promise: when all the other terminals in London are closed, Camden will still be open. That is the way we will run it. Camden will remain, you will have your jobs. Let the others close if they want to keep fighting. That's the deal.'

: It was put to the vote and I won by a tiny handful. The Divisional Manager could hardly believe it: 'My God, that's the first time we've ever won!' We changed lots of things, people had to work for the bonus. But traffic all around was falling away, just falling away.

:And my promise: all the other London terminals closed, Camden was the last. It's housing now; my office is still there, a house, and it's got the LMS notice, 1933, on it – rather funny really.

Cyril went on to do other things, leaving Camden in January 1967. It would be easy to express surprise at wheelbarrows and bonus fiddling but investing in modern equipment would probably not have made sense. The market was moving away from rail and the investment would never have been recovered. Shrinking a business is difficult.

Beeching had been appointed under a Conservative government. When Harold Wilson became Prime Minister after the 1964 election, he was initially kept on, but Labour politicians, inherently pro-rail, were out of sympathy. He was, it is said, fired – he was certainly asked to leave – and he rejoined ICI at the end of 1965.

His place was taken by Stanley Raymond. Raymond was a feisty, long-term railwayman, the first railwayman to chair it for a long time. It was he who asked Fiennes to leave Great Western in 1966 to become general manager of the Eastern Region and organise its merger with the North-East Region. The headquarters of the combined region was to be in York. Fiennes hated reorganisations. 'When you reorganise you bleed' is his famous remark.

SIR STANLEY RAYMOND

Born **1914**. Orphaned. Hampton Grammar School.

1931. Tax clerk in the Inland Revenue. Joined London Transport. Joined British Rail.

1957. Chief Commercial Manager for Scotland.

1960. Traffic adviser to Brian Robertson and then Dr Beeching.

1962. General manager of the Western Region which, as Gerard Fiennes explains, he shook up to good effect.

1965. Board chairman.

1967. Resigned. After British Rail, chair of the Gaming Commission.

Died **1987**.

What he hated even more was the stream of nit-picking directions from Raymond's board. Raymond loved too much the nitty-gritty of railway management.

Raymond had preceded Fiennes at Great Western. 'He had gone like a destroying wind through the traditional practices of the Great Western,' wrote Fiennes, and had a 'vast capacity for do-it-myself'. And that was the problem. His heart was in the rough and tumble of the front line, the ordering and cajoling and camaraderie and visibility of results. In the higher role, he did what he should not, and left undone that which he should.

Fiennes gave his people something to manage and an incentive to do it well, and let them get on with it. That was not Raymond's style. 'The BRB have laid it down', or 'It is the BRB's wish', or worse, 'It is not the BRB's wish' were the missives arriving weekly from headquarters. Fiennes resented them most deeply and began writing his book. The missives were bad enough but there was worse, he wrote:

> Among the subjects reserved to the centre, many were not going well. Diesel locomotives, electric locomotives, electric multiple units, wagons, the liner trains, cranes for liner trains, all in trouble, some of it deep trouble. The workshops authority was

> badly behind schedule in overhauls and badly over its target for costs. The staff boys have so far failed to secure an agreement on the open terminal for liner trains, or to enforce the year-old agreement on single manning of locomotives; or to produce the promised scheme for incentives on short distance freight trains. The commercial and operating people have produced no new major ideas since liner trains, merry-go-round, and the oil agreement of about five years before.

Fiennes was fired in September 1967. Extracts from his book, from which the paragraph above is taken, had been distributed to the press in advance of its publication. The papers lapped it up. 'Rail chief accuses his board' (*Sun*); 'Board shocked by finance criticisms' (*Daily Telegraph*); 'I don't take it back, says sacked rail chief' (*Daily Express*).

In September 1967 he left the railway. It was time to retire and he said he was happy to do so. His was the railway of the hands-on manager, the all-rounder, a railway where managers were able to bounce a derailed freight wagon back onto the track, and that railway had come to an end.

Stanley Raymond and Barbara Castle, smiling but not convinced (Alamy)

8 THE BARBARA CASTLE TRANSITION (1966–68)

With Wilson winning the 1964 election, Marples had to leave. His place was first taken by Tom King and then, in December 1965, by Barbara Castle. She brought a clarity of mind to transport matters and to her we owe many things.

She was appalled at the number of deaths on the roads: 'Hitler did not manage to kill as many civilians as have been killed on Britain's roads since the war.' She introduced the breathalyser and seat belts and made permanent the 70mph speed limit. And we owe her the first serious attempt to address railway problems.

We also owe her someone who would become a future chief executive of British Rail: John Welsby. We will hear more about him later, but in his words:

> Welsby: She was absolutely fed up with classic civil servants, they were standing in her way. She was a rather fiery lady and determined. She brought in two economists to leaven things up and guess who they were: my tutor from the London School of Economics, Michael Beasley, and my external examiner from Oxford, Sir Christopher Foster. They set up an economics outfit in the Ministry of Transport and I was invited to become a part.

With strong views of her own she got on no better with Stanley Raymond than did Gerard Fiennes. She was a moderniser, while he was steeped in the old ways and convinced of his ability to run the railway without the dubious help of the Ministry.

At the heart of government policy there remained the search for the 'profitable railway'. Despite it being deeply unpopular, she continued to support the closure of railway stations until, in a carefully thought-through presentation, Raymond persuaded her that the closure programme should be scaled back. It would not solve the railway's financial problem. He did not, however, persuade her that he knew what would.

There had in previous years been many attempts to improve the operation of the railway. 'At lower levels, changes in organisation between 1953 and 1970s were almost continuous. Sir Reginald Wilson inaugurated the 'Lines' within the Eastern Region, based essentially on traffic flows as constituting good business and management units. The concept spread to other regions; but the pendulum swung back and later the Lines were replaced by geographical divisions.'[45] Despite the experimentation, the changes failed to deliver fundamental improvements in efficiency.

The government stood back to consider and review the matter. Christopher Foster, Barbara Castle's adviser, noted at the conclusion of the exercise:

> The main outcome of the review was that the loss-making social services should be subsidised explicitly but that even if the government subsidised all the so-called social services, the railway would still make a loss. BR was less efficient in its use of people and assets than other railways. Administrative overheads were exceptionally high. It was a mammoth management task to turn it round..... The enquiry had shown up the painful inadequacy and lack of management skill and initiative of most of the BR top team.[46]

With that conclusion, Raymond's days were numbered. He was hustled out, complaining loudly, at the end of 1967. It was Foster's view that Beeching was partly to blame. By placing so much attention on station closure, he had obscured the bigger issue, that the whole railway was unprofitable and badly run.[47]

Much thought went into what would become the 1968 Transport Act. Barbara Castle left in April 1968 to go to the Department for Employment and Productivity, with her place taken by Richard Marsh, but what went into this Act was down to her.

As a first step there should be explicit acknowledgement of the cost of services that are both 'unremunerative and desirable for social or economic reasons'. These were to be supported by a grant. Richard Marsh, when Minister of Transport, listed the routes to be supported and the grant in respect of each according to a formula by the accountants Cooper Bros. The total paid in the first year would be £62 million. In reality, this did not go far enough. Other parts of the railway – late-evening trains for example, and much more – are desirable but uneconomic; but it was a start. A few years later, the 1974 Railways Act made provision for more comprehensive support, reflecting the European concept of the Public Service Obligation (PSO).

Also under the Act, the engineering workshops were transferred into a separate subsidiary. Thus British Rail Engineering Ltd (BREL) came into existence.

The need for a national ttansport plan was a central tenet of the Labour Party, but it never emerged. Someone given the job of producing one delivered only a few pages and wrote laconically but truthfully, 'there is little advice that I can usefully give'.[48] Castle settled on regional transport plans and set up five Passenger Transport Authorities to coordinate and operate public transport.

It was decided that any freight on the railway other than trainload would be better handled by an expanded and renamed National Freight Corporation (NFC) to which British Rail's Freightliner business was transferred, with British Rail retaining 49 per cent, as was British Rail's sundries business which by then made no sense at all. It was the business which had required two or three hundred men in the Station Hall in York, managed by Bob Reid in the 1950s. The NFC soon moved it onto road.

A further change to emerge concerned the working of the Board. Coordination and oversight was impossible so long as members had functional responsibilities. This had to change. The Board should stand back and hold those running the railway to account. It should become a 'planning board' and put the running of the business into the hands of an executive committee sitting below it with, for the first time, a chief executive.

The executive committee operated on an interim basis from February 1968 and was later formalised with the name of The Railway Management Group. According to Gourvish, 'The new organisation of 1970 was an advance on past practice in its enthusiasm for corporate planning, management by objective and the setting and monitoring of detailed business plans. The new executive management structure promised more effective control of the business from the centre.'[49]

In reality, it was not quite the planning board that had been intended. There were functional heads on it, though not the chief executive Bowick, but that was so that he could be paid a larger salary. And management, said Richard Goldson, by then Bowick's PA, was pretty seat-of-the-pants. Reams of computer printout, with those long, pale blue lines across it, would be delivered purporting to be management information, but it was not very helpful and largely ignored.

Besides, history demonstrates two things. First, at a high level, only the government can plan the railway. A planning board, however admirable and distinguished its members, even the grandly titled Strategic Rail Authority formed years later, is essentially a talking shop, a useful buffer. Second, a well-run railway is not achieved by 'more effective control of the business from the centre' – quite the opposite. It is what Raymond sought to do, and Marsh and Bowick through the Field Organisation as well. It is a most tempting conceit but fails in the face of the vast complexity and variety of the railway. Still, it is better than being badly run from the centre.

With Raymond on the way out, it would be the job of the next chairman to put the planning board and Railway Management Group into effect.

The task of finding such a person was not easy. Barbara Castle wanted Peter Parker. He was that rare thing, a left-wing 'businessman'. But Parker refused the salary offered, arguing, quite fairly, that it would put a ceiling on his ability to bring in good people and thus put him in a weak position from the start. At Parker's suggestion, Barbara Castle fastened instead on Henry Johnson, another long-time railwayman, who was duly appointed chairman in January 168.

SIR HENRY JOHNSON, KBE

Born **1906**. Educated at a private school, Bedford Modern School.

1923. Joined LNER as a traffic apprentice.

1962 – 1967 General manager of the London Midland Region where he got some order put into what had been the unsatisfactory programme for the first main line electrification, Euston to Manchester/Liverpool (completed 1966).

1968–71. Chairman of British Railways Board. Established the British Rail Property Board.

After British Rail, chairman of MEPC and other board positions.

Died **1988**

No. 55 January 1968 3d

LONDON MIDLAND

Rail News

The Newspaper of British Rail

All the signs show it'll be –

BR's YEAR OF DESTINY

45-year railman is chief

At the top . . . Mr H. C. Johnson

- *'Bill' Johnson speaks to Rail News –Page Seven*
- *Big re-think on rail jobs begins –Page Four*
- *Transport Bill summary –Page Seven*

RAIL NEWS REPORTER

IT'S GOING TO BE A MOMENTOUS YEAR FOR THE RAILWAYS. AND FOR ALL WHO WORK ON THEM. THE SIGNS SHOW IT. EVERYONE PREDICTS IT.

JUST LOOK AT SOME OF THE FACTS. GOING BEFORE PARLIAMENT ARE SOME OF THE MOST CONTROVERSIAL AND FAR-REACHING PROPOSALS EVER PUT FORWARD FOR THE TRANSPORT INDUSTRY.

They sweep away the morale-sapping burden of BR's multi-million deficit. They plan a full-scale reorganisation of passenger services in the densely built-up areas and a nationally integrated freight corporation

EVOLUTION OF THE RAILWAY ORGANISATION

1. Under the Big Four

Departmental under a general manager. Four departments (passenger, freight, civil engineering, and mechanical & electrical), each operating independently and reporting to the general manager. Limited coordination at intermediate levels.

2. Under Hurcomb and the Railway Executive

Highly functional/silo: the regional department heads reported up to functional heads in the Executive with little authority lying with the regional general managers, who hated the arrangement.

3. Under Robertson and the Commission, after absorbing the Executive

Re-established the authority of the regional general managers but with the department heads joint-reporting up to the Commission. No single person at the Commission controlling and directing the whole.

4. Under Beeching, under the British Railways Board

As above, plus financial analysis and work study, etc. Still no single person in overall control.

5. Under Johnson/Bowick

For the first time, a chief executive and management board. Below the Board, three levels: Region, Division, Area (newly created to absorb the ancient districts). Much greater coordination and focus.

6. Under Reid/Parker

Phase 1 (1982): Sectors – Control passed to sector directors heading the five market sectors (three Passenger, one Freight, one Parcels). Delivery remaining with the general managers and the Regions. The middle layer – the Division – soon removed.

Phase 2 (1986): Sub-sectors – Substantial control passed to the sub-sectors of each sector. Delivery remaining with the general managers and below them, the Areas.

Phase 3 (1992): OfQ – Both control and delivery passed to the sub-sectors, renamed profit centres.

BARBARA CASTLE'S TRANSPORT ACT 1968

(Extracts, highly truncated)

1. There shall be constituted a public authority to be called the National Freight Corporation to provide properly integrated services for the carriage of goods within Great Britain by road and rail.

5. The Railways Board shall separate into separate companies those parts concerned with the carriage of freightliner containers, and the carriage of rail sundries; and the collection and delivery of goods by road. There shall be transferred to the Freight Corporation fifty-one per cent. of the securities of the freightliner company and all the securities of freight sundries company.

9. The Minister may, for the purpose of securing a properly integrated and efficient system of public passenger transport, designate an area for the establishment of (a) a Passenger Transport Authority, and (b) a Passenger Transport Executive.

39. If, in the case of any railway passenger services provided by the Railways Board, the Minister is satisfied that those services are unremunerative ; and that it is desirable for social or economic reasons that such services continue to be provided; and that because of the unremunerative nature of the services the Board cannot reasonably be expected to provide them without assistance, then, the Minister may undertake to make grants to the Board in respect of such services.

41. It shall be the duty of the Board to perform its functions as to secure that its revenues are not less than sufficient to meet the charges properly chargeable to revenue account, taking one year with another.

45. The Railways Board shall undertake a review to determine whether the carrying on of its activities is organised in the most efficient manner. [This led to a dead end, The Field Organisation.]

Sir Henry, 'call-me-Bill', Johnson. Things got done
(Science & Society Picture Library)

9 THE JOHNSON/BOWICK PERIOD (1968–79)

MODERNISING THE RAILWAY

At last, under the chairmanship of Sir Henry Johnson – 'call me Bill,' he would say – an effective system of management was put in place. With it came a great deal of improvement. Things got done.

The reforms were picked up in a most interesting article in *The Times* in April 1969, headed 'New top-level board for British Rail in big shake-up'. They were the changes Johnson was putting in place.

> A new high-powered executive board will be established at British Rail's London headquarters with direct control through line management on a functional basis of divisional and local managers.
>
> Heading the board will be a new chief executive answerable to the main board for the entire system.
>
> Centralised control will give more decisive management and clearer lines of communication compared with the cumbersome and often woolly committee system that has ruled till the present.

W.G. Thorpe would be the first chief executive. He would be followed briefly by Wilson and then by David Bowick from July 1971 who would remain in charge for some years, until he retired to Malta and Ian Campbell took over. The next ten years are therefore the Johnson/Bowick period.

The top board, having passed the day-to-day job of running the railway to an executive board, became or was supposed to become a planning board, essentially a holding company with several self-accounting subsidiaries: hotels, hovercraft, shipping, Freightliner (in a joint venture with the National Freight Corporation), and workshops, land and estates.

AREA MANAGEMENT

Along with the change at the top was one at the bottom: the formation of Areas to replace the old Districts. Richard Goldson, whose training had earlier been overseen by Bob Reid, describes the change with some gusto.

> Goldson: Up until the advent of Area Management, the first duty at ground level was to carry on doing what you were doing. There was no managerial capacity for change; it was all about managing stability. When I say stability, I mean rigid, really rigid.
> : Throughout the 60s, every station, literally almost every station, had a stationmaster; if there was freight, a yardmaster and goods agent; if there was a motor power depot, a shed master; and they were, moderately, kings in their own castle. They had no incentive to change anything or to cooperate, just to carry on doing what they'd always done. There were manuals for everything. The objective was to comply with as many manuals as you conceivably could.
> : There was an expression, 'management by clerk'. What that meant was that the senior clerical grades effectively ran the railway by means of the thousands of written memoranda they produced. Everything was by memorandum. An awful lot of managers sat in their office and did nothing and left it to their clerks. It was a very strong ethos, right through the railway.
> : When Area Management came in in the late 60s or early 70s, it got rid at a stroke of all the stationmasters, yardmasters, goods agents, etc. – they were given 'special duties' somewhere else.

Area managers were appointed to be agents of change. They were to pull together within their hands the levers that most directly controlled the train service. That did not include the civil engineers looking after the track and permanent way who reported up to the regional head office, as did S&T. But the new managers needed proper control of drivers and rolling stock and had to dismantle the Motive Power Departments.

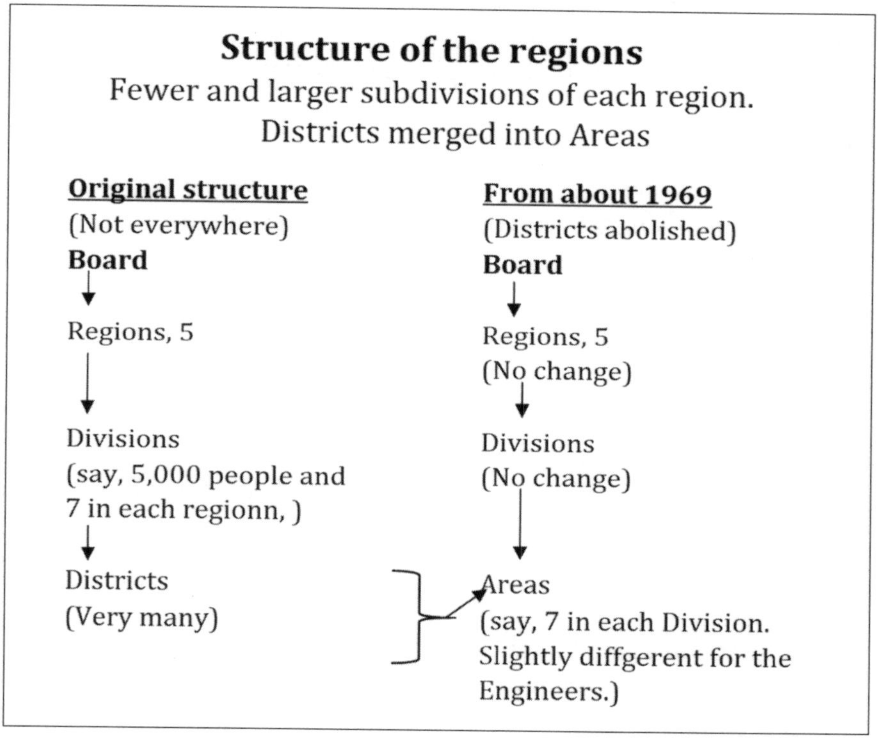

Goldson: At first the areas were quite small so there might have been only six or seven stations under an Area manager, but in the Leeds division of Eastern, as soon as they were first formed, they started being rationalised because there wasn't as much to do as had been thought.

: There was Scarborough, York, Leeds, Huddersfield, Northern, Bradford and Knottingley, where I was. That's seven. Some of these had diesel depots, motor power depots, S&T and M&EE.

: Area management undoubtedly brought the capacity and an incentive for operational efficiency, even for cutting staff numbers, though you were still graded according to the number of staff you had. There was management by objectives, and things like that, and work study.

> : That was one of the many good things Beeching brought in. The Grove became the training centre for work study and trained people in huge numbers over the years: a really good management tool, it rippled out across the railway till about the mid-70s. It forced into peoples' minds the idea that efficiency mattered.

There was certainly a lot to do: 'Mark 1's, regional enamels, gas lighting, fingerboards, semaphores and vacuum brakes were everywhere..... And working practices had evolved little from steam days.'[50]

John Nelson, in his book *Losing Track*, describes the jobs he was given as a young manager in the early 1970s and explains that railway management had become 'alive to commercial forces and concern to react to them'.[51]

If the Beeching period is characterised by station closures plus new ideas, the Johnson/Bowick period is one when things got done. Johnson's first two or three years were a little golden age. Sir Henry Johnson was one of those people on whose quiet watch sensible things got done.

For a start, in 1971 Johnson was able to declare a profit. Modest railway losses, mitigated by the grant for uneconomic lines, were more than covered by property profits.

This is from *The Times* in May 1971 under the headline, 'Terminal for Sir Henry after a good run':

> Most of these reforms, it is true, were given to Sir Henry.... rather than originated by him. Nevertheless, to him belongs credit for practical implementation of changes that have transformed BR from the government's biggest transport headache to one of the most effective, nationalised industries, in several respects world leader in its field.
>
> The railway Sir Henry will be handing over to Mr Richard Marsh in September will be in much better fettle than the one he took over.

And this from *The Times* in March 1972:

Richard Marsh. Most at home with a mic (Alamy)

> The past few years have seen a remarkable resurgence in the fortunes of British Rail's passenger business. Revenue has increased by 42% from 1968 to 1971 with volume rising from 17,700 billion passenger miles to 18,900 and an increase in market share of 1% every year.

But there were good reasons for the complimentary references in the Times. Bowick's executive board was grinding through the work. First was the completion of the InterCity network, a dramatic, exciting moment. Two great projects were involved, both given the go-ahead under Bill Johnson in 1970: first, the electrification of the northern half of the West Coast Main Line up to Glasgow and second, in parallel, the development of the finest diesel train ever built, the HST, for use on the Great Western and East Coast Main Lines.

It was not just the speed of the trains but the comfort of the coaches, indeed the entire experience led to its great success.

The huge significance of InterCity is shown in the chart. Its revenue grew by 50 per cent from 1967 to 1979 while revenue elsewhere remained largely flat.

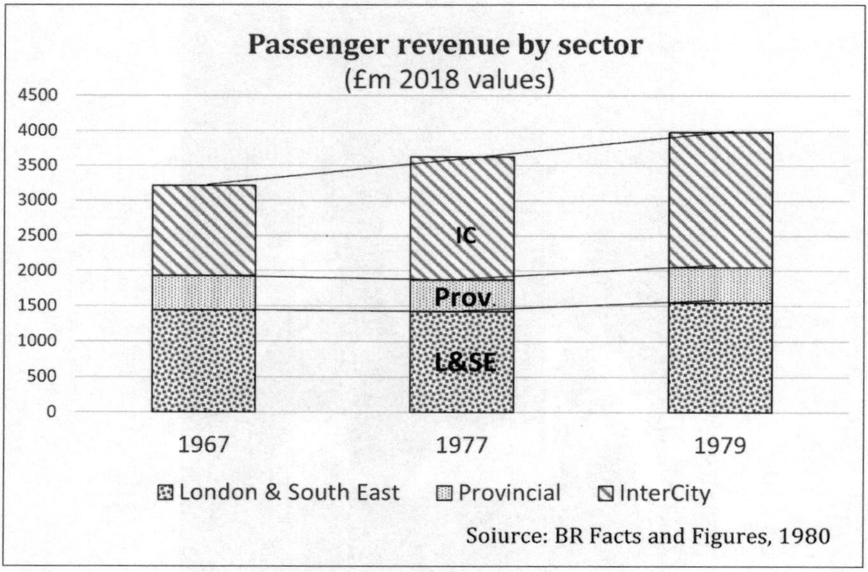

Passenger revenue by sector, £m, (2018 values)

	1967	1977	1979	Change
London & South East	1,441	1,421	1,546	7%
Provincial	487	452	502	3%
InterCity	1,287	1,749	1,928	50%
TOTAL	3,216	3,623	3,976	24%

Source: BR Facts and Figures, 1980

Bill Johnson's profits could not be sustained and Richard Marsh, the next chairman, ran into another bout of abuse and disparagement from politicians with yet another report contemplating a halving of the railway's size. Marsh, laughably described in his autobiography, devoted his time to the persuasion of the Treasury to increase investment in the railway. A great paper was prepared proving that Britain would then be better off. The Treasury could find no fault with the paper, Marsh says, but of new money, there was, of course, none.

10 RAILWAY DETAILS

INDUSTRIAL RELATIONS

If the railway had been a normal private company, it would have declared bankruptcy long before, laid everyone off, and started anew, but it could not. It had to work through within itself the vast changes in technology and working practices taking place.

In this, 1968 was a turning point in industrial relations. Till then there were disputes and occasionally strikes but with a degree of rationality as to how they were handled. After 1968, the mood darkened.

The story of ASLEF is well told in the most excellent book *Driven by Ideals: A History of ASLEF* by Robert Griffiths, published on the 125th anniversary of its founding in 2005. As the railway emerged from the war, it was socialism that union members thought would deliver a better world. ASLEF routinely passed resolutions aligning itself more with the Soviet camp than with the West, proclaiming solidarity with the peoples of Russia, Yugoslavia, etc., supporting communists in the electricians' trade union, denouncing Germany's proposed membership of NATO, deploring the bloodshed in Biafra, the war in Vietnam and the Soviet-led intervention in Czechoslovakia – a disillusioning experience – which demonstrated that 'the grim game of power politics still goes on in Europe'.[52]

There were, however, more immediate concerns: jobs and pay. Employment figures are stark. By 1968, half the posts had disappeared and another half would go in later years.

In the 1960s, the change from steam to diesel and the closure of stations cut a huge number of jobs. In the 1970s, the winding down of wagonload freight and the closure of marshalling yards and freight terminals and the change from small signal boxes to great power boxes cut more. There was little union resistance, pay was poor and there were reasonable redundancy terms.

It could however be sad for those who stayed. The second man on the footplate might wait years for promotion only to be knocked back as

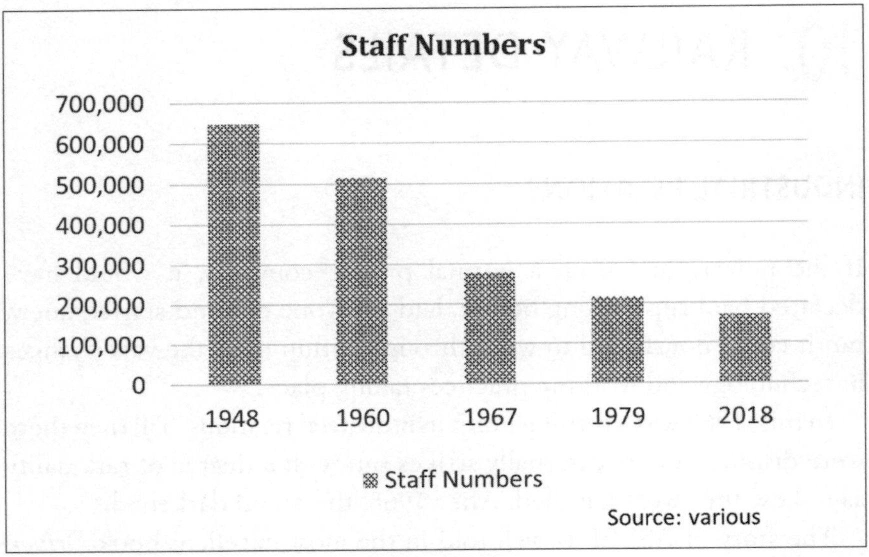

incoming drivers with greater seniority transferred from other depots that had closed down. The Guillebaud Report of 1960 confirmed the poor pay: pay was 8 per cent less than with comparable jobs elsewhere; for drivers it was 13 per cent less with 'generally unsatisfactory and frequently inferior facilities and amenities'.

The objectives of the unions – ASLEF, NUR and TSSA – were quite rational. First, preserve jobs, most obviously by holding on to traditional, labour-intensive ways of working, with elaborate stratagems for padding out the working day and resisting change. Any proposition affecting more than one station had to go to the sectional council, which met infrequently and was a great, most effective, blockage to any change.

Second, for ASLEF, hunker down and defend the footplate promotion ladder – it led to the best-paid jobs in the railway, defined in the Promotion Transfer and Redundancy Agreement – and fight to defend the spirit and traditions of the union. It was a craft union, a guild, a proud brotherhood of skilled people would decide for themselves how they would do their work. It had a spirit and soul greater than the people in it.

As *omerta* is to the Mafia, so is loyalty to ASLEF during a strike, with ostracism – being sent to Coventry – as the bloodless, but terrible punishment for those who break the code. In the book, it is never 'ASLEF' – this is not sufficiently respectful – but always 'the Society'. The Society does this, the Society does that. And the title of the book, *Driven by Ideals*, makes the point. Its general secretary, with respectful humour, is called 'the General' who, on taking office, 'dons the mantle'. People speak their minds in the meetings. The general must be a 'tough negotiator', be willing to use militant action when necessary – his determination must honour the struggles of those who came before – and he must be 'shrewd'.

No good comes from chaos. The General in 1970: 'History will show that our policy and actions in the last two years.... played a decisive part in preventing industrial relations from degenerating into shambles.' He must take care to husband ASLEF's influence and not share it too readily with its boisterous neighbour, the NUR, which should be kept at arm's length.

Third, negotiate pay rises, but generally without aspiring to do more than keep pace with inflation.

A few instances will illustrate the points of contention which would recur, year after year. They are taken straight from the ASLEF history book.

IN THE EARLY DAYS

1947. The working week is reduced from forty-eight hours to forty-four.

DURING THE ROBERTSON PERIOD

1955: The differentials dispute. In response to an NUR pay claim, the Commission, recognising the poor pay of those on lower wages, conceded advances of from 9 per cent for the lowest paid to 1 per cent for top-rate drivers. ASLEF rejected the offer, wage differentials being sacrosanct, and called a strike. It had to be suspended for further negotiation as it had been called just weeks before a general election. Negotiations to reach an agreement failed, Anthony Eden won the election, and the strike was back on. Britain's railways came to a halt, though some trains were able to run because a quarter of footplate staff were members of the NUR, which did not support the strike. The strike was long, seventeen days before agreement was reached, one of the longest in railway history. Brian Robertson remembered it as the worst time in his chairmanship.[53] Those few ASLEF members who refused to join 'became pariahs on the footplate and in the mess rooms. Many were not spoken to – or acknowledged – by their colleagues until the day they left the industry, which in some cases meant a period of 40 years.'

The flinty determination of ASLEF to defend its position was quite clear, even at the cost of damaging the Labour Party's chances in an election. The government considered changing the law to impose the now familiar pre-strike ballots, cooling-off periods and the banning of unofficial strikes. Fearing confrontation, ministers settled instead for an assurance from the TUC that it would encourage voluntary cooling-off periods: 'voluntarism'.

Similar proposals for legislation were made by Barbara Castle in 1968, dropped by Wilson, implemented by Heath in 1971 in a reckless manner and then abandoned, and finally introduced into law in 1982 by Norman Tebbit, where they have remained.

Spring 1956: The machinery of negotiation. Agreement was reached to revise the machinery into a form which would last for many years. The first stage was the Railway Staff Joint Council, with four autonomous sections, intended to resolve problems through negotiation. Next, the Railway Staff National Council. Finally, if no agreement, the Railway Staff National Tribunal. Its decisions were not binding but the machinery had to be exhausted before any party could take a grievance to an outside body such as an arbitrator or government minister. Later, the Board would propose that the decisions of the Rail Staff National Tribunal be made binding, but neither ASLEF nor the NUR agreed.

December 1957: Single-manning. The decommissioning of steam locomotives had begun and with it went the work of firemen. As with the introduction of electric trains, ASLEF maintained that a second man would still be necessary in the cab 'in case of emergencies and for safety purposes'. In December 1957 it relented somewhat and together with the NUR signed an agreement to permit single-manning on diesel locomotives for daytime trips of less than 200 miles or six hours, except for journeys of more than 100 miles without a stop. On other journeys, a second man, usually a former fireman, would ride in the cab with the driver. As diesel locomotives multiplied, so single-manning came to be applied on a wide scale.[54] These restrictions were relaxed over the years, in 1965 for example.

March 1960. The Commission accepts the Guillebaud recommendations, referred to above.

DURING THE BEECHING PERIOD

In the two years before Beeching unveiled his 'Reshaping Report', the unions achieved a lot: the Redundancy, Transfer and Resettlement Agreement, 'producing levels of compensation almost without equal in British industry'; and agreement to a 42-hour week for footplate staff. Beeching wanted peace with the unions for the launch of his report.

March 1963: Beeching's 'Reshaping Report'. The ASLEF General, forgetting his lines, welcomed the report. In a press statement:

> 'a very able document..... An entirely honest attempt to rationalise the railway system in this country..... While any would consider the plan ruthless, had it been less ruthless it would have been less honest..... It will be doing ASLEF members a grave disservice not to look practical necessities in the face.'

Tut-tut.

Within days the position was 'clarified'. The union would not 'stand idly by seeing the railways in this country largely destroyed'. Just four months later a different General would be donning the mantle. Nonetheless, ASLEF did not support the NUR in its call for strike action. The generous redundancy agreement helped the union agree to 'constructive engagement' with the Doctor.

1964: Various concerns. The union stepped up its campaign against rest day working. The Board should hire more drivers, it said, and not rely on rest days. It wanted reforms to the system of lodging turns whereby drivers stayed in British Rail hostels overnight after a long journey and were available to drive a train on the way back. This should cease so that a second driver would be required.

1965: Forty-hour week. The Board agreed to a forty-hour week.

1965: Single-manning. Agreement was reached to extend single-manning. Single drivers could run express passenger and parcel trains for up to 350 miles or six hours continuously, and stopping passenger and express freight trains on journeys of less than 250 miles.

By then steam trains were fast disappearing – the last from Bristol to Paddington ran in November 1965 but continued elsewhere for a few years – and the single-manning agreement came to apply to most passenger trains. Interestingly, some other railways, the Canadian for example, continued to carry second men and suchlike for far longer than in Britain.

1967: The brake van and the 'who sits where' dispute. This was most illustrative of ASLEF's concerns. The Board wished to eliminate the brake van at the rear of freight and parcels trains when fitted with continuous brakes, and therefore the job of the brakeman or guard. As part of a package, it agreed with the NUR that a new position would be created, a 'trainman' – who would sit in the locomotive, probably in the rear cab. The position would be open to displaced guards and promotion to driver would be possible. The proposal, inevitably, was rejected by ASLEF: 'It undermined the very basis of the Society's separate existence.'

As the book says, 'at the root of the problem was the competition.... for scarce train jobs and promotion opportunities'.

From ASLEF's perspective, the second man was part of the footplate promotion ladder: cleaner to fireman or second man and then to driver, the best-paid job on the railway, and getting scarce. Men climbed the ladder by strict seniority. Allowing older guards with seniority into the locomotive as a trainman obviously diluted the job prospects of firemen and cleaners with less seniority.

Nothing was resolved and the matter went quiet for twenty years. Brake vans were removed from such freight trains as had continuous brakes, and the guards sat, largely ignored by the driver, in the rear cab of the locomotive.

1968: The Penzance agreement. Described as 'far-reaching and momentous', the package included a substantial pay rise and the relaxation of a number of restrictions around single-manning and the second-man issue.

1969: Closed shop. The Board conceded the long-standing demand – which had come most insistently from the NUR – for compulsory trade union membership. ASLEF had been wary because the NUR still had some members on the footplate and feared that such an agreement would entrench its position and prevent ASLEF's goal of 100 per cent membership in the locomotive grades.

LATER PERIODS

1973: 100mph running. There was one further incident of interest in a later period concerning the high-speed trains, the HST and the APT. ASLEF had opposed the running of any trains at speeds above 100mph, but when the HST and APT appeared they had an agreement, so the book claims, that they would be double-manned and that ASLEF would be consulted about cab design, etc. But they were not consulted and both trains were designed and built with a single seat in the driver's cab. When a request was presented to ASLEF to test the new HST at speeds up to 125mph, it was turned down, and when the prototype APT was driven by someone, without ASLEF's permission, from a siding into a workshop for modifications, a national one-day strike was called. This forced those involved into action, and the concerns of ASLEF and NUR were resolved over the summer and autumn of 1973 and testing began.

Except for the last incident, this account takes the story to 1968, a pivotal year. Up until then, negotiations on the railway had been quite rational, with disagreements often resolved by negotiation. But from 1968 this changed.

For a start, traditions originating in the mists of time were being challenged. In many places, for example, the custom had been that trains and their drivers came as a package – somewhat as a cavalryman and his horse – delivered by the Motive Power Department. Drivers answered to shed masters, big characters who 'understood' them. These shed masters were in charge of both the footplate staff and the fitters who supplied a working train complete with driver for use out on the line. In the past, it was an arrangement that made sense, but it was one the new breed of Area managers had to unravel, often with much bad blood.

Change was everywhere. Issues broadened out and soon became entangled in the bitter, intractable conflict between Heath and organised labour.

THE BOMBSHELL

The change began with a 'bombshell'. The fuse of this bombshell was Lord Donovan's Royal Commission on Trade Unions which drew critical attention to the spread of shop-floor bargaining and the willingness of workers to take unofficial action without heeding their national officials. And the bomb: the Barbara Castle – a Labour Party member! One of us! – White Paper, In Place of Strife. Instead of voluntarism, new laws would impose ballots, postpone industrial action, make wildcat strikes illegal and deduct fines from strikers' pay packets: 'The whole repressive system would be presided over by a Labour Court'.

Harold Wilson supported the paper, but opposition in the Labour Party was so strong that it was abandoned. In its place, even greater efforts were promised to make voluntarism work. It did a bit, but it could never work for long. ASLEF and other unions did not believe that the chaos in the country was their fault and had no intention of cooperating. The talk in the unions was of the 'Gnomes of Zurich', of unions being made scapegoats for failed economic policies, and that Harold Wilson's 'great victory in the 1966 election had led not to a left-wing turn but to a floodgate of reaction'. The rhetoric indicates the darkening mood.

It was acknowledged that 'over the second half of the 1960s train drivers had seen the hourly basic wage rate climb by 38%, considerably more than workers in other industries'.[55] But this was no longer seen as an achievement. The redundancy agreement, previously welcomed, was denounced: 'catastrophic job losses that we have experienced from the productivity bargain.' Gains in pay had been achieved at the expense of fellow workers: 'For every output and punctuality scheme, they had sold the jobs of half a dozen colleagues and received two shillings and sixpence for every pound saved.'

From now on, every productivity initiative was to be opposed.

As the book says, 1968 'was the start of a period when organised Labour would find itself taking on the power of the state, requiring a response from union leaders which would be less sectional, more militant and more political.'

Conflict grew in intensity. De Gaulle rejected Britain's EEC membership, Harold Wilson was forced to devalue the pound, raise taxes and freeze pay.

Ted Heath won the 1970 election, and forced through legislation to implement his, reckless, version of in *Place of Strife*, with an Industrial Relations Court. In its sixth month of operation, it sent five dockworker trade unionists to Pentonville prison. 'As soon as the first trade unionist goes to prison, all hell will be let loose' said Vic Feather of the TUC.[56] He was not wrong. Lit up in lights was a target. Strikers, marchers and unionists went for it. They had a cause and an enemy, the government.

From then on, it was all over for Heath: chaos, unemployment, a balanced budget abandoned, money poured back into the economy, the famous U-turn, and inflation. The world too was against him. Bloody Sunday in Ireland, the Yom Kippur War and a doubled oil price all added to the sense of things falling apart.

Inflation, once established, is extremely difficult to remove and inevitably leads to strikes. Train drivers and guards struck over pay claims. Miners struck twice over their pay claims – a 20 per cent increase was the order of the day. Heath tried to fight. A state of emergency was declared, and the three-day week imposed from 1 January 1974 until 7 March.

Heath called an election for 28 February 1974 with the famous question, 'Who governs Britain?' The answer came back: 'Not you'. Wilson squeaked through with the most seats and formed a government.

But even he, with all his ingenuity and Double First from Oxford, could find no lasting solution to the problems: inflation, unemployment and constant disputes. January 1979 saw the biggest day of strike action since 1929. Rubbish piled up in Leicester Square and bodies were stored unburied in a shed in Liverpool when gravediggers went on strike.

It was the winter of discontent and the government, now with Jim Callaghan as Prime Minister, would face the electorate in May of that year, 1979.

INTERCITY ROLLING STOCK AND JOURNEY TIME

INTERCITY – DIESEL

The first good diesel locomotive in Britain was the Class 40, which went into service on the West Coast Main Line in 1958. Two hundred were built and operated across the country. It did, however, lack the power – 2,000hp at most – to maintain heavy trains at high speeds and offered little advantage over a recently built class of steam locomotive, the Britannia class.

The Class 40 was followed, from 1961, by the famous Deltic locomotive, with 3,300 engine horsepower. Only twenty-two were built, but they revolutionised intercity travel on the East Coast Main Line.

In due course, more power was needed, and so the Deltic was followed by the HST. As no diesel engine could be built to deliver more power than the existing Deltic without a great increase in weight, the HST was built with two power cars, one at each end; in this way, over 4,500 engine horsepower could be provided. Approval was given for its development in May 1970. The coaches were Mark 3, a more comfortable development of the Mark 2 coach, with air conditioning and air suspension, and were designed for 125mph travel.

Unlike the APT, the HST stretched but did not break the capabilities of the technicians. Progress was quick – just three years after approval, the prototype achieved 143mph on a run north of York in June 1973. As described earlier. Three years after that, in October 1976, the first HST passenger service capable of 125mph started in the Western Region.

With it, the engineers had revolutionised the InterCity business. It began service on the East Coast Main Line in 1978, travelling between King's Cross and Edinburgh in 4.5 hours. It would later move on to the Midland Main Line in 1982.

Roger Ford and Brian Perren in their book *HSTs at Work* describe the decision to support the HST development as the most important taken by British Rail since nationalisation. According to the authors, without the HST it is doubtful whether the InterCity business could have survived the 1970s, let alone aspired to profitability by the end of the 1980s.

THE TRACK

Gordon Pettitt talks about the track on which the HST ran.

> Gordon: When we introduced the HST at 200kph – well ahead of Germany at that stage – do not forget the track. Brian Davies was the chief civil engineer of Eastern. I've always said he would have been managing director anywhere else. If you talk to an engineer who has worked for Davies, you can trust him. He developed talent and of course created superb track.
> : Speed restrictions were eliminated on the East Coast for the HST. Brian Davies was behind that. He loved developing the East Coast Main Line and was very good at it. He might take track out of Lincolnshire, for example, and use it on the Main Line. He was putting in track for 100mph before it was needed – it's only a question of sleeper spacing and deep ballasting. He was a man who thought about the future and did not believe he was putting in track just for today.
> : Philip Rees, the chief civil engineer on the Western, was the same, only the thirteenth since Brunel!

The importance of track is beautifully illustrated by the following.

Before the war, the fastest time for travel from London to Edinburgh (by the streamlined *Coronation*) was six hours. After the war, with the same steam engine, the journey took seven hours and twenty minutes! A good part of the reason was track condition, frequent speed restrictions where the track was not sound enough to allow full line speed. Following improvements to the track and, wherever possible, the straightening and removal of sharp curves, the pre-war six-hour timing was again be achieved. It was therefore the track as much as the power of the Deltic that made this possible. From then on, with a good track in place, greater power did cut journey times. Most substantially, the HST cut the time for London to Edinburgh down to four hours and thirty-five minutes; the Class 91 electric train, which had twice the power of the Deltic, cut it, if the timetable allowed, to four hours.

Train	**Power Engine**	**Power Drawbar**	**Comment**
Steam – A4	–	2,000 hp	Realistically, the most that could be expected from steam – Gerard Fiennes
Steam – A4	_	2,500 hp	Duchess class – 'Frequently steamed up to such heights for short periods'.... 'To sustain such an output for any length of time would certainly need the efforts of two fireman', shovelling furiously. Maximum power reached at 40 or 45 mph. (Nock, page 31)
Class 40, diesel-electric	2,000 hp	1,500 hp	'Could not produce more than about 1,500 hp at the drawbar; but there was consistency about their work, which could not be said about steam at that time. And, maximum power reached above 10 mph.' (Nock, page 31)

Train	Power Engine	Power Drawbar	Comment
Class 40, diesel-electric	2,000 hp	1,500 hp	'Could not produce more than about 1,500 hp at the drawbar; but there was consistency about their work, which could not be said about steam at that time. And, maximum power reached above 10 mph.' (Nock, page 31)
Deltic, diesel-electric	3,300 hp	2,750hp	The equivalent drawbar horsepower was about 2,750.... 'But the very rapid acceleration from speed restrictions was an impressive feature of the running'. (Nock, page 74)
HST, diesel-electric	4,500 hp	3,400 hp	The power units of the HST, working at their maximum were according to careful calculation developing about 3,400 hp at 82 to 83 mph. (Nock, page 211)
Class 87, Electric used in pairs for freight		6,000 hp	North of Liverpool/ Manchester, heavy freightliners have to run uphill at about 75 mph. To do this requires, not one, but two Class 87 locomotives and a drawbar horsepower of nearly 6,000 ... (Nock, page 163)
Class 90, Electic	5,000 hp		Power output. Cyril Bleasdale's choice, see later chapter
Class 91, Electric	6,480 hp		Power output

The following table has been kindly supplied with help from a number of people.

EAST COAST SERVICES: LONDON – EDINBURGH

Six Expresses (excl. dated trains)

Year	**Traction**	**Daily Trains** (Day+ Night)	**Journey Times** (day trains)	**Line Speed***	**Comments**
1922	Steam	4 + 4	8hr 30 – 9hr 45	75mph	
1939	Steam – A4	5 + 4	6hr 00 – 8hr 30	90mph	Streamlined 'Coronation' gave 6hr journey time from 1936
1951	Steam – A4	5 + 4	6hr 45 – 7hr 33	90mph	Post War track conditions Loco-changes en route
1962	Diesel – Deltic	5 + 4	6hr 00 – 7hr 35	100mph	First Deltic timetable with continuous line speed upgrades
1976	Diesel – Deltic	9	5hr 43 – 6hr 22	100mph	Impact of track improvements and 3,300hp traction
1986	Diesel – HST	13	4hr 35 – 5hr 09	125mph	Full HST accelerated timetable
1993	Electric – CI 91	15	4hr 01 – 5hr 07	125mph	East Coast electrification 1990 Further track improvements
1991	*Electric – CI 91*	*Record run*	*3hr 29 – nonstop*	*140mph*	*26 September 1991: Loco+6 140mph where available*
2019	Electric – IEP	18	4hr 20 – 4hr 46	125mph	CI 800 Hitachi bi-mode
2022	Electric – IEP	32	4hr 10 – 4hr 30	125mph	*Full IEP timetable including Open Access London–Edinburgh*
2030	Electric – H52	n/a	2hr 40	215mph	New infrastructure London to Wigan with very high speeds
Speed records on East Coast Infrastructure				**Speed**	
1938	Steam – A4	–	–	126mph	3 July 1938 test down Stoke Bank: fastest steam in world
1991	Diesel – HST	–	–	147mph	1 November 1987 down Stoke Bank: fastest diesel in world
1991	Electric – CI 91	–	–	162mph	1991 test run down Stoke Bank: UK speed record

* Fastest line speed available on East Coast at the time

NOTES TO TABLE ON PAGE 145:

A. Sleepers were a significant part of Anglo Scottish market 100mph track/traction 1962
B. Continuous track improvements 1960–1990 maximised benefits of traction upgrades
C. Test runs listed above show awesome speed potential but . . .
C. Maximum Line Speeds plateau at 125mph 1986 – limits of mixed traffic railway with more trains
D. Post 1990 electrification priority has been on frequency rather than speed (eg half-hourly Edinburgh)
E. Future journey time improvements require new & faster infrastructure: HS2 around 2030

INTER-CITY – ELECTRIC

When the first leg of the West Coast Main Line – the southern leg – was completed in 1966/7, the new service was a revelation as to what rail travel could be.

The principal locomotive from 1965 was the electric Class 86, with a power output of 3,600hp, well above that available from diesel or steam at the time. For the first time in Britain, 80mph average start-to-stop timings were possible. Its Mark 2 carriages were more comfortable than before and ran on continuous welded track. Passenger numbers soared and the InterCity brand was launched.

The second leg – the electrification of the northern half of the line up to Glasgow – was approved in 1970 and completed in May 1974. By then, the Class 87, built from 1973 to 1975, was available, with a power output of 5,000hp.

Ten years later, the Class 87 was joined by the Class 90 (the design which Cyril Bleasdale insisted upon). Built from 1987 to 1990, it replaced all the original locomotives (Classes 81–85) on the West Coast Main Line.

Both the Class 87 and Class 90, both electric, had a maximum speed of 110mph, which drivers said seemed to keep the trains 'happy'. This was fast, but business managers wanted 125mph, as could be delivered by the two-engined diesel HST.

Approval for the electrification of the East Coast Main Line was not given until 1984. For the launch, the Class 91 was built, with a power output of 6,480hp. Thus came about the fixed formation InterCity 225 train, composed of a Class 91 with nine Mark 4 coaches and a driving van trailer. It was able to run at 140mph (around 225kph), although in practice the top permitted speed was slightly less (125mph).

In summary:

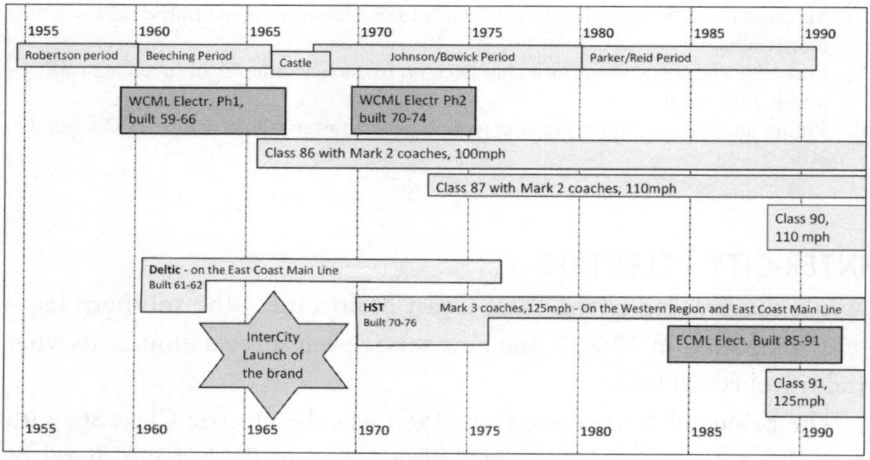

FREIGHT

The second element of work done during the Johnson/Bowick period was the efficient handling of freight.

There was a great expansion of trainload freight: Merry-Go-Round coal trains, which were very profitable, and Freightliner. Both Merry-

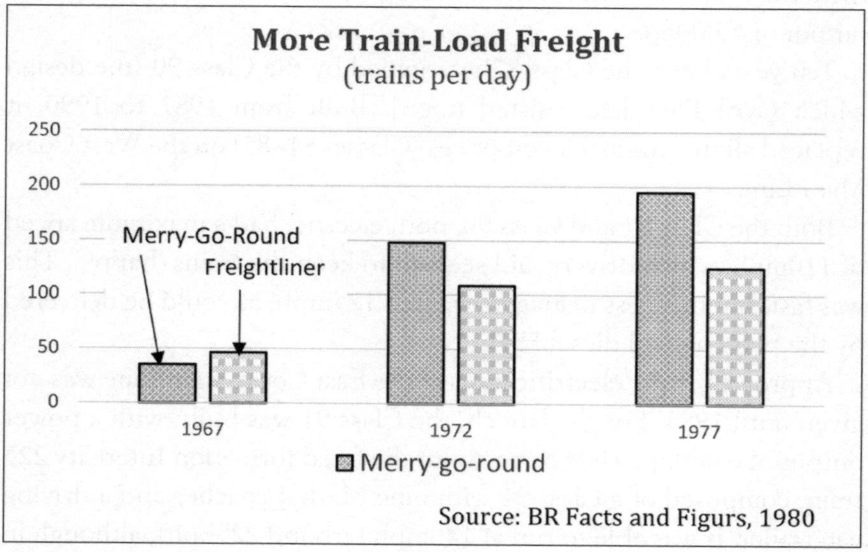

Go-Round and Freightliner had been begun under Beeching but under Johnson/Bowick were greatly expanded.
As for wagonload, the 1968 Freight Plan committed the company to continue such business. Considerable effort was put into the development of a more focused and efficient service, launched in 1972 and relaunched under the Speedlink name in January 1977. It worked for a while and allowed the old wagonload network with thousands of wagons and hundreds of freight terminals to be cut right back.

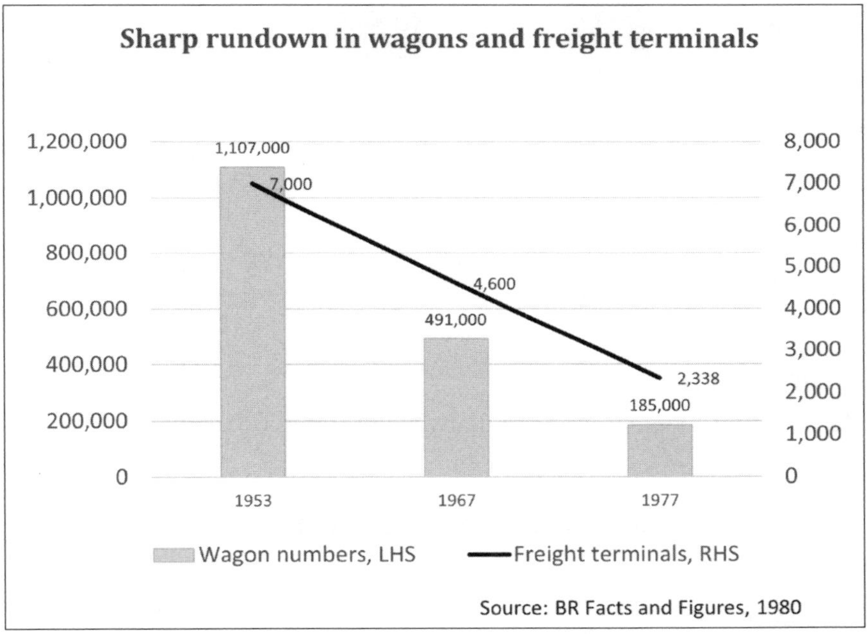

Impressive though the increase in trainload freight was, freight as a whole continued to fall as a percentage of revenue. From 52 per cent of total revenue in 1967, it made up only 35 per cent in 1977.

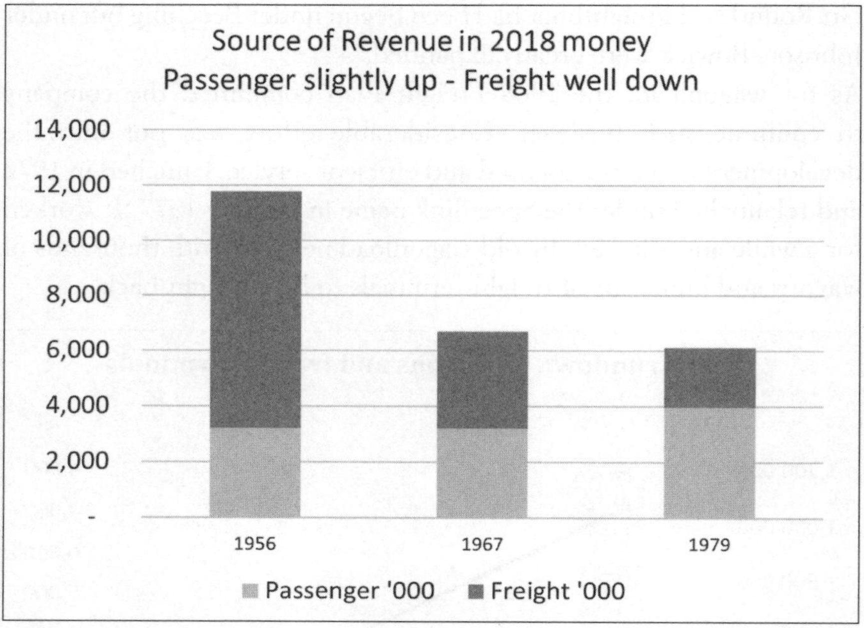

RESIGNALLING

Resignalling schemes allowed many small signal boxes to be closed.

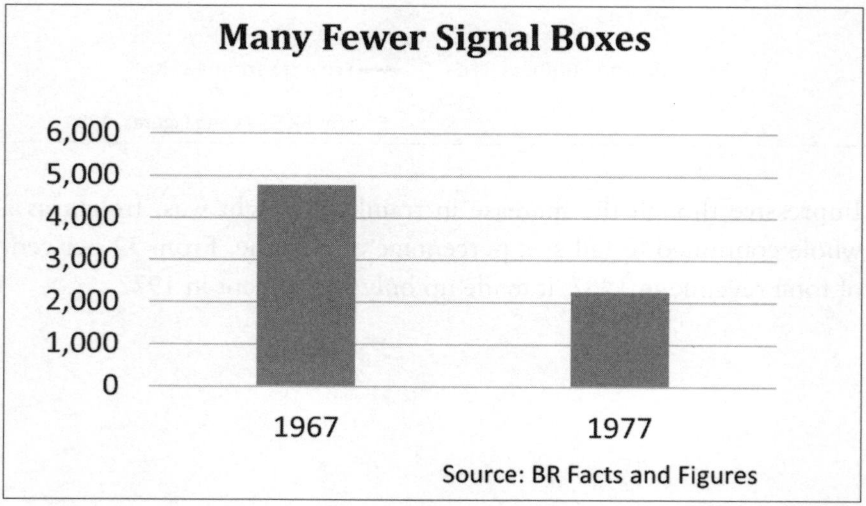

STAFF NUMBERS

A consequence of these and other measures was a substantial reduction in staff numbers, down by 23 per cent over the ten years between 1967 and 1977, from 279,000 to 214,000.

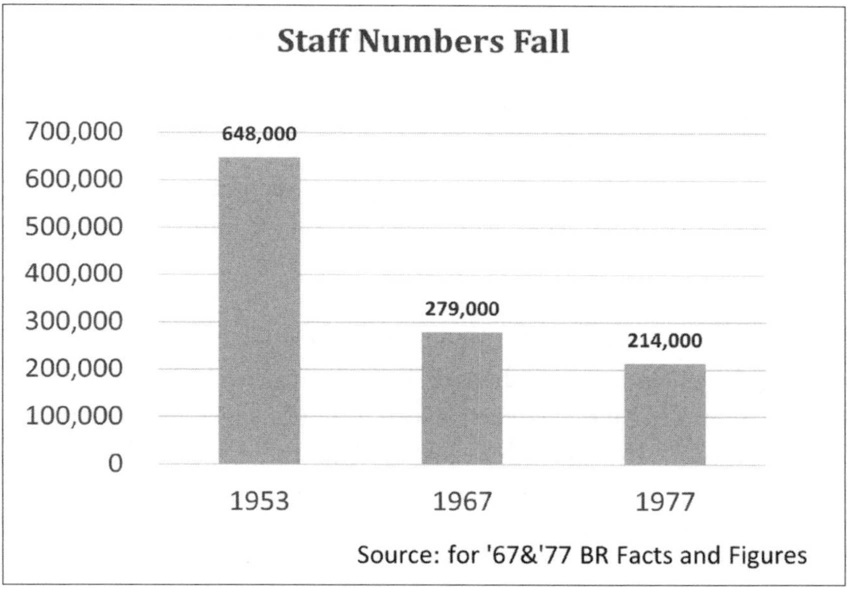

The completion of the InterCity network, the growth in passenger revenue, the increase in trainload freight and the large-area resignalling schemes were substantial achievements in the Johnson/Bowick period.

SIGNALLING: THE HEART OF THE INFRASTRUCTURE

SOLID-STATE INTERLOCKING

The power signal boxes being installed in the 1970s were remarkable constructions. They covered large areas but there had to be a less expensive, more reliable way to have them built – Solid-State Interlocking (SSI) was that way.

If the HST stands out as a triumph of British Rail engineering, so also should SSI. The development of the HST was not high science, just good engineering, but SSI was. Its development took ten years. It was first installed in 1985 and was still being installed in new signalling systems in Britain and overseas thirty years later. An installation life of thirty years.

Alan Cribbens tells how it came about.

> Cribbens: I was doing postdoctoral research at UCL in 1969, sponsored by the railway research department. They were interested in communication with moving trains, which in those days was a challenge. After working for two years on this, Sir David Davies, who was then the assistant director of research at Derby, recruited me to join their signalling section. This was right at the end of 1970. They were working on an improved version of AWS.

Note – AWS (Automatic Warning System) is a device in the cab which alerts a driver to the fact that his train is approaching a signal and informs him whether it is clear (green) or not clear (double yellow, yellow or red). It was widely installed in the 1950s following the dreadful Harrow and Wealdstone accident in 1952. It is a good system, but not ideal for the density of traffic in the Southern Region.

> Cribbens: We started to develop an improved version to address the problem in the Southern Region. We began to develop what was essentially an in-cab signalling system.

An in-cab system is one that presents detailed signalling information within the cab, thereby avoiding the need for the driver to watch out the window for the 'lights on sticks', and usually includes some system to automatically stop the train before it runs through a red light.

> Cribbens: We were making progress, but the system needed three large boxes of relays in the train and track conductors laid along the Four Foot (the space between the rails), all very expensive and cumbersome. While we were doing this work, the first commercially available microprocessor appeared called the Intel 4004. It was a four-bit machine with very limited capabilities, but it did what we needed. We got it programmed. What is more

important, we developed a system that did everything twice and unless the two halves agreed with each other, the system would fail to a safe condition. It was failsafe. We developed what I think was a rather novel technique for doing that. It was important because it was eventually used in SSI.

: As it happened, the development failed. We had made a complete mess of connecting the system to the outside world and the Southern Region decided to install conventional AWS anyway.

: When the project was cancelled, this must have been about 1975, I pressed for research into the use of microprocessors for interlocking in signal boxes, to replace the relays.

So began solid-state interlocking.

A word about interlocking. From its earliest days, the railway required a system to make sure that a signalman in a signal box, pulling the levers which operated the points and signals out on the track, did not send a train into the path of another. An ingenious, mechanical, most complex contraption built underneath the bank of levers made sure this could not happen. It came to be called interlocking.

Mechanical signal boxes gave way to electrical signal boxes, but interlocking was still required. It is the heart of a signal box. Interlocking in signal boxes covering large areas with four, eight or more tracks approaching junctions becomes extraordinarily complicated and must be totally reliable.

Electrical signal boxes began to appear in the 1920s and 1930s. Electrical relays replaced the mechanical devices of the past. By the late-1950s, technology had advanced. Relays and communication systems had become more sophisticated and it became possible to build signal boxes to control large areas. Their insides are a familiar sight, with long displays on the wall showing the track layout and the state of every signal. The relays, fundamental to their operation, were small, rectangular electromechanical devices, about 8in x 5in x 2.5in. Wired up correctly, they controlled the signals and points out on the track and made sure one train was not routed into the path of another. The 1970s was the high point for the installation of large power signal boxes, with many still in use.

When the northern half of the West Coast Main Line, from Crewe up to Glasgow, was electrified, it was controlled by just three such boxes, and possibly one or two more. The one at Preston was/is enormous. It replaced over 80 manual signal boxes. Alan Cribbens estimated that it contained 30,000 relays. It controls 460 colour-light signals and 360 point machines, and much else.

The London Bridge power signal box, another example, opened around the same time, and there were more. Their significance lies not only in the signal box but in the work done when they were being installed to improve the layout of the track in the vicinity (and indeed, sad to say, to take out capacity, not then needed). The aim, if it can be done, is to separate trains going to different destinations well before they reach the main station so that their paths do not have to cross within it.

The track layout was changed for trains from Kent approaching London Bridge, some going to Cannon Street and some to Charing Cross. They were separated out in the New Cross area, well to the east of London Bridge.

The number of trains every hour heading the short distances from London Bridge to Cannon Street and Charing Cross is very great. To allow such a density of traffic, the signals are placed close together, one or two hundred yards apart. In the morning or evening peak, trains follow each other, not fast, but close together. The working timetable showed thirty-two trains an hour passing these signals: just one example of what can be done with simple equipment.

But to return to Alan Cribbens, talking about the mid-70s.

Cribbens: We worked away on the interlocking project for a couple of years. One of the problems was communication. We had to send signals along the track. It sounds a bit strange but at the time the Americans had developed a databus for the B-1 bomber with a very promising-looking coding technique. They were doing it at 2mb a second and we were doing it 10kb a second. They were only sending it 50m and we wanted to send it 10km, so we had a lot of adapting to do. But we did it and were well on the way to producing a prototype solid-state interlocking when there was a big interruption.

: A storm had blown down forty miles of the telegraph poles along the railway in the north of Scotland, from Inverness to Wick and Thurso. Wires on these poles carried information between the signal boxes, and without them trains couldn't run. The cost of replacing the poles was so great that the line was under threat of closure.
: We suggested a way of connecting the signal boxes by radio. This was jumped on and we produced a system which worked very well. Basically, it replicated what the wires had done, and incorporated our failsafe design. Years later it was replaced by a better system, Radio Electronic Token Block (RETB), but our system worked well.
Cribbens: This is a picture of a circuit board from our control unit. As far as I know, it is the world's first failsafe microcomputer.
: Our success made an impression on the S&T people at the Board, particularly Armand Cardani, so I was given my own section to run and went back to developing solid-state interlocking.
: We set up a tripartite agreement between ourselves and GEC

World's first failsafe microcomputer

Signals (later merged with Alstom) and Westinghouse Signals (later acquired by Siemens). We were to do the design and software and they were each to turn it into an engineered product that could be reliably installed out on the railway. There were to be two different versions, but they were required to be interchangeable, which happily they were.

: We got the basic machine built quite quickly but had to add a lot of bells and whistles around it. It needed a technician's terminal, of course. The biggest engineering challenge was to devise a safe method of connecting to the signals, points, track circuits and such things out on the track. We designed a signal module and a points module to handle this function. Both had to be designed so that the points could never be moved in error and the signal would be held at red if anything failed. This was one of the biggest engineering challenges. The modules were located at the trackside and connect to the interlocking by the data links I've mentioned already.

: I ought perhaps to clarify that SSI is a fixed set of software, which contains all the necessary signalling principles, and doesn't change from place to place. You tell it what to do at any particular location, what the signalling engineer wants to happen, using the SSI design language. This language uses signal engineers' terminology but in a highly structured form. We built a data compiler which took the textual description of what was required and turned it into computer code. It was quite a challenge but fundamental to the success of the product.

: The pilot scheme went live at Leamington Spa in September 1985. We wasted a bit of time because the S&T people wanted us to run it off-line for a year and compare it with what the existing system, the great manual lever thing, was doing. But we couldn't see any way of doing this. So the system went live over Saturday night and Sunday morning, 7th and 8th September. On Monday, they knocked down the old signal box. No going back.

: What SSI did was to replace the relays in a power signal box with integrated circuits – by then we had a much more powerful processor, the Motorola 6802 – and the mass of electrical wires along the track with just one or two.

: The system was a success and went on to become the standard method of resignalling. At first the engineering companies were worried about SSI, worried that they would lose revenue for it was so much less expensive. But the opposite was the case. SSI went on to be exported to a long list of countries: Brazil, South Africa, Australia, Hong Kong, even France and Belgium. Five years ago, it was estimated to have generated £5 billion of exports.
: Then a sad thing happened. When Railtrack was formed in the early 90s we had a forward-looking R&D programme which included a second generation of SSI. But one day we are all summoned to a meeting in London, people from the whole signalling industry, and we heard these words: 'SSI is dead in the water.' The business was to be opened up to competition.

It was the high point of competition mania.

Cribbens: They contracted Ansaldo to do the Manchester South resignalling – it was a nightmare to get working – and Siemens (Germany) to do Portsmouth – which was a mess of wires and years late – and Bombardier to do Horsham – they had so many problems adapting to British practice that it had to be abandoned.
: Eventually they came back to SSI. Only in the last two or three years has it stopped being installed. It has had an installation life of thirty years.
: There are new systems now, but the good news from my point of view is that they are using the same basic data structure that was in SSI.

One of them is Westlock from Siemens. 'This builds on many of the features that made SSI popular in the United Kingdom including re-use of SSI's programming language and its external hardware.'[57] Another is Smartlock from Alstom, which is much the same.

INTEGRATED ELECTRONIC CONTROL CENTRE (IECC)

Interlocking is not all you need in a signal box. You need signallers, you need displays they can look at to see what is happening out on the track, and you need switches or buttons they can operate to control the signals and thus the movement of the trains. In the 1980s, Derby developed a system aimed at automating some of this called the Integrated Electronic Control Centre, or IECC. It was an early use of computer screens for showing track layout, and it contained within its software a system called Automatic Route Setting (ARS), which automated some of the decisions previously made by the signalmen. The normal path to be followed by each train is stored in the system and ARS instructs the interlocking to set the sequence of signals required.

In principle, when there is disruption, instead of having to leap into action and work out the best way to recover the service, the signalman can sit back and let intelligence within the ARS do that for him. In practice, things are often not so simple and signalmen can have a busy time.

The IECC, the interface with the signaller, sits on top of ARS and SSI. The first one was installed at Liverpool Street Station in 1989 and another around the same time in York. It became widely used in Britain, in about thirty signal boxes in one form or another.

The Liverpool Street installation was not entirely without problems. Chris Stokes was deputy director at Network SouthEast at the time and was worried about introducing it for the first time at such an important location.

> Stokes: I went up to Derby to quiz them on the potential risks in some detail and came back more, but not entirely confident. In the event, the initial operation was disastrous. The IECC worked fine from day one but the SSI modules which had been installed at the same time started failing all over the place. When we got to the bottom of it, it was because it was the first SSI installation in a 25kv overhead area and they proved highly susceptible to high-voltage interference. It was resolved reasonably quickly. For my part, I had the right instinct to challenge, but I had worried about the wrong piece of kit.

Just as Derby research developed the IECC, railways elsewhere developed their own systems. Signallers on the continent like to see 'train graphs' while those in Britain are accustomed to looking at 'track layouts'. The systems look different but do much the same thing.

The one thing other railways did not develop as well as in Britain was SSI; hence its great success in the export market.

Progressively, more and more of the old signal boxes were converted to newer forms. Recently, Network Rail announced a major reform, the planned replacement of all signal boxes with twelve Rail Operating Centres, controlling very large areas. Software of the most challenging kind – traffic management systems – is required if their benefit is to be exploited to the full.

A modern signal box in 1957 at Cowlairs and a modern signal box and control office in 2016 at Three Bridges controlling, inter alia, the Thameslink core with ERTMS. (Cowlairs from the National Railway Museum, and Three Bridges, by Muir)

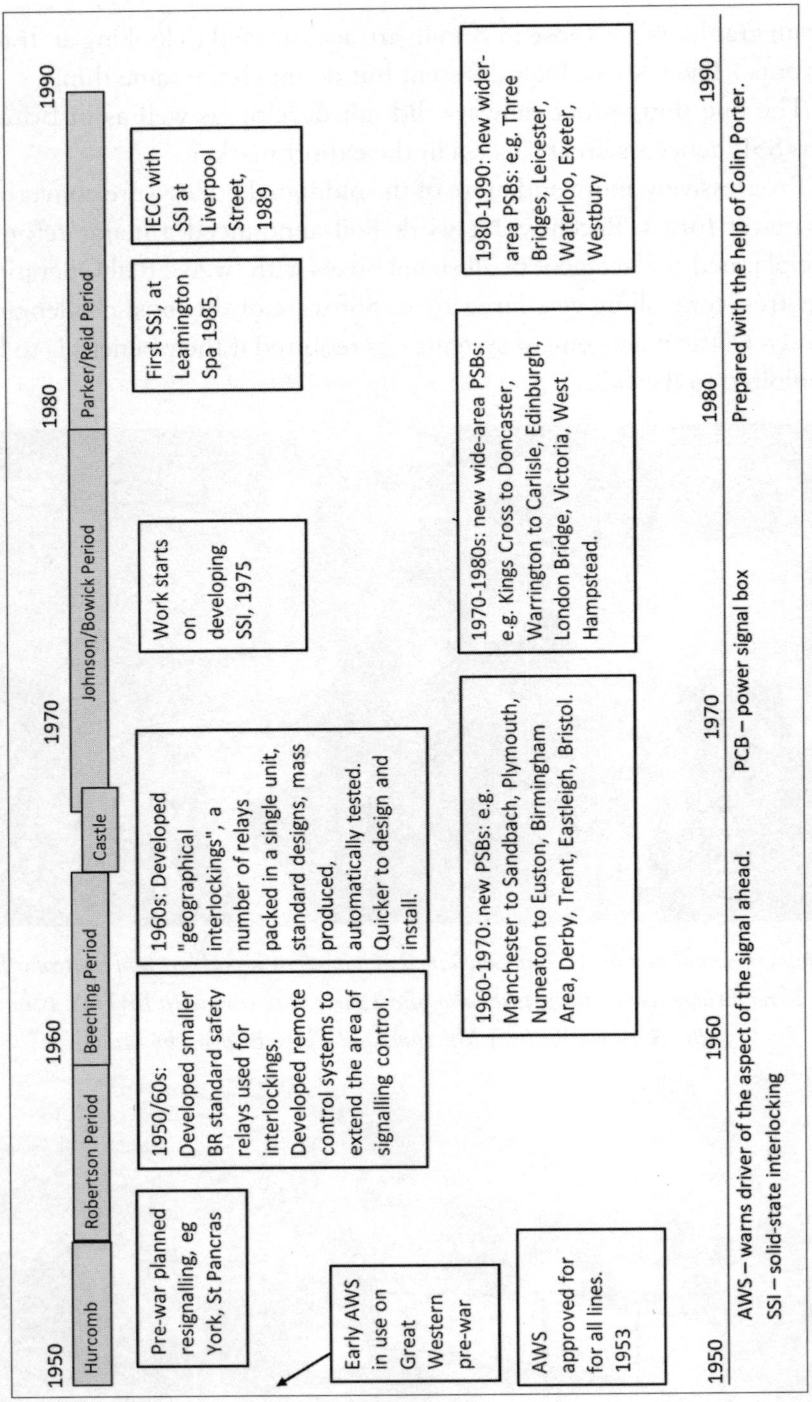
1950
1960
1970
1980
1990
Hurcomb
Robertson Period
Beeching Period
Castle
Johnson/Bowick Period
Parker/Reid Period
Pre-war planned resignalling, eg York, St Pancras
1950/60s: Developed smaller BR standard safety relays used for interlockings. Developed remote control systems to extend the area of signalling control.
1960s: Developed "geographical interlockings", a number of relays packed in a single unit, standard designs, mass produced, automatically tested. Quicker to design and install.
Work starts on developing SSI, 1975
First SSI, at Leamington Spa 1985
IECC with SSI at Liverpool Street, 1989
Early AWS in use on Great Western pre-war
AWS approved for for all lines. 1953
1960-1970: new PSBs: e.g. Manchester to Sandbach, Plymouth, Nuneaton to Euston, Birmingham Area, Derby, Trent, Eastleigh, Bristol.
1970-1980s: new wide-area PSBs: e.g. Kings Cross to Doncaster, Warrington to Carlisle, Edinburgh, London Bridge, Victoria, West Hampstead.
1980-1990: new wider-area PSBs: e.g. Three Bridges, Leicester, Waterloo, Exeter, Westbury
1950
1960
1970
1980
1990
AWS – warns driver of the aspect of the signal ahead.
SSI – solid-state interlocking
PCB – power signal box
Prepared with the help of Colin Porter.

IN-CAB SIGNALLING

As he explained above, in the mid-70s Alan Cribbens had been working on a form of in-cab signalling for the Southern Region which was not taken forward.

His system would have used wires running along the track carrying an electrical signal to be detected by equipment on the train. Depending on the frequency of the signal the equipment on the train would know the aspect of the signal ahead: red, yellow or green.

Compared with continental railways or some in America, British Rail was rather late in seeing the need for in-cab signalling.

Line-side signals have been found to be quite satisfactory for speeds up to 125mph (Britain is unusual in allowing such high speeds with the system); at one time it was even thought safe for trains to run at 140mph with line-side signals. That was the speed it was hoped would be possible on the East Coast Main Line with the Class 91 locomotive. An extra aspect, flashing green, was to be added to give the driver more time, but common sense or perhaps caution prevailed.

Germans, more cautious, were not comfortable relying on line-side signals for speeds above 100mph. Consequently as long ago as 1965 the Germans demonstrated an in-cab signalling system called LZB, which used a pair of wires running along the track, just as Alan Cribbens's system would have done, carrying an electrical signal which could be picked up by the train. That system has been progressively developed, and is used today to signal the high-speed German trains.

At the same time, when the French started work on their high-speed trains, they too developed an in-cab signalling system. Their system is called TVM. Instead of wires running along the track, TVM uses the rails to carry the electrical signal to be detected by the train. TVM was ready for the launch of the first TGV, the Train à Grande Vitesse, on the route from Paris to Lyon in 1981. As with the German system, it has been progressively developed and now signals Eurostar through the Channel Tunnel and up to St Pancras International.

In Britain, after the Clapham accident in 1988, it was decided to pilot two slightly different in-cab systems, somewhat similar to TVM/LZB, and called automatic train protection (ATP). They were installed on the Great Western Main Line from Bristol to London and on Chiltern Railways. These worked well enough, but were not rolled out any further.

The Ladbroke Grove crash in 1999, ten years after the Clapham accident, led to renewed pressure for train protection. The enquiry was much taken with the idea of a nationwide, fully automatic in-cab system, but was persuaded that any such system, if it ever worked, was twenty years away, which remains the case twenty years later!

With the authority of Sir David Davies, Alan Cribbens's previous boss at Derby, the enquiry mandated a much simpler solution: the Train Protection and Warning System (TPWS). While AWS simply alerts the driver to an upcoming signal, TPWS detects the speed of the train and, if travelling too fast approaching a signal, applies the brakes automatically. The combination of AWS and TPWS, now installed in all trains in Britain, has been shown to lead to a safe railway without the need for an in-cab signalling system.

On the continent, the proliferation of national systems led to a second objective, a standard Europe-wide system so trains could more easily operate between countries.

But also, the great increase in passenger numbers and the filling up of the network led to a third objective: capacity, the squeezing of more trains onto the track. For this, direct control from the centre of the speed at which the trains are driven is required.

In Europe, teams have been working for thirty years on such a system, the European Rail Traffic Management System (ERTMS), but it has proved remarkably difficult to bring to fruition other than on new lines with a simple layout. The Thameslink core, the part of Thameslink running through central London, is such a simple layout and has been equipped with ERTMS with great success. Direct computer control of the trains allows them to run closer than would be possible if the drivers were in control – so delivering high-capacity. Now, with more experience in its use, ERTMS is planned for the far-from-simple southern end of the East Coast Main Line.

PART THREE

REID AND PARKER (1980–90)

11 THE SOUTHERN REGION (1974–90)

In 1974, aged 53, Bob was promoted to one of the biggest jobs in the railway, the General Manager of the Southern Region.

He had been in his previous job only briefly, Deputy General Manager in York, which had not been a happy appointment. Bob had his own ideas for how things should be done and had little sympathy for the prevailing culture as exemplified by his then boss, Ian Campbell, the General Manager.

It was a difficult time, too, for him personally. His wife Isobel was seriously ill. They could not, for a long time, find a house which they liked in London so Bob lived in the Charing Cross Hotel and came back up north when he could.

As Janet explains:

> Janet: It was all very difficult. But eventually we moved. I think it might have been Christmas Eve. By that stage my mother was very ill with cancer, and in hospital. She had been unwell for a bit, but she really was unwell by then and Dad had been working in London for a year.
>
> : My mother had spotted a house in Purley early in the summer of 1974 and we finally moved from Doncaster on Christmas Eve 1974. Dad, my brother and I organised the move between us. Purley had been chosen because it was near friends of my mother who were very supportive and near the hospital where she became a patient so we could visit easily.

It was a comfortable looking house, in a narrow tree-lined cul-de-sac up the hill to the west of Purley town centre, with the railway station, visible over trees and roofs, in the distance.

And the job?

> Janet: Dad really enjoyed it. Somebody once said that it must have been difficult. I remember his reply: 'Well actually, the

> Southern Region is not difficult. It just needs strong management.' The unions were very strong. That was more of an issue. There were the Waterloo drivers and drivers in another depot who were particularly militant. Dad spent a lot of time dealing with unions. He talked with them and would go out on tours. Dad was always good at talking to people. He was a good people person and would always make sure he talked to the most junior. That probably came from his background, and the army and the POW camp. I remember seeing him once, years later, at some reception or other when he was chairman. Dad was there right in the depths of a little crowd talking to somebody obviously quite junior. The other senior person present was just talking to his senior colleagues, he was not talking to the people who mattered on the ground. Dad was always good like that. People responded to him.

On one occasion, he secured the union's cooperation for cost savings, cutting about £1.7 million a year. It was achieved by collaboration but the exception rather than the rule.[58]

> Janet: 1975 was a lovely summer, the year we settled into London. I remember it well because I was home from university and Mum was still okay. She was not well but she was in remission. We had a nice summer. It had been the right thing to move and Dad was okay because we were all together. Then Mum died at the beginning of January 1976. It was hard for all of us. Dad looked after my brother and me, of course, but he had his work, so he just plunged himself into that. One of his colleagues told me that she knew it was affecting him because he would fall asleep during meetings. It was simply the strain and his way of dealing with it.

Frank Paterson (who had worked years before near Bob on the Deeside line in Scotland) can add colour to Bob's time in the South. He had been appointed divisional manager of the Central Division in the Southern Region before Bob arrived. It was a big job Frank had, very hands-on.

In Frank's words:

> Frank: Lance Ibbotson was the general manager who appointed me. He was followed by David Binnie and he by Bob Reid. They were all different.
> : Ibbotson was a real character, one of the Whitemoor elite. They were the LNER traffic apprentices who invariably had a spell as Assistant Yardmaster at Whitemoor (a vast marshalling yard in the Fens). They were people like Bill Johnson, who became chairman, David Bowick who became chief executive and Bobby Lawrence, once head of the London Midland Region. Big characters.

Christopher Foster remembers lunching at London Midland with Bobby Lawrence. A big character indeed: 'Silver on the table. Port. It was like an officers' mess. Lots of people sitting around. Very long lunch. It was absolutely stunning.'[59] Later, Bobby Lawrence joined the Board, overseeing property, and on the Board was the last no-drink-at-lunchtime refusenik: 'I just remember Bob clutching a glass of something strong and saying in justification, 'I'm the only bit of your railway that makes a profit."[60]

> Frank: Ibbotson would come out to the divisions once a month and we would take him on a tour. He saw what was going on and was full of ideas and criticisms and so forth: very old school, very, very robust. He would arrange lunches; he had a great penchant for incredible menus and apart from the local managers would invite the mayor and the councillors and people like that. That was certainly not Bob's style.
> : David Binnie I had known for donkeys' years. He too was a very social animal and encouraged social activities, but more for the staff than for local dignitaries.
> : Then Bob came along. Bob was like neither of them. Nothing registers about his divisional visits – which is interesting in itself. He really came out to educate himself and not to tell us what to do.
> : He was a hard person to get to know, private, not warm. We had

had some dealings together and I did not think he had much time for me, but one night I got a call from him, I was then a divisional manager, and he just said, 'I would like you to know that the Board has decided to appoint you as deputy general manager.' That was it. I asked some quite reasonable questions about other people and what was happening to them but he just said, 'None of your business.'

: He was not a man for the details, but he did like to prepare. Perhaps, somehow, there was a lack of confidence. When state visitors flew into Gatwick, nothing should go wrong. They went by train to Victoria which had the paraphernalia for their reception and a royal waiting room with decoration chosen by the Queen. Ibbotson and Binnie knew this would all go just fine. They were comfortable with the hurly-burly and with what might, or might not, go wrong. Bob was not like that and would require dress rehearsals.

: It was the same for the opening by the Duke of Edinburgh of the huge resignalling of London Bridge. In that case, two dress rehearsals.

At the opening the re-signalled London Bridge. The Duke of Edinburgh congratulates Frank Paterson with Reg Peat and Bob Reid looking on. It had all gone smoothly. (BRB)

> : I can imagine that Bob might have said that the Southern Region 'was not difficult, it just required firm management'. Perhaps his severe style and refusal to get stuck in was what was needed. He was not at all comfortable if things went wrong and made sure that his managers were not either.

Finally, Frank tells the story of Bob's first meeting with Peter Parker.

> Frank: When Parker was first appointed, Bob organised a dinner in the Charing Cross Hotel for the Southern Region management to meet their new chairman. Parker must have said something, it was some organisational matter, which Bob disagreed with. An argument flared up. Bob, who was never particularly articulate, got more and more heated. Hunched over, head down, he seemed angrily to be lecturing his placemat, and the back of his neck got redder and redder. With a glass or two of wine, he was quite capable of 'going for it' and did so.

Parker, rather tolerantly, describes the same occasion like this:

> I met him first in 1976. We had a flaming row – I had not taken as part of my briefing that Bob had once had red hair and a flaming temper to match. He believed rightly that opposition is true friendship, and sparks flew. I immediately asked his help to establish the innovation of marketing at Board level in BR.
>
> He had just lost his wife, after a long illness; he told me that he was contemplating stepping out of the rail scene altogether.[61]

Parker did indeed pull Bob away from the Southern Region and on to the Board to establish the novel discipline of marketing – a broader idea than 'selling', which is all that had happened before.

Christopher Foster was not wrong, the London Midland table silver was stunning. (NRM)

Chairman Sir Peter Parker with the 1983 Corporate Plan containing investment commitments he could never have secured till Bob was in charge. (Alamy)

12 PARKER AND HIS NEW BOARD (1976–1979)

Parker, when he became chairman in April 1976, could see that he needed a more hands-on board than existed when he arrived. The following January he brought four new people onto the Board. Ian Campbell came on as head of engineering and research, James Urquhart as head of operations, Clifford Rose as member for personnel and industrial relations and, finally, Bob Reid, appointed board member for marketing. Campbell, Urquhart, and Reid all had Scottish roots: the McMafia.

Three people would report to Bob: the head of freight, the head of passengers and the head of parcels. They were to generate business and plan the future shape of their service – classic marketing.

Freight was a problem area. Bob asked Frank Paterson to take it on. For Frank it was an exciting task, working with the Central Electricity Generating Board on Merry-Go-Round and with British Steel and their 20 million tonnes of steel freight. The assault on the loss-making wagonload freight was under way; one third of marshalling yards were closed and the number of freight wagons halved. Speedlink, the focused and more efficient wagonload service, was relaunched. Frank loved the work but Bob, said Frank, seemed curiously detached from all this activity. Urquhart was far more involved.

In truth, Bob was out of sympathy with much of the thinking at the Board. It is not hard to imagine why. The financial position was terrible. But his colleagues were responding as they always had, cutting costs where they could and trying to run a better railway, the relaunch of Speedlink an example, none of which, Bob felt, was the true answer.

In the previous five years, from modest requirements for government support, the requirement had tripled to £563 million, and this for a business generating customer revenue of about £1,000 million.

Bad as it sounds, the reasons were not entirely to the discredit of the railway. Inflation had led to strikes which caused disruption.

On one occasion a 29 per cent pay rise had been required to bring peace. Railway costs had risen but the government had prevented the necessary fare increases.

Further, through action begun under Henry Johnson, there had been real improvements: more wagonload freight, a reduction in staff numbers, fast inter-city services on four routes, computers in use to manage the wagon fleet, resignalling schemes.

As Parker said, he was a great booster of morale: 'We now have the smell of success in our nostrils. We know what winning feels like.'[62] You could argue that it was the high point of good conventional railway management. But was good conventional management enough?

Peter Parker certainly thought it was. The only problem he could see – or at least the only one he talked about – was that the railway was starved of investment. 'Freeze to death', 'piling up problems for the future' and 'struggling to work within the fiscal constraint placed on them'. In this, he was no different from Dick Marsh, merely more personable. The 'crumbling edge of quality' became one of his mantras.[63]

The 1977 Transport White Paper saw things rather differently, certainly as regards freight:

> Rail offers no real alternative for most of the goods that now go by road'[64] and 'Substantial diversion of freight traffic from road to rail is not therefore immediately possible.'[65]

It goes on to say:

> The choice ultimately rests with the railways – whether they continue to provide a traditional freight service which can barely pay its way and is gradually eroded because it cannot earn enough to renew and develop the business. Or whether they support a strategy which involves some radical change.

Over the years, two 'solutions' were repeatedly proposed for the railway's problems. The first, that it should be cut in size, well beyond what Beeching did. The second, that it should be improved and expanded with greater investment. Neither was realistic. But around this time, thinking began to emerge amongst a small group of people, some in the new strategy unit, that it should be managed in a different way.

Bob knew that change was needed. We know this from Paul Watkinson, as he explains below. He describes a walking holiday at that time, 1978 or 79, in the Lake District.

> Paul: It was a semi-jolly. I was doing public affairs at Euston. David Binnie, the general manager, organised a visit by Peter Parker to the Lake District to meet local leaders and tourism people. Bob Reid and Cliff Rose were in the party.
>
> : After seeing the Ravenglass and Eskdale railway, we took some time off, and headed by minibus to Windermere by way of the Hardknott Pass and Wrynose Pass. The little bus stopped at Hardknott, some hung around drinking coffee, but Bob, Cliff and I went for a walk to the site of the Roman fort.
>
> : Bob and Cliff were talking. Bob seemed quite frustrated; he was pondering his own future and I think he did not agree with what was happening at the Board, even though he was marketing director. He seemed to me to be a dissatisfied man. He didn't feel he could have the influence he wanted; I remember that very clearly.

A happier appointment for Bob was chairmanship of British Transport Hotels. He was joined by Prue Leith, then the charismatic young restaurateur, and Sir Alexander Glen, a remarkable soldier/diplomat who had fought with Fitzroy Maclean in Yugoslavia, the inspiration, it is said, for James Bond.

With no one to defer to, Bob and his colleagues were able, or at least could try, to breathe new life into the group. It was an early candidate to be sold off, which it was in 1983.

In Prue Leith's words:

> Prue: He was probably the least talkative member of the Board, but when he spoke, it was always to the point and worth hearing.
>
> : We could have made more of a difference, but year after year the profits we made disappeared to prop up other parts of the railway so the hotels were constantly starved of cash. Bob would have

> been pragmatic about this, his loyalty, I think, being to BR, but I watched the hotels estate gradually getting shabbier, the telephone system more out of date, and I had huge battles to introduce less stuffy and more trendy bars and restaurants.
> : The sale of the business when it came was a fiasco, sold well below its market value. The sale was a very strange affair.

Difficult it was, but Bob enjoyed the work.

In June 1978, David Bowick, who was not well, moved up to vice chairman with his position as chief executive taken by Ian Campbell. By then Peter Parker and Bob Reid had got to know each other much better. It was Bob who Parker asked to join him when they went on a visit to Washington. Parker knew that the appointment as chief executive should really have gone to Bob – he and John Palmer at the Department for Transport agreed as much – but, Parker said, he could not buck the consensus on the Board which was for Campbell.

Peter Parker's most vivid memories of his childhood, when his character was formed, are of Shanghai, J G Ballard-land, in 1937.

> 'If God allowed Shanghai, he owed an apology to Sodom and Gomorrah.'

The road swarmed with crowds, the girls sheathed in silks and brocades, and gleaming in their dresses…. Between the International Concession and the French Concession was another world apart, the Chinese city of Shanghai. The feudal contrast of conditions made an indelible impression on my mind. Bliss it was to be European but to be Chinese was hell. Teaming poverty and unhappiness. The breeding ground for revolutionaries…. But then, that bloody day, the Japanese moved in. The show was over. Shells showered shrapnel on the roof of our exclusive, sacred Bath club…. Within days, we were in long queues, holding our hand-luggage, all we could take aboard the British destroyer. We were refugees. (His autobiography.)

13 MARGARET THATCHER, PRIME MINISTER

It was surprising, when the election came in May 1979, that the 43-seat majority for Margaret Thatcher was not larger. But she offered a disquieting vision: success should be rewarded and, by implication, failure should suffer the consequences; people should stand on their own feet and, by implication, those who could not should expect little support; and the protective blanket provided by trade unions should be pulled away.

The message in her party's manifesto is more tactfully phrased, with these commitments:

> To strike a fair balance between the rights and duties of the trade union movement.
> To restore incentives so that hard work pays.
> To concentrate welfare services on.... those who are in real need.

There was more to Margaret Thatcher than this harsh message suggests, but at the time that did not matter. People were fearful. After seeing Britain's position in the world slip steadily back, year after year, and seeing so many other attempts to provide solutions fail, there was little confidence that anything different would work. Thatcher's vision was unproven. Things were a mess, but it was our mess. Besides, even if her vision was right it would come at great cost to many.

There remained, therefore, a strong, lingering attachment to the soft socialism of the Labour Party: a planned economy, nationalised industries, government ownership of public services, bailouts when things got difficult, and a view that unions should have the means to force compliance with their wishes – with invitations to Number 10 for beer and sandwiches.

Thatcher had entirely different ideas. There would be no more invitations to Number 10 for union leaders, let alone beer and sandwiches when they got there. Five weeks after the election, Geoffrey

Howe, Chancellor of the Exchequer, presented his first budget. It would unleash a storm over the country blowing over anything weak or unsupported and generating fierce opposition.

The railway would be at the centre the storm. Out went all the previous devices for controlling the economy – prices and incomes policies, voluntary social contracts and whatnot – and in came one simple idea: control the money supply and hang the consequences. Only in this way, said Howe, would inflation be got under control, and only when inflation was under control would the economy start growing.

The consequences were indeed dire. With cash made scarce, interest rates shot up, indebted households lost their possessions, and activities which made little commercial sense went to the wall. Support for British Rail was cut. At a time of inflation, the seemingly small cut was in reality a savage reduction.

Other countries faced similar problems and had taken similar action, sharply reducing their governments' spending. Economies shrank across the whole world. Britain slid into a deep recession and unemployment rose. Nine months after his first budget, Howe presented his second. Previous governments would have responded with a financial stimulus – the traditional Keynesian remedy – but Howe's clampdown continued. There would be no U-turn, Margaret Thatcher saying, famously, 'You turn if you want to; the lady's not for turning,' a reference to Heath's disastrous U-turn ten years before. Jim Callaghan, leader of the opposition, called the budget 'the most socially divisive since 1931'.

For his third budget, eighteen months after the first, in March 1981, Howe faced extraordinarily difficult circumstances. Things were not going well. Despite the medicine, the promised fall in inflation was nowhere to be seen. It was running at 13 per cent. Interest rates were even higher, at 17 per cent. Millions of people were out of work. It was about as bad as it could be.

But Howe pressed on. Taxation was in fact increased for there was still a government deficit. He was roundly criticised on all sides. Famously, 364 economists signed a letter to *The Times* saying he was wrong and that his measures would push the economy further into recession.

But it was the economists who were wrong. Unemployment did continue to rise, reaching 12 per cent, but the economy was already beginning to turn and a few months after the letter had been signed it started to grow again. The recession ended. Inflation came down to a more reasonable 5 per cent and the economy motored away, growing at 2–5 per cent for some ten years.

But this was in the future. The early 80s were not happy times. With such high levels of unemployment, with bankruptcies and the closing of businesses, and cuts in public services, people suffered. Riots broke out in Brixton, Birmingham, Leeds and Liverpool. The cover story for *Time* magazine was headed 'Why Britain burns'. *Der Spiegel* wrote: 'At the time of the marriage of Prince Charles and Lady Diana, England is on the verge of civil war.' The Toxteth riots in Liverpool lasted nine days. Petrol bombs were thrown, buildings set on fire, seventy so badly they had to be demolished. Police were injured and hundreds of arrests made. For the first time on the British mainland, CS gas grenades were used.

The Geoffrey Howe medicine did work, but it did not work for everyone. In Liverpool, unemployment remained above 20 per cent for nearly twenty years.

It is hardly surprising that there was resistance to Thatcher's policies. Many thought they were immoral and inhuman. Others simply that they were the wrong way to run the country. But a growing number accepted the logic and in dogged, stoical ways worked to turn their businesses and personal lives around.

This is the background to Bob's first three years as chief executive of the railway.

14 BOB AS CHIEF EXECUTIVE (1980)

Bob as chief executive

Thatcher's first appointment as Secretary of State for Transport was Norman Fowler. Peter Parker remained chairman. Below him, two people were running the railway: David Bowick, vice chairman-rail, and Ian Campbell, the chief executive. By then Bowick was ill and wished to retire; his wife, it is said, insisted on it. His retirement was announced, and he left late in 1979.

Ian Campbell moved up to take Bowick's place as vice chairman, but with narrow responsibilities. Now was the time for Bob Reid to be appointed chief executive and be given a free rein to run the railway. His appointment was announced in January 1980, with the award of a CBE in the New Year's honours.

His last words as marketing director, in the December 1979 *Railnews*, were these:

> In marketing terms the most important achievement of the 70s has been the evolution of a range of soundly researched products, each with clearly defined financial objectives, based on the separation of the things we want to do commercially from the things we are required to do by government.
>
> InterCity, trainload freight, Freightliner, Red Star parcels and Speedlink form an outstanding quintet of transport products unmatched in their respective fields by any other operator.
>
> For the 80s the big test of the marketing function of BR will be harnessing the opportunities presented by advanced technology, by productivity gains and by the energy crunch to consolidate the rail mode as the natural and most cost-effective choice for bulk freight and InterCity transport.

JUST PEOPLE

Bob Reid, on his last day in the office, 30 March 1990, photographed by Jim Collins

Frank Paterson, joined LNER 1946, and below, his favourite photograph with Grace

Katy and Cyril Bleasdale, joined BR 1950

Ursula and Gordon Pettitt, joined BR 1950

Paul Watkinson, joined BR 1961

Mitzie and Chris Green, joined BR 1965

Sue and Chris Stokes, joined BR 1967

Pauline and John Nelson, joined BR 1968

Stephanie and Alan Cribbens, joined BR 1970

Catherine, his daughter, and Richard Goldson, joined BR 1970

Gail and Jim Collins, joined BR 1971

Christine and Peter Field, joined BR 1973

Antonia and George Muir, the author, joined the railway 1996

In these dry words, you can see where his heart lies. It lay in financial objectives, in doing things commercially, in products which can stand up to competition – and in expecting subsidy only for things specifically required by government.

The word 'product' is important. It suggests something designed in order to be sold to customers, in contrast to something designed to be a better railway.

Parker in the past had talked about there being a 'manifest destiny for the railways in this country'.[66] In Bob's mind, there was no such thing. There were products, and if a product did not sell it would be discontinued – 'manifest destiny' be damned. The difference between a product and a good railway is fundamental.

THE CASH CRISIS

The first three years of Bob's appointment were extraordinary. There was danger on every side. On taking up his position, in January 1980, he faced an immediate crisis. Cash was running out. The Board did not have enough to get through the next three months till the new financial year in April.

Government funding had been cut and inflation had taken off, this time reaching 21 per cent, a level hard nowadays to imagine. The fuel bill rose by £50 million. On top of inflation, a three-month strike in the steel industry damaged BR's freight business. Fewer cars were transported, less coal went to steel works, fewer steel products needed transport.

Parker worked to keep spirits up. 'I have no grounds for pessimism, strong, firm, grounds for optimism.'[67]

Memories of Parker are entirely favourable. He was hands-on. He went down to Euston station to get involved in de-icing doors; he would talk to anyone, plate layers or general managers, and get the pitch right without condescension or awkwardness. He was rightly popular.

To avoid a dispute with rail unions at the same time as the steel strike, the government pressed the Board to agree quickly a pay rise of 20 per cent, matching inflation. To pay for it, the January fare rise was set at an equally large 20 per cent. Such a rise fed inflation elsewhere in the country. Price rises drove pay claims, which drove price rises. Inflation did not come down quickly.

There were also the normal things to contend with. It was a particularly cold and snowy winter and life was difficult for everyone. Bill Bradshaw, then Chief Operations Manager, broadcast the appeals known so well: update emergency plans, keep the batteries in locomotives and power cars charged, keep water systems drained or lagged, check electric point heaters, check snow ploughs, carry out rehearsals and call out staff as soon as possible when bad weather threatens. These were difficult times.[68] Everything was sacrificed to survive.

Stock levels were reduced, debtors pressed for payment, investment postponed and new recruitment put on hold. Even part of a pay award was delayed and rolled forward till April. It was cash that mattered. The Board had no authority to borrow beyond its external financing limit, the 'EFL'.

The Board squeaked through past April 1980, keeping within its financial limits.

In truth, the railway is a fairly resilient affair from a cash point of view. The business, much changed since Beeching's day, was then 60 per cent traffic passenger and just 40 per cent freight and parcels. Freight was down, but passenger volumes were steady, indeed slightly up, so the fare rise of 20 per cent brought in enough cash to keep pace with inflation, and with a depreciation charge of £128 million, if investment is cut right back, survival is possible.

In reality, the immediate cash-saving measures just scratched the surface. Much more had to be done. In the following year, administrative costs were cut, trains shortened, vehicles scrapped to avoid maintenance, jobs eliminated and services cut. Hundreds of locomotives, coaches and freight wagons were broken up or mothballed. Three hundred of the oldest InterCity coaches were scrapped. A manager at the time recalls gross overstaffing, unproductive jobs and too many deadwood managers, which Peter Parker's five years at the top had still not eliminated.[69] The number of freight marshalling yards was cut to thirty-seven, only three being 'major yards'.[70] The business of collecting and delivering parcels was retained – though not for long – but parcels depots were to be cut from 220 to forty-one.

Such action takes time to work through, and by September of Bob's first year the Board was again facing a cash crisis. Some Board members wanted to break through the cash limit. Parker lobbied for more money. Circumstances were indeed so bad that a small increase in the EFL was agreed by government. But action to save costs intensified and the following January's fare rise of 16 per cent was brought forward to November 1980.

The Board squeaked through again past April the following year, keeping within its financial limits.

It is often said, 'never let a good crisis go to waste'. Most of what was done should have been done years before.

NORMALITY ALONG WITH THE STORM

A feature of the railway – so large and diverse – is the mixture of crises and normality. Despite cost-cutting and the turmoil in the country, normal things were going on. HST trains continued to be built and put into service. BREL continued its programme to speed up the repair of rolling stock.

Hopes resurfaced for a Channel Tunnel. Norman Fowler told Parliament, 'I have been examining preliminary proposals by BR and French railways for a single-track rail-only Channel Tunnel.' The projected cost seemed quite reasonable (about one third of what, when it was finally built, the tunnel did cost) and Norman Fowler was positive – easy to be when you know no serious decision is needed.

Another report addressed the electrification of the two InterCity routes, East Coast and Great Western. Again, Norman Fowler was positive, telling the Commons, 'The report presents several broad issues which the government will need to consider. In economic terms it presents a favourable assessment.'

One modest electrification was approved and was going well: the Bed–Pan line, the electrification of the 50-mile line between St Pancras/Moorgate and Bedford. It was on schedule for completion in 1982, but without any agreement with the unions for how it would be worked.

Less happy was the Advanced Passenger Train (APT) with its great 'ability to disappoint'. A prototype achieved a record speed of 162mph in December 1979 – a real achievement – but, seeking to forestall a government refusal to sanction further investment, the Board, with Bob Reid's full approval – he wanted faster trains to compete with cars on the motorways – arranged for this prototype train to be put into passenger service.

The decision led to one of the most infamous events in rail history. On 7 December 1981 the press was invited aboard the APT for its first official run from Glasgow to London. Technically it was a triumph. It set a record for the journey of 4 hours 15 minutes. The press, uninterested in triumphs, were offered instead a disaster: the sickening sensation experienced by passengers as the train tilted to go round a corner. The 'queasy rider' it was christened. The whole thing became a joke and was said, most unfairly, to typify the incompetence of the railway.

Development limped on for far too long. Eventually, in about 1986 Bob Reid, listening to yet another presentation explaining what was going wrong, lost his cool and yelled. 'I don't want to hear about it again. Put it in the railway museum in York.'[71] And that was that.

BOB BY NELSON

During this time, Bob was living in Purley, as he had since he had come down from Yorkshire. He would travel up to London every day by train and arrive, not especially early, at his office in front of Euston station.

We have a good description of Bob's early years as chief executive from John Nelson. In John's words:

> Nelson: I was the Divisional Passenger Manager in Sheffield, a sort of junior-to-middle manager at the time. As I was considered, I suppose, to be going somewhere, I was appointed for a two-year stint as the chief executive's personal assistant. This was late 1981.
> : I was in trepidation because this guy had a fearsome reputation.
> : He was an austere man in the way he looked and in the way he came across. An austere Scot in appearance, if you know what I mean. But he had a soft centre; he was a humane man. He was hard-edged but he also had a lot of empathy. He was quite liberal-minded, interestingly, although he did not have that reputation.
> : Even though people say he liked a drink, he was not a great drinker. He might have a glass of red wine but that was about it

and he did not drink at lunchtime or anything like that. And he did not like the 'mess' culture. I think this was a Scottish thing. He was disdainful of people who thought they had made it and should be in a mess with people serving them lunch and glasses of wine. He did not like it at all and found an opportunity to ban it. The occasion was the industrial disputes going on. He decided it was completely incongruous for management to be wining and dining themselves while turmoil went on out on the real railway. He got one or two anonymous poison pen letters as a result. I was asked to investigate. It was quite a surprise when we learned who might have written them and the matter was not pursued.

: Bob would have wall-to-wall tasks most of the day. He would meet a lot of people, often one-to-one, and he spent a lot of time on the phone, sometimes calling people outside the formal structure. He had a good relationship with the Mayor of Peterborough who was also, strangely, a driver and a member of ASLEF. Charles Swift was his name, most respected for his integrity.

: The formal management structure was distrusted because of its hierarchical nature. He regarded it as an impenetrable bureaucracy and did not always trust what the general managers were telling him.

: He went out regularly on tours of the regions to talk to managers, to meet the staff on the ground and see for himself what was going on. He used these tours, or any meeting with groups of managers, as means of making a point.

: The tour of a region would start off with a dinner with the whole management team. Over dinner, Bob would hold forth, initially, but then choose a subject – he might ask whether a commercial man could overrule a safety decision – and then pick a fight, pick someone to argue with, deliberately. He did this almost wherever he went. He wanted a point to be made for everyone to see. It was interesting psychology.

: Bob chaired the Railway Executive Group. He was the boss. On it were the regional general managers and the functional heads: the chief engineer, the operations director, the commercial people. One of my roles, as secretary to the group, was taking the minutes.

: As minutes secretary of the group, I did the seating plan. There were a huge number of people, twenty or more. They sat round an oval-shaped table. I put out nameplates, specifying people by title. Bob sat on one side in the middle. Sometimes, if there was someone he was gunning for, it seems often to have been the engineering director, I would be told to change the seating plan and put that person opposite him. Bob would then choose a moment in the meeting, always talking quietly, to point out for everyone to hear what this hapless person was doing wrong. At times it was a bit embarrassing. He never raised his voice. His austere manner, the way he came across, was enough. He was softly spoken; you might struggle to hear what he was saying if you were at the end of the room.

: These meetings, of course, were not to take decisions, though it may have seemed that they were. He made all the decisions.

: There would be separate meetings on, for example, industrial relations, and the Railway Executive Group would have little impact on that.

: He was a very determined individual. In his mind, he knew what was right. I cannot think of a single occasion where he compromised. Well, there was one, privatisation, where he made gestures which he thought might buy off the politicians. But in terms of running the railway I cannot think of a single thing that he wanted to do that he did not achieve.

: Major productivity initiatives were forced through like driver-only operations, flexible rostering for drivers and getting guards off freight trains.

: Sector management was steamroller in, against opposition.

: My job was fascinating. It brought me into contact with all the senior people and I could see how Bob was fighting a number of really significant battles. They were mould-breaking things he did, all of them.

The next two chapters will describe the forcing through of the productivity initiatives and the steamrollering in of sector management.

PETER PARKER

But first a word about Peter Parker. Peter and Bob got on well together. They were comfortable with their different roles: Parker the communicator and Bob the doer. But there were differences in their viewpoints.

In the first place, Parker thought it his job to campaign to persuade the government to spend more on the railway. He kept talking about the 'crumbling edge of quality' and ran an advertising campaign: 'How long can we go on running the most cost-effective major railway in Europe?'[72] Bob took a different view. The money was the money. It was the railway's job to operate within whatever the government provided. Parker's campaign might seem harmless, it certainly achieved nothing, but it sent out the wrong message to railway managers; the solution, Parker implied, was more money not better management. Bob had no patience with this.

Secondly, Parker thought that the productivity battle with the unions could be won by persuasion, by argument, by inclusive meetings, by warm personal relations with their leaders. They could, he thought, be persuaded of the need for change. Parker was not naïve, nor soft, but he did believe in the power of communication. His autobiography is filled with stories of suppers with union leaders and their wives. Bob did not share this view, and cosy meetings with union leaders dried up when he became chairman. Parker was not entirely wrong and Bob not entirely right. Parker's efforts never resulted in any union agreement, but they did let people understand the way things were heading.

Cyril Bleasdale puts it well.

> Cyril: I think we underestimate Peter Parker's achievements. He gave a great fillip to morale in the railway. This is not a dead-end organisation, this is not a railway that is going to close, it has got a future. He was a very gifted person. He was articulate and approachable. Parker had the vision. The implementation and doing was Bob Reid. Bob wasn't a visionary. He was 'show me what the problem is and I'll solve it.'

That view of Bob is Cyril's. Bob did have a vision, it just wasn't theatrical.

15 THE ASLEF STRIKE (1982)

PRODUCTIVITY

For years past, the Board had sought to agree productivity improvements as part of the annual pay round. Each agreement was accompanied by the union's assurance that they would 'consider' – a key word – changes to the established working practices. With the rarest exception, no change was ever agreed.

The unions had a point. They wanted to trade their agreement for improved pay. But none of the pay rises did more than keep pace with inflation. Unions therefore held on most tightly to those practices which the Board most wanted to remove.

Both sides were in a bind. Pay and conditions, hours of work, etc. had indeed fallen behind those elsewhere. There were many vacancies which could not be filled. But an across-the-board pay rise could not be afforded without improvements in productivity, which the unions would not agree to. Neither side could move.

The changes required were well known. They featured particularly in a document called 'The Challenge of the 80s' launched at the end of 1979. It was filled with facts and figures and thoughtful analysis, a document very much in the Peter Parker mould. Its premise was that a rational discussion with the unions about the needs of the business would secure agreement. But not a bit of it. There was an outcry when the document came out. Bill Ronksley at the ASLEF Annual Meeting shouted, 'This is not productivity – it is slavery.'[73]

The 1980 pay round, following the 'this is slavery' outburst, contained the usual union assurances about productivity. There was a long list of topics to consider. As both the country and the railway were facing a most obvious crisis, there was some hope that this time, at last, change would be possible. There was much expression of goodwill.

But the front page of June's *Railnews* demonstrated the idiocy of the whole thing. A vast system of meetings, 'carefully monitored by a sub-committee of the Rail Staff National Council' was required. In breathless prose, *Railnews* proclaimed, 'Hardly had the ink dried on the signing of the deal, which gave rail staff a 20 per cent pay rise, when meeting dates were being fixed to begin detailed talks on the proposals.'

It went on: 'So complex and heavy is the undertaking that most of the days left in 1980 have been earmarked for one meeting or another.' Each of the five regions was involved and, within each, four sectional councils had to be catered for – twenty groups in all. Each would require an introductory meeting, a meeting to discuss the substance, and follow-up meetings.

No one could seriously believe that such a process would achieve anything – and it did not. The union leaders were commendably clear. Ray Buckton for ASLEF and Sid Weighell for the NUR both declared they would not contemplate any of the changes the Board wanted. Buckton, writing in *Railnews* in August 1980, said that while ASLEF was comfortable with some types of change – he mentioned only a willingness to drive more powerful locomotives carrying heavier loads at greater speed – it was not happy with others.

> Because unions do not accept every crackpot scheme put before them', he wrote, 'there is a popular misconception that they are opposed to change. While we are not opposed to the efficient deployment and utilisation of manpower, we cannot permit a breakdown in our members' health in management's pursuit of that mythical break-even balance sheet figure.'
>
> He goes on, 'There is a call for a greater degree of flexibility of working, but it is clear that what is being sought is a relinquishing of conditions of employment which have been hard won over the years.

Not much chance of agreement there.

Sid Weighell of the NUR was, on the surface, more amenable. Most helpfully, he was prepared to agree flexible rostering, but on the issue most affecting guards the NUR would not move. The 'disappearance of guards' from freight trains could not be placed on the agenda.

Knowing that this farcical consultation would get nowhere, Bob changed tack and set about the matter in his own distinctive way. Instead of inviting discussion, he spelt out, clearly and politely, the six specific changes he required. Set down in a September 1980 *Railnews* article, they were as follows.

ONE. THE TRAINMAN CONCEPT

Hitherto, the career paths leading to becoming a train driver or a guard were entirely separate. When you joined the railway, you were heading in one direction or the other. The trainman concept was a proposition to create a new post, a trainman, for junior staff but from which people could be promoted either to become guards/conductors or to become drivers.

It was not particularly controversial, but ASLEF was reluctant to agree – they feared it would lead to their being swallowed up by the NUR. As it was not a priority, it was left on the backburner and implemented some years later in modified form.

TWO. ONE-MAN OPERATION OF SOME FREIGHT TRAINS: A DRIVER BUT NO GUARD

This was controversial. With continuous brakes, brake vans were no longer required. Nonetheless, guards still rode on such trains, in the rear cab of the locomotive, with almost nothing to do. Thousands of jobs were at stake and the matter was clearly a problem for the NUR. The Board put it off until some years later.

THREE. ONE-MAN OPERATION OF SOME PASSENGER TRAINS: A DRIVER BUT NO GUARD

Unlike on freight trains, guards on passenger trains had things to do. The guard controlled the doors, opening and shutting them at stations, and was 'in charge of the train'. If the train broke down and was stranded away from the station, the guard would escort the passengers off the train. If there was an accident, the guard would take steps to warn other trains. There was the job of checking tickets and looking after passengers with, traditionally, the title of conductor.

While on rural and long-distance lines these tasks were important, this was less so on commuter lines. With the train stopping every few minutes and staff at most stations, there was an argument that the driver could close the doors and that other tasks could be carried out by the station staff.

Safety was an issue so, if on-train guards were to be dispensed with, the train and station had to be properly equipped. There had to be sliding doors which the driver could operate, radio communication between signalman, driver and passengers, and either staff on stations to wave to the driver when it was safe to shut the doors or mirrors and cameras so the driver could see the full length of the train.

This too was a problem for the NUR. Indeed, it still is.

The intention was that the Bed-Pan line (St Pancras/Moorgate to Bedford) then being renewed and electrified, would be equipped for driver-only operation. New electric trains, fitted with all the necessary equipment, had been ordered. But the NUR had not agreed to the change and the trains would remain stuck in the sidings when they arrived.

FOUR. EASING THE CONDITIONS FOR SINGLE-MANNING: ONE PERSON IN THE DRIVER'S CAB

Following the single-manning agreements of 1965 and 1968 it was accepted that the second man could be dispensed with in most circumstances, and by this time 80 per cent of train services were single-manned. But Bob wanted single-manning on all trains. It was never a major issue and the second man did not fully disappear from all InterCity trains until after privatisation.

FIVE. FLEXIBLE ROSTERING

In a famous agreement in 1919, after many bitter disputes, the shift length for drivers was set at a fixed eight hours, irrespective of the work required. Though clearly inefficient, the eight-hour shift was sacrosanct, a symbol of past victories which could not be traded away.

Bob wanted this changed so that shifts could be of different, but not unreasonable lengths, reflecting the work required, but still averaging forty hours a week over a full roster. On the face of it, agreement should have been possible – no one was to lose their job or lose money.

The Board chose it as the issue it would first seek to win. For such a small change, the struggle generated enormous, disproportionate hostility and a damaging strike eighteen months later.

It should not be supposed that the eight-hour day means eight hours in a driving cab. There is inevitably a lot of sitting around. The average train-working content of the eight-hour day was just 3 hours 20 minutes.

SIX. THE OPEN STATION CONCEPT

This was a proposal to do away with ticket barriers at stations for InterCity services and to move revenue protection and customer service onto the train. It was implemented and in due course extended, for example, to London suburban trains. Years later it became obvious ticket examination on suburban services did not work. The trains were too crowded and the journeys too short. Ticketless travel mushroomed and could not be ignored. Except for InterCity stations, from the mid-90s the idea was put into reverse, and ticket barriers were commonly re-installed.

These were the six changes Bob wanted to see.

We therefore end 1980 with a vast schedule of meetings, the union's red lines, Bob's six points and, after nine months of negotiation, no changes agreed except for the open stations.

THE STRIKE

The next year, 1981, saw a fresh determination by the Board. Any pay increase was to be held back till changes were specifically agreed. Starting in April, bitter negotiations got under way. The expressions of goodwill of the previous year died away.

Across the country, it was a time of great conflict. It was the summer of riots in Liverpool, Manchester and Brixton. The atmosphere was very bad. Eventually, in August, the Board, in a desperate financial position, offered a small rise, 7 per cent (when inflation was 12 per cent). The offer was rejected, and no increase in pay was made. A tortuous struggle between the Board and the unions began. The first skirmish was an appeal by the unions to the tribunal chaired by Bill McCarthy. The tribunal sympathised with the unions and concluded that there should be an immediate 8 per cent rise with a further 3 per cent paid later in the year, taking the increase to 11 per cent, roughly matching inflation. There was, of course, another commitment by the unions to consider changes to working practices but nothing was agreed.

The Board did pay the 8 per cent. But in December, when the 3 per cent rise was due, it hardened its position and determined that the matter be brought to a head. It set its mind on achieving this one specific item, flexible rostering. Until it was agreed, the 3 per cent would not be paid, neither to ASLEF members nor NUR.

Without the 3 per cent, an enraged Ray Buckton led ASLEF on an immediate campaign of industrial action. Seventeen strike days stretched over January, February and March of 1982. It was misery for passengers.

Sidney Weighell for the NUR was equally outraged. He had accepted flexible rostering. Why should his members not get the 3 per cent? His red line was the removal of guards on freight trains, which the Board was not pressing.

While this was going on, the TUC leader, Len Murray, got the two unions together to discuss a merger – a long-standing idea, never likely to happen. The meeting did not go well. Sidney Weighell accused ASLEF of being 'devious' and 'liars' over the matter of the merger. In reply, the ASLEF president, Derek Fullick, yelled at Weighell, 'You're a traitor to the trade union movement; you did nothing during our dispute but give comfort to the British Railways Board and their political masters in Whitehall.' At this Weighell jumped from his seat and called Fullick a liar, thereby eliciting a response which came to be celebrated in trade union circles. 'If you call me a liar once again, I'll get you by your braces and drop you down the lift shaft.'[74] Thus ended the merger attempt.

To add to the atmosphere of crisis Argentinian 'scrap metal dealers' landed on South Georgia, indicating that an invasion of the Falkland Islands would soon follow.

The dispute over flexible rostering ground through the dispute resolution machinery. Eventually it reached the highest body, the Rail Staff National Tribunal.

The hearing got off to a rowdy start with a standing ovation for Ray Buckton, and the chanting of 'We Will Not Be Moved'. Buckton: 'The locomotive man of the day considers that the eight-hour guaranteed day is the bed-rock of his agreements and that he will not relinquish it whatever the consequences.'[75]

The inquiry dragged on through April with British Rail despairing of the result, viewing McCarthy as a 'compulsive fudger of any issue put before him'.[76]

On 7 May, to the horror of ASLEF and unlike most previous hearings which had sided with the union, the tribunal decided that the Board was right: the sacrosanct eight-hour day should go and be replaced by flexible rostering. 'Totally unacceptable' was ASLEF's reaction. The June issue of its journal carried the proclamation 'We will not bow to BR's blackmail.'

The Board pressed ahead. On Tuesday 29 June, it informed ASLEF that managers were being instructed to issue new flexible rosters from the following Sunday, 4 July. A national rail strike loomed, and over an issue the importance of which no one could comprehend.

The national press poured scorn on ASLEF and its leadership. Even the *Guardian* tore into the union. 'Now it is ASLEF'S turn to bluster its way to the brink of disaster. It is for the union and not BR to back off by withdrawing the strike threat. ASLEF leaders merit ritual humiliation for not bargaining in good faith – flexible rostering will come what may.'

Sidney Weighell of the NUR tore into ASLEF: 'That mob ASLEF. We agreed to negotiate and then I'm told 'the eight-hour day was sacrosanct because my grandfather had worked it'. It was a farce.'[77] His union, however, decided that in all conscience its members would not cross an ASLEF picket line.

The Sun carried a huge front-page quotation supposedly from Peter Parker: 'I will smash ASLEF' – and urged the Board to 'Crush Buckton's militants'. Parker was in more of a rage than anyone: 'Pigheaded, anarchic, brutal, savage, abrupt, suicidal, selfish, stupid, foolish, muddled' was what he was telling the *Evening Standard.*

But people under pressure dig in. ASLEF would not budge. From midnight on Sunday 4 July, the railway network fell silent. At picket lines up and down the country there was optimism that the Board could be brought back to the table, that the disruption to the country was so great that the Board would be told to back down. But they underestimated the government. The Minister of Trade, Cecil Parkinson, declared: 'Today, a little more than a week after the liberation of our British people on the Falklands there are trade union leaders and a minority of politicians apparently intent on bringing Britain to a halt.'

Troops returning home from the Falklands were not impressed by what they were hearing. Over the side of a troopship arriving in Southampton waters was a huge banner saying, 'CALL OFF THE RAIL STRIKE ... OR WE'LL CALL AN AIR STRIKE.'

Support for the strike could be found in some places, however. The *Morning Star* argued that the government was using the Board to cripple all organised trade union activity. Some nurses joined the picket lines. Tony Benn congratulated ASLEF in the Commons on their 'principled and courageous stand in defence of the eight-hour day' and told the Durham miners' gala that the Conservatives 'want to smash the unions and create a servile workforce'.

Gratifying though such solidarity was, ASLEF realised that the government was in too strong a position and the trade union movement too sceptical of its case to allow it a victory. On the Sunday, at the end of the first week, ASLEF went to ACAS again proposing a compromise which was, again, rejected by the Board.

At BR headquarters, a crucial question, asked every day, was whether there was any weakening in the resolve of drivers to stick with the strike or would some begin to drift back to work. Not many did. The pressure on drivers was immense, both ways. Bob Reid talked to as many people as he could to get a sense of what was happening. As John Nelson describes:

> Nelson: Bob made a point of reaching right down to grass-roots level and talking directly to people on the ground. He used to get me to do a lot of that as well. If he wanted to know what the drivers at Southend Victoria were thinking – they were particularly militant – then he would speak directly to people there. He did that all over the country.

THE STANDARD
CLOSING PRICES
Monday, March 15, 1982. 15p. Incorporating the Evening News

Defiant Buckton tells tribunal:
8-hour day is here to stay

'WE WILL NOT BE MOVED'

by John Williams

TRAIN DRIVERS' leader Mr Ray Buckton today stood firm on the issue of flexible rostering as Lord McCarthy's tribunal got off to a rowdy start.

Outcome 'crucial'

THE STANDARD
LATE PRICES STOP PRESS
Wednesday, June 30, 1982. 15p. Incorporating the Evening News

SIR PETER PARKER'S BROADSIDE FOR ASLEF
'Pigheaded, anarchic, brutal, savage, abrupt, suicidal, selfish, stupid, foolish, muddled'

RAGE OF THE RAIL CHIEF

BRITISH RAIL chairman Sir Peter Parker today branded Ray Buckton and his ASLEF executive as savage, suicidal and stupid.

by John Williams

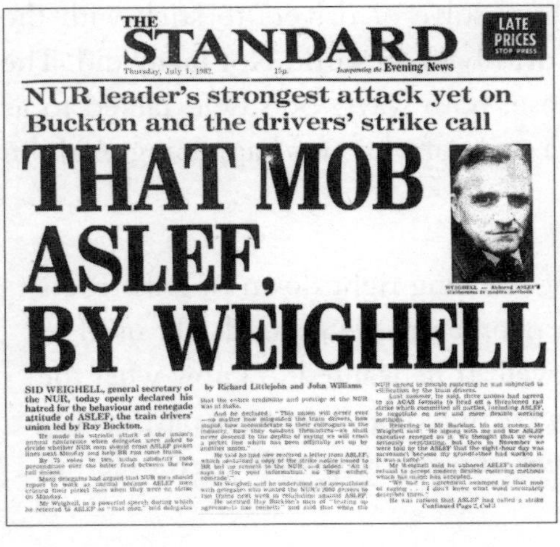

THE STANDARD
LATE PRICES STOP PRESS
Thursday, July 1, 1982. 15p. Incorporating the Evening News

NUR leader's strongest attack yet on Buckton and the drivers' strike call

THAT MOB ASLEF, BY WEIGHELL

SID WEIGHELL, general secretary of the NUR, today openly declared his hatred for the behaviour and renegade attitude of ASLEF, the train drivers' union led by Ray Buckton.

by Richard Littlejohn and John Williams

: He was involved in all the details of how the strike was handled. I slept overnight in the office in a sleeping bag on the floor. There were rooms upstairs for Board members so that is where Bob slept. There was a canteen in the morning for breakfast, so it was not too bad.

Was he a hawk?

Nelson: He was. He was very determined. He knew what was right.

The Board pressed forward. In a letter signed by Peter Parker, sent to home addresses hoping for support from the wives, the Board issued an ultimatum saying that the entire railway would be closed from Wednesday 21 July unless there was a return to work, and that all striking employees would be dismissed.

The union urged its members to 'stand firm' and sought help from Michael Foot, leader of the Labour Party. But of help, there was none.

In those days, the Trades Union Congress (TUC) had an influential role in advising trade unions and assisting them in their disputes. What one union might do could help or harm other unions. Union leaders would meet therefore and offer support and advice and on rare occasions urge restraint. This was one of these times.

On Friday 16 July, at the end of the second week, the general secretary of the engineering union, Terry Duffy, convened a meeting of the TUC Finance and General Purposes Committee, on which sat Ray Buckton of ASLEF. Duffy did not support the strike. He had already told Buckton so. Other committee members argued that flexible rostering could actually improve the conditions of workers. ASLEF was left therefore to argue not that flexible rostering was wrong, but that management should not be able to impose changes without agreement. It is a telling point. The merits of the dispute had long ago ceased to matter. At its heart, this was a dispute about power.

The meeting at the TUC went on all Friday, stretching until 1 a.m. on Saturday morning, when it finally broke up. Just hours later at 7:30 a.m. that Saturday morning, ASLEF was summoned again to the TUC and presented with a document which its president described as 'one of the greatest betrayals' in union history. While the meeting at the TUC the previous day had ground on, representatives of the TUC and the BR Board had been meeting in secret at ACAS without ASLEF being present – an extraordinary procedure. The document handed over that Saturday morning, agreed in secret between BR and the TUC, required that ASLEF call off the strike and work the seventy-one rosters issued so far on the basis of an undertaking that the Board would not issue any further rosters for two weeks.[78]

The ASLEF members were appalled. They returned to their headquarters in Arkwright Road, Hampstead, for a long discussion, lasting all Saturday afternoon. They were being required to swallow a bitter pill, and having done so, left over the back garden fence to avoid the press at their front door. The next day, Sunday18 July, the union's executive noted the failure of the TUC to assist in their struggle and called off the strike.[79]

What stands out from this story is that despite a weak case and overwhelming public hostility, ASLEF had not readily given in. They had stuck to their position for six months, striking on numerous occasions, including a national strike lasting two weeks. Some drivers had gone back to work, but not many. ASLEF was a very determined brotherhood and very bitter it had lost.

A meeting of 400 footplatemen in Glasgow erupted in anger when their representative reported the decision. Similar anger was expressed at mass meetings in Sheffield and Humberside. A bedridden past delegate telegrammed saying, 'Remember always John Bromley's spirit', referring to a doughty union fighter of 1920s fame.

With the strike over, the executive sought to discipline members who had worked during the strike. Fullick described them as 'scum' and a 'cancer in our midst'. Fear of litigation prevented expulsions, but the matter rumbled on for a year, and some strike-breakers were ostracised in their locality for the rest of their careers.

The Board pressed ahead with the issue of new rosters. One might wonder why the Board chose this item, flexible rostering, as the first to pursue. Manpower savings were small and offset by a pay rise to secure peace. But the matter had the advantage of being winnable. The public, unable to fathom ASLEF's objections, were wholly on the side of the Board.

THE FUTURE FOR THE UNIONS

It is worth observing that there have been no other disputes of a similar kind involving ASLEF since then. There have been many disputes, but generally over pay and hours of work, with perhaps two exceptions: first, should Sunday be in the working week, not the trivial point it seems; and second, are drivers prepared to cooperate with driver-only operation if that is being opposed by the NUR?

For the NUR, the future was far more threatening. Their membership had halved. In 1955 it had been over 350,000; it was now down to 140,000, and two big battles lay in the future: preserving guards on freight trains and preventing more driver-only operation. The former would soon come to a head; the latter went quiet for many years as it is costly to implement.

At heart, the two issues are different. The first is simple: it is about jobs. The second is more interesting, for it is not about jobs for often on a driver-only train there is still a job for a guard, looking after passengers, but not a job required for the running of the train. Some say it is about trade union power, the ability of the union to stop trains running if they withdraw their labour. But there is more to it. It is also about dignity, about the gradual deskilling of industrial labour. Not so long ago, guards used to be 'in charge of the train', and they had authority. If an accident threatened, they got down on the track, put down detonators, put on track circuit clips, and escort passengers off the train. It was set out in 'the black book'. From being broad-based 'industrial' jobs requiring training and technical knowledge, they were becoming people jobs. The jobs are responsible, but they require little technical knowledge. It is easy to say this should be of no concern if the pay is right, but deep down it is. It is a railway example of the deskilling of industrial jobs and the discontent that can arise.

Something similar but less obvious had been experienced by drivers. The drivers were unhappy when the Areas were established in the 1970s and the Motive Power Departments dismantled. Previously, they and their train came as a package. They reported to the shed master and signed on in the shed. They and their locomotive were a partnership, a single thing. Gordon Pettitt describes his father, a driver, wearing white gloves as his train was so clean. Note the word, 'his train'. The coming of the Areas led to drivers being separated from their trains. They became a fungible resource. A skilled one, of course, with precise but limited technical requirements. A modern driving cab has been so simplified that it has been described as being like a Fisher-Price toy but, Fisher-Price toy or not, it remains the control panel of a sophisticated £15 million piece of moving equipment carrying a five hundred people and there is dignity in being in its control.

All in all, ASLEF should be content, but the circumstances facing the NUR were very different. Weighell, a moderate, was voted out of office and succeeded by Jimmy Knapp. He talked a fighting talk but was careful, canny, a realist. He remained general secretary for 18 years until he died in 2001, aged 61, being replaced by Bob Crow in 2002. He too was canny, 'Don't start disputes which you don't know how to get out of' was one of his sayings. He also died young, aged 52 in 2014.

16 SECTORISATION

The problem of a profession-led railway and the relative weakness of general management had been recognised for a long time – Bill Johnson recognised it, Cyril Bleasdale says that Peter Parker recognised it – but the dominance of the professions was so ingrained that till Bob Reid arrived, no one had the determination for the task of putting it right.

Bob Reid had been divisional commercial officer in Glasgow and had come across decisions by the engineering professions which, as he saw it, obstructed what would make good commercial sense. Bob wanted a 'business-led' railway – a phrase he would use again and again. The focus had to be not on signalling or rolling stock or operations – the professions – but on the total service as perceived by the customer.

Determination would certainly be required. Plans to focus on 'products and markets' began to be drawn up in the strategy unit from the summer of 1978. Details were fleshed out, but often hidden from the regional general managers so as to postpone their opposition. And opposition there was when the details emerged in 1980 and 1981. Frank Paterson, then at Eastern, was a sceptic, and Lesley Lloyd at Western a 'vocal critic'.[80] They argued that the new appointments were unnecessary and a distraction and, anyway, that they, the general managers, were quite able to develop products and markets if that was what was wanted.

But, by then, 'Reid was leading the charge and in no mood to compromise.'[81]

The idea that emerged was that the railway should be conceived of not as five regions but as five business sectors: InterCity, London and South-East, Provincial, Freight, and Parcels. To reorganise the railway on these lines would have been too disruptive so instead a plan was developed to place an overlay on top with authority to prepare plans and budgets for the entire railway, in the light of the requirements of each business sector. It would be the duty of the regional general managers to operate within these plans and budgets.

Budgetary control and planning

Before 1982	From 1982
The Board	The Board
↓	↓
	Sector directors: three passenger (plus freight and parcels)
↓	↓
Regional general managers, 5	Regional general managers: (5)

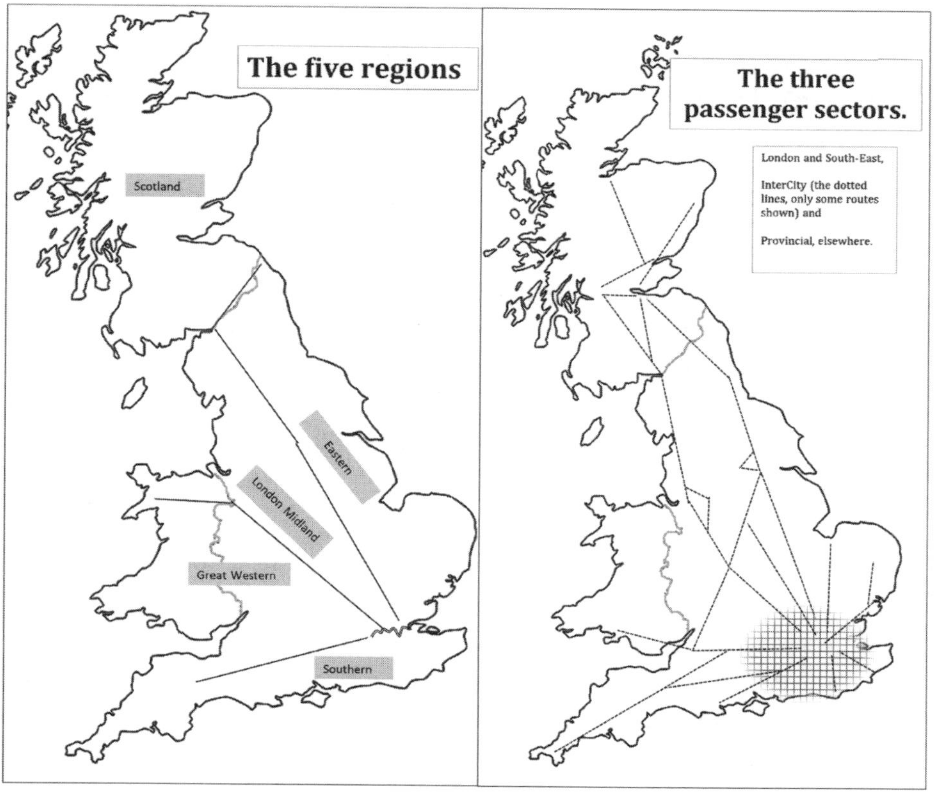

Each sector had to deal with all five regions, except the L&SE sector and the Scottish region. And deal with head office directions – a 3-D matrix, not easy.

This most radical idea faced heavy criticism. A memory of one meeting between Bob and the general managers is of very hostile body language from some general managers which translated into 'let's see this daft proposal off'.[82] There was reason for the objection. The general managers were drenched in work to keep the railway afloat and the proposal would divert good people onto a task which was bound to make the life of a general manager more difficult – which it did.

It took two years to work through the details of what came to be called 'sectorisation'. The biggest job was the accounting system, which had to be redesigned so as to allocate cost and revenue correctly and allow the business sectors to know how well they are doing. Till then, in the famous phrase, the only place where cost and revenue came together was on the chief executive's desk.

The main accounting problem was the allocation of infrastructure costs between the users of the track: freight, local passenger or InterCity passenger. There is no 'correct' way to do this but a workable solution was found.

INFRASTRUCTURE COST ALLOCATION

After much cogitation, two different theories emerged for the allocation of the cost of shared resources, for example the costs of a four-track route shared by InterCity, Provincial Passenger Services and Freight. The two theories were: Prime User and Sole User.

Three people alive today understand the difference, Richard Goldson is one of them.

> Goldson: Under Prime User and considering a four-track route, the main user (probably InterCity, even though it only uses two of the tracks, the two high-speed tracks) picks up the entire cost of the route, offset only by the assessed short-run incremental costs caused by the additional operation of other trains. That incremental cost will be very low for other passenger trains, possibly more substantial for freight.
> : Under Sole User, the main user (again InterCity) pays only the assessed costs which would be incurred if it were the sole

user, usually the cost of a plain two-track railway with no junctions, etc. The rest of the cost of the four-track railway and its associated junctions, fast/slow crossovers, etc. are then divided between the other users. This results in a much larger charge to other passenger operators, and a somewhat larger charge to freight.

Sole User seems more fair but it leaves no single person in charge of the route. Under Prime User, it is clear who is to manage the totality, but under that system InterCity could never make a profit. Sole User had to be adopted.

Once revenue and costs are allocated to a market sector, it is possible for them to be managed as one, on the desk of someone with a realistic ability to manage what he or she sees. In this way, both of the two problems identified 30 years before by John Elliot can be addressed. Responsibility can be devolved from the centre to a local level and coordination between the professions becomes possible.

When the announcement of sectorisation came, it was very low-key. In Bob's column in *Railnews* in January 1982 it was the fifth item. At the end of his column, Bob wrote this:

> December also saw the announcement of the appointment of the five directors who will be responsible to me for the results of InterCity, London and South-East, other Provincial passenger services, Freight and Parcels.
>
> Briefly their responsibilities will be:
>
> 1. Accountability for the financial performance in each sector against the objectives that are set.
> 2. The preparation and endorsement of plans and budgets for each sector.
> 3. Obtaining through geographical and functional management a product of the quality and cost required.
> 4. Initiating corrective action as necessary to ensure targets are met.

> This is an important move as it changes our present hierarchical form of management to one which is based on integrating geographical as well as business responsibilities.
>
> The appointments do not signal a major reorganisation.
>
> [.....]
>
> The responsibilities of the general managers of the railway regions for day-to-day management on a geographical basis remain unchanged.

Three of the sectors were designated as the 'commercial' railway: Freight, Parcels and InterCity; and two as the 'social' railway: London and South-East, and Provincial. The former should be operated so as to make a profit, the latter so as to live within the amount of support provided by the government through the 'public service obligation' (PSO) funding system.

The five new sector directors were:

- Henry Sanderson. He was already Chief Freight Manager and was confirmed as the Sector Director for Freight.
- Mike Connolly. He was already Chief Parcels Manager and was confirmed as Sector Director for Parcels.
- Cyril Bleasdale, whom we have already heard about, became Sector Director of InterCity. He had most recently been managing director of Freightliner.
- John Welsby, whom we will talk about later, became Sector Director for Provincial Services. He had most recently been in the strategy unit.
- David Kirby, who had been a successful manager of Sealink, was made both Sector Director London and South-East and general manager of the Southern Region. Gordon Pettitt, by then a most experienced railwayman, was made his deputy in both roles. That sector, London and South-East, was very large. It covered the Southern Region, south of the Thames, and railway services up to about 30 miles north of the Thames, the London end of three other regions.

That the announcement was low-key is not surprising. The February *Railnews* front page read:

Ice, blizzards and strikes hammer BR
TEST OF ENDURANCE
ASLEF action: cost runs into millions

John Nelson, Bob Reid's PA, describes what happened.

> Nelson: The first sector directors were appointed soon after I arrived and, all of a sudden, the Railway Executive Group completely changed its orientation, almost overnight. The key people, the people who were being encouraged to do things, suddenly became the commercial people.
> : The general managers opposed what he was trying to do. They, literally, had territorial control and behaved like gods in their own fiefdoms. They could not see why this change was needed. And they were strong personalities: Frank Paterson in Eastern, Lesley Lloyd in Western, Leslie Soane in Scotland and the London Midland general manager Jim O'Brien. The only one sympathetic to what Bob was trying to do was Jim O'Brien. He later became board member for marketing and was the person to whom the sector directors reported for a while.

As many confirm, the sector directors had at first little more than a secretary to help and had to find their own way, both a place to sit and which battles they should fight.

Bob had chosen them well and each got on with the job in their own way. John Welsby describes how he, a one-time economist, came to become a sector director and what he did.

> Welsby: Sometime in the late 70s, the Board had become less than enamoured with what was happening within the management of BR. It wanted a strategy unit – and that for that to work properly there should be some grit in it.
> : I was then in the Department for Transport in charge of the

economics unit looking after railways. My unit pretty much always said 'no'. It was very much the period of Parker and the 'crumbling edge of quality'. Public relations and all that stuff. 'No' was usually the right answer. Someone told the Board that the grittiest thing he knew was Welsby.
: I moved across as part of the strategy unit. We had a lot of home truths to tell, which did not go down well. When Bob was chief executive, the power of the general managers was really amazing. Bob called them barons. Before the Board executive meetings, they would have their own informal meeting and would come to the Board executive absolutely lined up on whatever it was they had decided they wanted. Bob was in a very, very difficult position.
: The majority of the guys said, 'This is the way we do things round here; just leave us to run the railway Bob. You go off and keep the government quiet.'

John Welsby goes on explaining the type of person appointed.

: Bob deliberately brought in people who were not of the standard railway. He wanted grit in the system. Cyril Bleasdale was brought in from Freightliner to cover InterCity, David Kirby from Sealink to cover London and the South-East, and he brought in an economist – what does he know! – to cover Provincial.
: The man was extremely perceptive; he knew he could only go so far so fast. There were some people who opposed him he could shift but getting rid of a general manager was an entirely different kettle of fish. Over the years he started to ease some of the old barons out of their halls and replace them with people, mainly younger – but that was incidental – who were more imaginative in following through what he wanted to do. But it would take time.

From being an economist, John Welsby suddenly became a manager. How did he go about the job?

Welsby: I looked around and the first thing that struck me was how unfortunate was the equipment we were using. The idea of cascading stuff from first line services in the south and have them end up thirty-five years later on my patch did not seem a good way of doing things. The DMUs were terribly unreliable. I went to Derby and said, 'I would like to spend some time with your engineering intelligence section,' and they said 'What?' And I said, 'Talk with your engineering intelligence section,' and they said, 'Oh, we don't have one of those.' I had to talk to Jim, who said one thing, and then I had to talk to George, an equally proficient engineer, who said something different.

: I have been criticised a lot for Pacers, but they were ready to go and the only thing available. Derby Research was working up something new, the Sprinters. I talked with them a lot. My experience of the road haulage industry suggested engines should last a quarter of a million miles and could be married with the right transmissions to give proven and reliable powertrains.

The first Pacers arrived in West Yorkshire in November 1983. They were, basically, a Leyland bus body attached to a railway chassis: lightweight, inexpensive trains designed for low-volume commuter services. They got a bad name later but were better than what they replaced.

Welsby: You might ask why the general managers had not pressed for better rolling stock before. But procurement was never their job. Obviously, they were consulted, but rolling stock was a centralised function; but even those at the centre found it difficult to get things done. They held the levers, but the levers were not connected to anything.

: Anyway, the GMs did not think like that. They were controlling costs, not the passenger experience. Besides, the PTEs were beginning to have a big say in what happened. The Pacer was invented for the West Yorkshire PTE.

While Welsby was getting on with his job at Provincial, Cyril Bleasdale was doing the same at InterCity. His was the prestige appointment. His task was to show that InterCity could be profitable.

An early win for Cyril concerned the allocation of the HST fleet, the fastest and most comfortable trains and most suited for InterCity. There were some in the Western and the Eastern Regions. The general managers of these regions had allocated them to their most important routes.

None ran on the Midland Main Line serving Sheffield. Its city council and chamber of commerce were crying out for a fast service to London. The Master Cutler was their prime train and they wanted it to be an HST. They even offered to pay for it. But Sheffield's route to London was partly in Eastern and partly in Midland, and so was not a priority for either region. The cries of the city council had been ignored.

The Midland Main Line, however, was an InterCity service, and it was for Cyril to decide what should run on it. He could see that taking a small part of the HST fleet from the Western and Eastern Regions and putting it on to the Sheffield run would make sound commercial sense.

Armed with the figures which came out of the new accounting system, he was able to make this happen, and it worked. Passenger revenue went up by a third in the first four weeks. It was a decisive step, noticed across the railway: commercial considerations were supreme. Sector directors had clout.

Cyril Bleasdale also got involved with engineering as had John Welsby. A new locomotive was about to go into production. Cyril went to Germany.

> Bleasdale: The Germans asked me, 'Why are you planning to build the wrong locomotive?' Back in Britain, I consulted around. 'Cyril, the Germans are right, this is the wrong locomotive – but don't quote me.' So I went to Ian Campbell, the Board Member Engineering. 'I'm afraid we're not going to go with the Brush six-axle Co-Co. It's not the one that I'm going to recommend. I am going to recommend a new design, a Bo-Bo four-axle.' Ian Campbell hit the roof. Face reddened up. 'I've spent £4 million on this prototype! Who is this guy telling me what to do?'
> : Campbell's decision-making was awful – he jumped around too much – but I'm biased, I suppose.

The Bo-Bo four-axle it was. It was at first called the Class 87/2 (the

'Super Class 87') and later the Class 90, as many design improvements became incorporated into it. It powered the East Coast Main Line for many years. It is still in use, a most versatile locomotive, employed on many different routes.

A Bo-Bo and a Co-Co are different only in the number of axles on each of their bogies: the Bo-Bo has two axles and the Co-Co three. Cyril wanted the one with two, the Bo-Bo. Three axles may be useful for pulling heavy freight, but for passenger traffic, two are ample and weigh less.

The locomotive Ian Campbell wanted was the Class 89. A prototype was built and it ran briefly until 1989. One of its last tasks, in October 1989, was to pull a special train to take Margaret Thatcher to Sandy in Bedfordshire. Lovingly restored Mark 1 coaches were procured from David Ward's special trains outfit, with refreshments served in the traditional silver service manner. Margaret Thatcher loved it.

> Bleasdale: The interesting thing is that during the argument Bob Reid stood aside, never tried to get involved. But somehow, very quietly, you knew you had his support. The same happened with quite a different matter. I wanted to paint InterCity trains with a different livery. It was a big step. It got turned down by the Railway Management group that's great super. After the meeting Bob just said, 'You'll be back.' And back I went a few months later and it went through.

We have a good description of Cyril's task from a speech he gave to the Railway Study Association in December 1982, at the end of his first year, fully reported in *Railnews*.

The need for sector directors, Cyril said, was perfectly clear: to put the requirements of the market, in his case InterCity travellers, in the driving seat. But he was not finding the job easy. He talked of three frictions: friction between himself and the engineering directors at head office, whose decisions affected Cyril's cost base; friction with other sectors, each of whom competed for space on the track and had conflicting requirements; and friction with the regional general managers, who had their own ideas of what should be done.

Friction was no criticism, Cyril said. That there was friction showed there was a job to do. Bob Reid was much involved in helping to resolve the issues.

Previously, Cyril said, decisions had tended to swing from extreme cost reduction, almost regardless of its revenue impact, to the extreme of maximising revenue yet ignoring long-running costs. In the future, profit would be used consistently as the objective.

Being part of the 'commercial railway', InterCity had to make a profit, but Cyril was losing £100 million a year (costs were about £500 million and revenue about £400 million). Some cost savings were immediately clear: cutting 25 per cent of the locomotive-hauled coaches with a better use of HSTs, rerouting a service to avoid renewal costs, cutting back a resignalling scheme, and reducing the cost of a train maintenance depot programme. Altogether Cyril could see a quick saving of £50 million.

Thereafter things would be more difficult. Five task forces were set up to work out plans for each of his sub-sectors. These were the five main lines: West Coast, East Coast, Great Western, Midland and IC Cross Country. Their aim was to improve net revenue by 10 per cent (about £40 million). This, together with the short-term savings, would come close to the £100 million turnaround required.

17 THE TURNING POINT (1983)

The year 1982 was truly the lowest point in the railway's fortunes. It had endured six months of dispute with ASLEF and suffered from chaos in the country. Passenger numbers and freight volumes continued their long, slow decline.

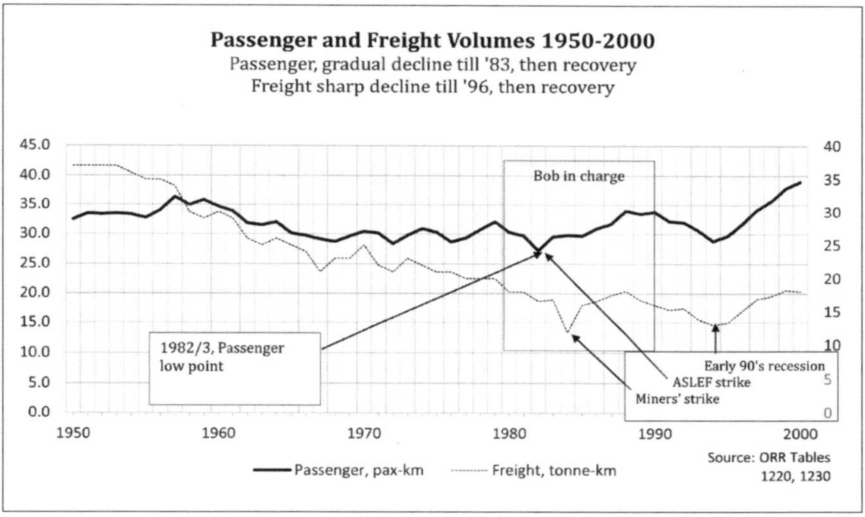

The financial results tell the story.

- **1980.** A loss of £77 million. But, more important, the Board kept within its cash limits.
- **1981.** Parker: 'We battled through 1980 – a grim year – and this year will be grimmer still. The harsh reality is that we are running a railway through the worst recession in fifty years.' Result: a loss of £37 million but, again, the Board kept within its cash limit.
- **1982.** The railway would have broken even but for the ASLEF strike, which cost £170 million. Result: a loss of £174 million.
- **1983.** Then, gloriously, a year with no strikes, no disruption, no chaos. 'Best results for six years'. Profit of £8 million.

1983 was the turning point. 'Breaking even' or 'making a profit' does not mean the Board operated without government support. Far from it. Support totalled £934 million for a group with a turnover of £2,255 million. But it does indicate accurate financial management, no strikes and no surprises throwing things off course.

But before moving on, there was some tidying up, some loose ends to tuck away.

LOOSE ENDS

SERPELL REPORT

The first such loose end was the Serpell Report. Fascinating it might have been but it had to be kicked firmly into the long grass.

Sir David's review of the finances of the railway had been commissioned by David Howell, the Transport Secretary. Sir David had been a permanent secretary in the Ministry of Transport and was a part-time member of the Board, so was well informed of the issues.

The report made a compelling read. For the future shape of the railway, there were three options to consider: Option C, a railway network as it then was with 11,000 route miles; Option B, a somewhat smaller network; and Option A, a very much smaller network with just 1,630 route miles. If commercial viability was required, no government support at all, it had to be Option A. Any larger network would always need government support.

In reality, it was the same conclusion that half a dozen other reports had come to, but in this case it was well illustrated by maps, and money being so tight, there was a fear that Option A was a real possibility.

Outside the London commuter belt and some services to the south coast, the Option A route map had very little on it; it was largely blank. Beyond the south-east there were only the four InterCity lines: London to Norwich; Great Western to Cardiff; the West Coast Main Line up to Glasgow and Edinburgh, with a few lines running off it on the way; and the East Coast Main Line as far as Leeds and Newcastle, but not beyond. There were no commuter services outside London, no service even between Edinburgh and Glasgow, and as for rural lines none at all.

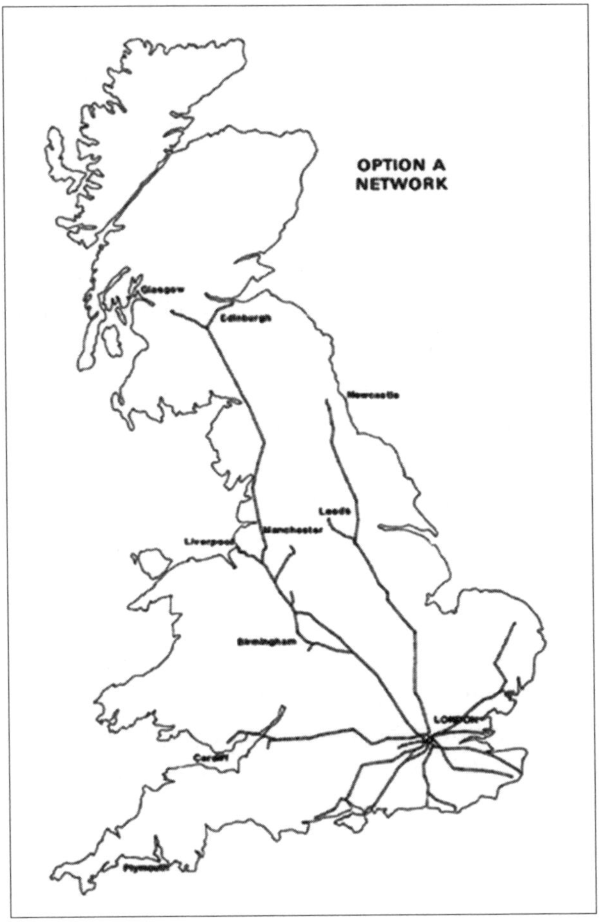

In dealing with this report, Peter Parker was in his element. Grandly, he dismissed it as 'a disappointing document.... offering little advice on the key question of the long-term strategic objectives which BR and the government should be pursuing'.

Parker's efforts were in fact unnecessary. In the eighteen months since David Howell had commissioned the report, a marked change had taken place in the government's attitude. When she came to power, if she thought about it at all, Margaret Thatcher would have lumped the railway in with all the other antiquated and un-reformable features of British life which required pruning. But the determination Bob Reid had shown that to cut costs, to tackle the unions and to live within its financing limit convinced her the railway was worth saving.

Even before the report's publication, the government had approved some investment schemes: the electrification to Weymouth, the Anglia electrification, the Pacers, the Glasgow–Ayr electrification and new ticket machines.

In reality, the Option A route map did the railway a service. Its stark appearance drove home to anyone who saw it that a subsidy-free railway was a non-starter, quite likely David Serpell's intention. Certainly, David Howell, the Secretary of State, rowed back from any interest in 'extreme plans'. 'Option A', he said, 'was a valuable illustration but not a practicable option.'

Eight months later, the Board had the confidence to deliver a corporate plan with increased investment, and the government gave it support.

BED–PAN

A second loose end was the rolling stock lying idle in sidings at Nottingham. The trains were ready and waiting to run on the newly electrified Bed–Pan line, which had been equipped to operate without guards. It was to be driver-only operation. The trains had sliding doors which the driver could operate, the stations had mirrors so the driver could see when it was safe to close the doors or staff on the platform to indicate the same, there was radio communication between signal box and driver, and a facility for the driver to make announcements to passengers.

The entire concept was anathema to the NUR. For seventeen months the trains had lain in the sidings waiting agreement from the unions. No progress was possible during the ASLEF flexible rostering dispute, but that was now out of the way. Eased by various promises and an additional payment to the drivers and guards, agreement was reached and the trains ran in August 1983. It was a big day, a significant change to how the railway might operate.

AIRPORT LINKS

It was not all retreat or standstill. Bob had pushed the upgrade of Gatwick

Express, which became a good profit-earner. Norman Payne of British Airports Authority was a friend and the new line to Stansted Airport and indeed the line to Manchester Airport were pushed through.

CUTTING OUT THE DIVISIONS

Also about to get under way was cutting the cost of administration. Leslie Soane was brought down from Scotland, given the title of Deputy Chief Executive, and asked to carry out a review.

In the past, the regions, all six of them, had each been divided into Districts and below the Districts into Areas. It was an expensive three-level structure with administrative staff in each one. In Scotland, the middle layer, the Divisions, had been cut out years before, in 1966. Bob announced in his column that the same was to happen in England. Eight thousand jobs were to be cut within two years.

This happened as planned – by January 1984 in London Midland – with seemingly little dispute, in stark contrast to the introduction of flexible rostering, a change which brought no job losses but closed the railway in bitter dispute with ASLEF. A strange world.

From then on, in the regions, there was a headquarters and a number of Areas. These Areas became the core operating unit of the railway. In mid-1984, there were 85 across the country.

Structure of the regions

Fewer and larger subdivisions of each region.

Districts abolished from 1969, Divisions from 1984

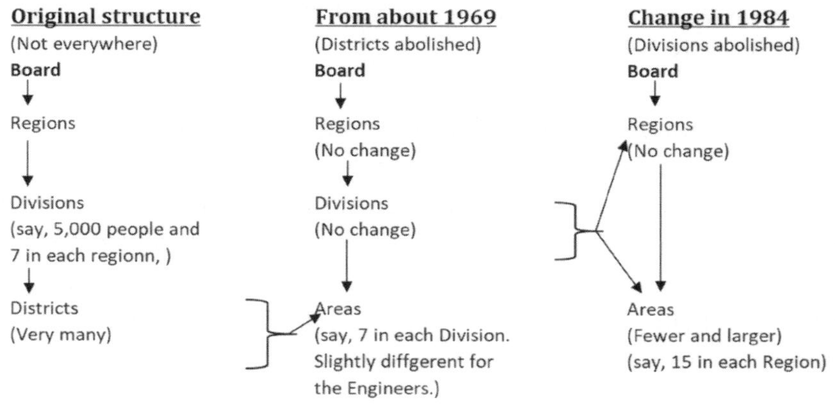

PAUL WATKINSON

The sector directors had been appointed, and were working away, but what now? What next must be done? Paul Watkinson, we have introduced him already, throws light on Bob's thinking.

> Watkinson: When I was Divisional Manager in Leeds in the early 1980s, I began to have contact with Bob again. He was a great friend of John Batley, my predecessor, who had moved to Board HQ as secretary.
> : Bob's tailor was in Leeds and he would sometimes drop in on me when he went to visit him. This usually happened on a Friday and he would sometimes then stay overnight with John in Ilkley, where I lived too. Bob, John, me and our wives would have supper in a wine bar in the town and talk of endlessly about what we would change.
> : We didn't want to talk about the railway all the time. We had long conversations about plants and vegetable gardens; and he talked about his family, young Bob and his daughter, Janet. He was relaxed and came across as a kind cultured person, a side not always seen. However, he felt deeply about the railway and the task of restructuring which was at hand.
> : The regions were over-managed, but it wasn't in his mind, at that point, to get rid of them. What was in his mind was to develop InterCity, and the others, into full-blown businesses and manage the railway through the businesses. You can't carry on running this as an operational-led railway. That was his agenda, definitely, in the early 1980s.

Bob Reid brought Paul Watkinson down to the head office in 1984 for he wanted to stir up the personnel function in the headquarters. The people were good but set in their ways. They knew the machinery of negotiation back to front and were close to the unions and the sectional councils, but the vast, labyrinthine negotiating machinery just perpetuated resistance to change. Paul was to be the 'fox in the hen coop'. Unfortunately, the hens were too strong to be troubled by a single fox.

Not being able to make progress in the personnel function, Paul began working on another matter.

> Watkinson: Between '84 and '86 I worked in very closely with John Welsby, a good guy, clever. Bob was putting a bomb under the mechanical engineering side of the railway. He was not at all happy with the status quo. He wanted it dealt with firmly and chose John for the job. John was remitted to sort out the expletive, expletive mess. Bob would not have used our current swear words. He was a gentle man, but in this matter, I saw Bob's steely side. Ruthless when he had to be.
> : He trusted Welsby, so he and I and David Blake slaved long and hard and eventually got the BREL structure sorted. It had to be. The concept of just-in-time was unknown to it.

The light maintenance depots, required for the day-to-day running of the railway, were taken out of BREL and brought within the main railway. Heavy maintenance and manufacturing remained in BREL. Not being time critical, these could be procured through competitive tender, and BREL could itself be put up for sale. When Bob first heard of this plan he raged at John Welsby: 'You're nothing but Thatcher's lackey.' He feared anything that would interfere with the ordered running of the railway. But when that did not happen, he came to appreciate what had been done.

> Watkinson: In about 1988 I became director, employee relations. We were pushing hard in the late 80s for reform and trying to engage with the unions about a modern agenda. We could no longer regard the railway as this great big thing, the same everywhere. The new structure, the rise of the sectors as businesses, demanded a change to the negotiating machinery and to the structure of pay and conditions.
> : You didn't need to be a genius to see that running a business with low basic pay, half what it should be, topped up by an impenetrable web of overtime and allowances was no way to proceed.
> : If this was to change, and basic pensionable pay improve, there

had to be more flexible and productive working arrangements. Pay and conditions had to move down to a local level, so it could be different in different places. Attempts to push this through took a lot of time and led to the bitter, protracted dispute 1989 about pay and the breaking up of national bargaining. It was a very stressful time for me personally.

: Eventually, in 1992, after a huge amount of hard negotiating by my personnel team, the sacred agreement, the National Machinery of Negotiation, was abolished and a new framework put in place, for the most part, it is still in use in today's railway.

: It was a turbulent time, but I'm happy I was part of it. We restructured many working practices and got through the privatisation process without any serious labour relations difficulties aside from the skirmish with the RMT about pay in 1993 and, of course, the awful Railtrack signaller strike in 1994. How did we do it? A lot of hard work plus reassurance about pensions and free travel, matters close to the heart of all staff.

: In terms of their pay and conditions, the train drivers were always going to be the winners from privatisation and ASLEF knew it. The RMT was always going to be difficult, as it has proved.

GOVERNMENT AND THE 1983 ELECTION

Two years after coming to power, the government's reputation was as low as it could be. Its economic policy was widely detested. It had left many people out of work, impoverished and destitute. Death was threatened by the IRA, with no solution in sight. Two bombs exploded on one day in Hyde Park and Regent's Park, killing eleven, and bomb threats closed train stations. With Arthur Scargill in a powerful position in the coal miners' union, another confrontation threatened. Ken Livingstone, the new Mayor of London, mounted a rival economic policy. He snubbed the Chancellor and halved fares on the Underground, casually arguing that the increased patronage would cover the cost.

It seemed the end of an era, and that all the familiar structures would collapse. But they did not. The wave of strikes petered out, the

High Court took a different view from Ken Livingstone and forced him to back down over the tube fares, Scargill remained too weak to call a strike, and with luck and heroism the Falkland Islands remained British.

It had seemed that the Conservative Party would surely lose any future election, but Geoffrey Howe's economic policy began to work and Thatcher's robust attitudes, the vigorous virtues of a grocer's daughter, struck a chord with many people.

Opinion polls turned in the government's favour – aided in that direction by victory in the Falklands and what was happening in the Labour Party. Michael Foot swung his party to the left and presented an election manifesto promising to reverse everything Thatcher had done, famously described as 'the longest suicide note in history'. Instead of facing defeat, the question became how big the Tory majority would be. It was 144.

With the election out of the way, the government had to decide who should take over from Peter Parker.

18 BOB AS CHAIRMAN (1983)

BOB BECOMES CHAIRMAN

There is a story told by Cyril Bleasdale that Bob and he, on a trip across the Atlantic, sitting together on the aeroplane, started talking about who would get the chairman's job when Parker retired. Cyril encouraged Bob to put his hat in the ring. 'Put yourself forward,' he said.

This was in 1982, well before Bob Reid had established his reputation, and it was not at all obvious that a career railwayman would even be considered.

Bob was interested. 'What can I do?' he asked.

Cyril suggested he develop some ideas and put them forward in a speech. He should give himself a profile, make himself more than a 'Mr Fix It', make himself seem like a chairman in waiting.

The conversation made an impact. They spent the night in New York. The next morning, Cyril was touched to find, delivered to his room, a handwritten note from Bob thanking him for his advice in the aeroplane.

Bob worked carefully to put his ideas together. He hired a speaking coach, for he was not confident about speaking in public. The speech was given at the Chartered Institute of Transport with a dinner afterwards for influential people and officials who Bob had invited, Cyril amongst them. It was a success.

By the beginning of 1983, Bob was certainly in the running, but Thatcher had not yet grasped the truth of the man and was still trying to bring in an outsider – a hatchet-man – who she assumed would be more effective at cutting costs.

By then, John Nelson's place as Bob's PA had been taken by Robert Walters.

Walters: 222 Marylebone Road was being refurbished. Bob

stopped that. He had spoken with John Harvey-Jones, the ICI chairman, who persuaded Bob that culture lives in the walls, it's buried there. He could modernise Marylebone Road as much as he liked, but the old culture would live on, including the five management dining rooms, four of which had free alcohol every lunchtime. The refurbishment was jettisoned, and we stayed in the offices at Euston Square.

: I had been warned against the job. 'Be careful, Robert, he's a fearsome man. He doesn't suffer fools. A lot of people dislike him greatly.' But the truth was the opposite; he was an enigma. He was a fabulous boss on a personal basis. He had high expectations of you. If you delivered, he was hugely appreciative. If you didn't, he'd give you a steer perhaps or get you to think about it a bit more, but if you tried to pull a fast one or even tell a white lie, his reaction was gruesome. I remember one gentleman, senior man, pretended he'd done everything necessary on some job when he hadn't and was going to Paris the next day. Bob said, 'No you bloody don't. You're staying here until you sort this cock-up out.' Man came into my office next door in tears.

: One of my jobs was to draft Bob's monthly column in *Railnews*. His burning theme at the time was the evil, the iniquity of subsidy, which he saw as a huge source of confusion and muddled thinking about efficiency. I don't think the specifics of hardware, signalling or trains or whatever, featured in his day-to-day thinking. He was driven entirely by a more responsive style of management to the marketplace and improving business performance.

: In matters like the introduction of the new trains on the Bed–Pan line, he was very careful to avoid treading on the toes of his directors or general managers who, so far as he was concerned, were fully capable of dealing with the issues. Although he led very strongly, he didn't do so by drawing power to himself. Behind the scenes, he ensured discipline, that press releases were entirely consistent with the management plan; there was to be no chink into which someone could drive some bloody-minded wedge.

: He was meticulous about preparation for his meetings. If there were meetings with trade unions, obviously Bob wouldn't be there, but the previous evening the management team would be in his office and they would go through every nuance, every possible outcome of any particular question, so they could plan and not be caught out by the events of the meeting. On that, he was the most methodical person I've ever known.

The June election held things up. But even after, Thatcher dithered, time slipped away and Bob, not wishing to hang around waiting for news, went on holiday to the Alps, 'to a nice little unpretentious hotel run by Italians. He'd learnt Italian as a POW', explained Janet.

Over the previous months, he had refused the suggestion of a two-year appointment while they continued to look for a 'big-hitter' as chairman. Bob was adamant, he needed five years to do what he wanted to do. 'Five years or nothing.'

In the Italian mountains, in September 1983, he got a message to call the Secretary of State, Tom King.

As the story goes: 'He was offered the chairman's job when, still dripping wet after walking in the Italian mountains, he telephoned Tom King from a public call box in Val d'Aosta.'

John Palmer, the deputy to the Permanent Secretary in the department, was listening in. Tom King explained that the government would like to appoint him as the new chairman and Bob replied that he would be pleased to accept. Tom King went on: 'I have two questions for you. First, do you support Serpell?' (By this, he was referring to Serpell's views about waste and inefficiency, not to the famous options A, B, C.)

Bob replied, 'Yes.'

'Second,' asked Tom King, 'are you going to promote a programme of electrification?' This was a difficult question. Clearly, Tom King did not wish to be faced with demands for the vast sums that electrification would require but, equally, electrification was thought to be fundamental to an efficient railway. Bob replied simply that he would like to see the electrification of the East Coast Main Line. That, happily, satisfied Tom King.

On 3 September, under a newspaper headline, 'Deputy takes BR 'hot seat'', Tom King announced the appointment, saying, 'Bob Reid has shown himself as a most effective chief executive for the railways and has earned the right to lead this major national undertaking.'

Ray Buckton of ASLEF thought differently. He piped up in a BBC interview.

> Well, I'm extremely disappointed..... Of course he knows the problems because he created them..... He was a party to what took place in 1982..... Any man who threatened to sack all the drivers in the industry because they wouldn't accept conditions of service imposed on them by such men as Mr Reid and Mr Urquhart and Sir Peter Parker – those are the three I hold responsible – doesn't look very well for the future.

Appointed as deputy chairman – just in case Bob wilted in his attack on Serpell waste – was Sir Richard Cave, 'a big man in personality and physique', and the founding chairman of Thorn EMI. Happily, Bob and Richard Cave got on well together; they knew each other from summer holidays together on the Suffolk coast.

The coverage in the papers was sparse. Outside the railway, Bob was entirely unknown. The front pages, besides, were filled with other things. The shooting down by the Soviet Union of a South Korean jumbo jet filled with passengers which had strayed into Soviet airspace.

Inside the railway, however, he was very well known. Many, many letters of congratulations were written and sent to him. They seem at first quite routine. But as you turn them over – there are two full ring binders – reading some and listening to Janet explain who they were from and why they were his friends, something more comes to mind.

What you are seeing is a picture of a person's life, not a list of things done, but a record of the friendships he has made and the impressions he has left on people's minds. What is in these ring binders is a rich, rich picture with detail and colour and variety. Austere and shy perhaps, but he had made a deep impact on many people.

> Janet: He had a twinkle and a very dry sense of humour, as did my grandfather. He could make jokes with a completely straight face. And in his private life kept his friendships throughout his life. That

generation, who served in the army or the air force or the navy, had a rapport with all kinds of people for they had experienced the grim and the less grim together.

At the top of the pile was a letter from Robin Brockbank, a general in the army, a very old friend, said Janet; they had been in the Westminster Dragoons together. They had got into a fight – teenage boys – and thereafter remained close friends all their lives. Bob's reply, 'I'm still trying to get used to the character described in the newspapers. Buckton did me the best turn ever by his clearly expressed misery at the news. Three and a quarter years is not long to complete what I want to do, but I'll have a go.'

That was the gist of most replies; that and 'Let us hope I can do the industry some good during my term of office.'

There were letters from railway people: from John Nelson, Cyril Bleasdale, Frank Paterson, and many more. One from Bobby Lawrence, a 'great' of the old railway, the Whitemoor elite. One from Gerard Fiennes, who wrote simply, 'We wish you very well indeed.' Henry 'Call me Bill' Johnson wrote, as did David Serpell, John Palmer and Bill McAlpine. So many people wrote.

Peter Baldwin, a former permanent secretary, wrote, 'I've seen your qualities in the glare of very intense fires indeed and I'm greatly comforted that you are there.'

Sidney Weighell, a real star, wrote in quite opposite terms from Ray Buckton's grump on the radio: 'Railway staff should be delighted that you have been asked to take over the chairmanship.'

Relatives and family wrote, An Aunt Margaret wrote. His goddaughter wrote, 'Dear Uncle Bob', and many agreed that 'Isobel would be proud of you.' She would indeed.

A clergyman who knew his family wrote, '…like father like son – wouldn't he be proud of you….. I've been reading John Buchan's *Julius Caesar*. Caesar had been certain he would get to the top. So I wonder when you first thought you would. You have aye been so unassuming, never showed this to the outside world – but you may have been quite different to your peers and seniors in the railway.' To which Bob replied, 'To tell you the truth, I never thought that I would get anywhere near the top..... I think my driving force has been an abhorrence of working under people that I felt were not quite as good as I was!'

He was remembered by a fellow pupil from Malvern – 'I remember you as a shooter'.

Bunty wrote, 'What luck, the rolling stock will have your initials on them so that no one else can pinch them.' To an Oxford friend Bob joked, 'reminds me of your enjoyment trying to dispense drink without taking the cork out'.

Some people who knew him long ago on the railway wrote: a stationmaster from Cowlairs in Glasgow; a railway plumber whom Bob had got to know and had kept in touch with. People from Hull; he had made a great impression in Hull. And the Bishop of Staffa and Iona.

A Nancy Walker wrote. A chatty letter. She had been a clerk in the district superintendent's office in Edinburgh thirty years before. 'I was supposed to familiarise you with the district relief timesheets.' Since then, she had travelled on railways all over the world, but 'L.N.E.R was THE Railway dear to all of us.' Bob replied most sweetly: 'I have very pleasant recollections of a clerkess in that office, which must have been you..... I do remember enjoying very much your good company.'

His friend and colleague on the railway, Cliff Rose, had died recently at a young age, leaving a widow, Maureen. It was not Maureen who wrote, but Maureen's mother, for she had grown to love her son-in-law. She congratulated Bob, of course, but she was really writing to say, 'I seem to miss Cliff more each day, he would be so happy for your future.' And 'keep in touch with Maureen from time to time.' Bob replied, 'Don't worry, I'll look after Maureen as much as I can.'

You can never tell the footsteps you leave behind. This is one letter Bob did not expect: 'Dear Bobby.... hard to believe that Sept 3rd is 44 years since the outbreak of the Second World War. You may remember we used to take tea and whads to the troops along the Thorpeness road – and at Aldeburgh – while you were waiting to join up! I kept wearing your Tank Corps brooch for *ages*!' Bob replied: 'I have the most vivid memories of you as one of my earliest and most beloved girlfriends who I had to leave behind because of the war.'

Among his friends was the family in Italy who had given him shelter when he had escaped from the prisoner of war camp. He had visited the Guasti family in gratitude after the war. In later life, when he visited the Italian Alps each summer, he always spent a few days with the family at the end of his holiday.

Taken as a whole, what does the picture show? There is little sign of chums, just an occasional reference to going to the rugby in Edinburgh. The letters were from the world he inhabited: from family and railway and government people. Their real respect is quite evident, as is their warmth and affection.

Three score years and ten we are upon this earth. This is what you leave behind.

THE TRIUMVIRATE, FROM '83

To run the railway, Bob, now the executive chairman, established a triumvirate consisting of himself and two joint managing directors: Geoffrey Myers and Jim O'Brien. Reporting to Bob were the general managers, reporting to Jim were the sector directors, and reporting to Geoffrey were the functional heads of engineering: civil, mechanical, signals and projects.

The triumvirate from September 1983:

- Bob Reid – general managers.
- Jim O'Brien – sector directors.
- Geoffrey Myers – engineering functions.

> Walters, Bob's PA: Geoffrey Myers was a civil engineer. He was larger-than-life, he was an ebullient character. He spoke an enormous amount of common sense. I remember he was the person to whom Bob would turn first in discussing an issue. He was his anchor. He was a damn good, well-rounded railwayman. If there were two people who worked as a team it was Bob and Geoff.

Though chairman, Bob could not have stepped back from the day-to-day business; there was too much to do: a miners' strike looming and the need for approval for the new corporate plan.

Tom King was Secretary of State for only a few months after the June election. In October, Nicholas Ridley took his place, a most felicitous change. The two men, Bob and Nicholas, both with the manners, style and interests of naturally born patricians, understood and trusted each other.

Bob Reid and Nicholas Ridley, two peas in a pod. (BRB)

Peter Lazarus, permanent secretary at the Department, explains:

> Lazarus: He and Nicholas Ridley each had the supreme good fortune to arrive in their respective offices at just the same time. They clicked as no minister and chairman had clicked before; the only possible comparison was the excellent relationship between the late Lord Marples and the late Lord Beeching, and that lacked the personal warmth and friendship which, I believe, started from the discovery that they both cared passionately about fishing.

THE '83 CORPORATE PLAN

The corporate plan, published in August 1983, just weeks after the election, envisaged new investment, modest in scale but significant, and only small changes in the size of the network. Settle/Carlisle was to be closed to passenger trains – a decision reversed - but not freight, and there was a question mark over Marylebone station.

No. 247 OCTOBER 1983

Railnews

InterCity 125

THESE ARE MY TARGETS

IN FULL ON PAGES 2-3

BOB REID, former chief executive and a long-serving railwayman, has set a range of objectives for himself, the industry, its managers and staff at the start of his BR chairmanship.

In a special question-and-answer session with Railnews he predicted a "bright" future for British Rail but warned it would only come about if the industry earned it.

He said: "We have to step up the pace of change and develop a whole new set of attitudes.

"We have to sharpen our marketing skills, develop our response to the needs of the customer and realise that if we want to sell a product it has to be a good one.

"We shall have to rely more on our own efforts than perhaps ever before."

The WEAKEST aspect of BR's service was the way it treated its customers. "We don't do enough as individuals to make our customers welcome."

Its STRENGTH was the popularity of rail as a means of transport with good prospects for growth.

Mr Reid stressed that the Corporate Plan, published in August, represented the minimum improvement expected in the next five years. He was confident its targets could be met. "We have to maintain our financial performance in getting costs down and investment up." But he was certain the railway had a continuing role into the next century.

Mr Reid said the strikes of 1982 had left behind some bitterness between management and the unions and he called for a renewal of "the sense of a railway community working together . . . We must fight the competition, not each other."

'We have to step up the pace of change'

BOB REID, chief executive, railways, has been appointed to succeed Sir Peter Parker as chairman of British Rail.

He took up the three-year appointment on 19 September.

Sir Richard Cave, chairman of Thorn EMI, has been appointed part-time deputy chairman with effect from 1 October.

Mr Reid, 62, heard of his appointment by telephone from Transport Secretary Tom King while on a climbing holiday in Italy.

A professional railwayman since joining the LNER as a traffic apprentice in 1947, he has been general manager of both Eastern and Southern regions and a Board member since 1977.

He has held the post of chief executive — BR's "managing director" — since March 1980 and was appointed Board vice-chairman at the beginning of this year.

Mr Reid, a regular Railnews contributor, is currently president of the Chartered Institute of Transport. He is a widower with a son and a daughter.

But – a subtle point but an important one – this was a plan to build a better railway and not simply one that cost less. Bob, in his column in *Railnews*, pressed the point: 'We have to step up the pace of change.... we have to sharpen our marketing skills, develop our response to the needs of the customer and realise that if we want to sell a product it has to be a good one..... We do not do enough as individuals to make our customers welcome.'

Because Ridley was so 'dry' Thatcher trusted him, so he was able to support the plan on the basis that the target for reducing financial support be brought forward by two years. Bob accepted the new target and was unequivocally determined to meet it.

> Peter Lazarus: He began his chairmanship in the late autumn of 1983 and immediately set about restoring the bond of trust with ministers. Crucial to this was his skill, diplomacy, realism and vision in negotiating a three-year target for the level of government grant, which he committed himself to cut by 25 per cent over three years. At that time, many people inside and outside the railway believed that this would be impossible to achieve. In fact, he did better, and so won an increasing reduction in the degree of interference and over-sight from Whitehall.[83]

Gloriously, in the following year, approval was given for the long-hoped-for electrification of the East Coast Main Line. In John Nelson's words:

> Nelson: He secured the electrification of the East Coast Main Line against all opposition, really. The government did not want it, the civil servants did not want it, but he persuaded them to do it. That was a huge achievement. I mean the East Coast Main Line has been criticised because it is not a terribly robust form of overhead-line construction, but people forget what a triumph it was to get it built at all.

To match or indeed exceed the 125mph of the HST diesel trains then running on the East Coast Main Line, approval was given for a prototype of what would become the Class 91: the InterCity 225 electric locomotive, which was to be capable of 140mph, and, though non-tilting, be capable of pulling tilting coaches.

With the corporate plan approved and with the East Coast Main Line electrification going ahead, a clear sense of enthusiasm can be felt, a desire to drive things forward, a sense that the railway had turned a corner.

But things would have to wait. A miners' strike loomed and if it were to happen, the priority for the railway would be not customer service or even profit, but continuing to carry coal.

MINERS' STRIKE (1984–85)

The hatred of Thatcher, the dream of a socialist Britain and the threatened closing of coal mines all contributed to the miners' strike. It was bound to happen. Arthur Scargill had got himself to be leader of the National Union of Mineworkers and the great, heroic King Canute-like struggle to prevent the closure of loss-making pits began in March 1984.

Bob Reid was asked to keep peace with his unions. Some coal traffic was blocked on rail but, on the whole, practical support for the miners was limited. Bob had a daily phone conference with the general managers, the ones with their fingers on the pulse, close to the ground, to make sure nothing was done to inflame feelings. The railway had to be seen to be impartial between the government and the miners and, in carrying coal, just to be 'doing its job'.

The absence of a ballot caused miners to lose their entitlement to social security and free school meals. Hunger and poverty became rife, with many relying on handouts and donations from charities. The dilemma for miners was most unpleasant: stay out on strike and live in great poverty or return to work and be viewed as a scab, perhaps forever.

For the country, the strike was damaging. There were blackouts, but not sufficiently so to bring down the government. The miners were not able to win, and after a bruising year, the strike was called off in March 1985.

Throughout, pressure on Bob had been intense. Though reserved and austere, he was human. Simon Jenkins, a long-standing board member, describes an incident:

> Jenkins: I chaired the environment panel, it was really about the architecture of our buildings, and had a small budget to improve things. We had done a good job painting and renovating a station,

a particularly interesting station, and had won a RIBA prize, just a little silver cup. I took it to a board meeting.

: Bob was really quite down at the time – some bad things that happened and there was some awful publicity – he was really an emotional man. I put the cup down in front of him as we were assembling. 'What's this?' he growled, dismissing it with a hand. 'It's a prize.' I said. 'What is this bloody prize?' He was very peremptory. I persevered: 'Our environment panel has got a RIBA prize for the best such scheme in Britain. The railway has won a prize.' As the message sank in, tears came to his eyes. I always remember that. It was as if someone loves me after all.

: After that, I got my million pounds to set up the Railway Heritage Trust, got Bill McAlpine to chair it. Been a great success. I'm very proud of it.

The Board, of course, supported Bob Reid in what he was doing but not, it seems, with great enthusiasm. Simon Jenkins was convinced that the way forward, the way to recapture the spirit of the old railway, the private railway, was not sectorisation but building on the regions. The regions were the way forward he thought. It was people like Frank Paterson, at the Eastern Region, for whom he had respect. It was they who made the trains run, day after day, it was they who knew the passengers.

Jenkins: Bob thought the only thing to do was to reorganise the railway as a business. He was obsessed with the word 'business', used it all the time. For what it's worth – it's in the history book – I disagreed. But Bob was a big enough operator, he had huge authority, utterly in control of the chain of command, no rivals or competition, so the Board basically backed him.

KNAPP'S GUARDS DISPUTE (1985)

With the miners' strike over, the Railway's Board was able to press hard for further productivity. The priority was the removal of the requirement for guards to ride on freight trains, for which there was no possible need, and on those passenger services where the trains and stations were properly equipped to enable driver-only operation.

Weeks after the end of the miners' strike, the Board wrote announcing the extension of driver-only operation to the line from King's Cross out to Welwyn Garden City and Royston, and that driver-only operation would commence in Strathclyde/Glasgow by the end of the year. This was progress on the third of Bob's six points.

A further letter stated that pilot schemes for the removal of guards on freight trains would soon begin. This would be the second of Bob's six points.

Dispute with the guards' union, then led by Jimmy Knapp, was inevitable. Some on the NUR executive committee wanted to strike straight away but Jimmy Knapp, though equally angry, persuaded the committee to first hold a ballot, which he was sure he would win. A strike, and a legal one at that, was a near certainty.

In response, Bob Reid was at his most implacable. This is what he was saying in interviews:

> Reid: It is a great disappointment to me that I've been unable to get the cooperation of union leaders in furthering our industry.[84]
> : They want a government-protected monopoly. British Rail, when I joined, had 40% to 50% of the transport market, now it is 10%. There will be reform or decline. That realisation is only now dawning among the generality of our employees.[85]
> : There is a two-year-old NUR conference resolution stating that the union is 'not to enter into any further talks on productivity.' We tried persuasion and we failed, so we have to say: 'Right, we're going to do it.'[86]
> : The railways have been protected for too long, and in the past management just kept on compromising and running away from the real issues. This time we are determined that will not happen. This time we must get a clear-cut solution.[87]
> : We have got a union totally opposed to my policy, and we have got to fight it through or else the railway faces a long and painful decline.[88]
> : Freight is in dire trouble because it lost a lot of business during

the coal strike. We simply cannot afford to have men doing damn all at the back of the loco. There are bound to be job losses but we really have to shake the industry up so it has a long-term future.[89]
: One day perhaps they will come to believe in the determination of this management because this management is absolutely determined.[90]
: Oh, heavens yes, I will sit it out all right.[91]

Graham Turner, writing in the *Daily Telegraph*, in an article entitled 'Bob offers his railwayman a march or a lament', concluded his piece by saying, 'The truth is that if the troops will not follow a leader as patently decent as he is, they do not deserve a future.'

Remarkably, and against everyone's expectation, the railwayman chose a 'march'. Possibly tired of strikes and wanting a normal life, possibly seeing the failure of the ASLEF strike and the miners' strike, the ballot came down against a strike by a small margin. The troops had decided to follow Bob Reid. True, strikes broke out locally, but the Board took a hard line and refused payment of any pay rise until agreement was reached and signed.

From that time on, freight trains would no longer operate with guards. On the passenger railway, driver-only operation was introduced on the trains in Strathclyde/Glasgow and on the two lines out of St Pancras and King's Cross as the Board had planned.

With the end of this dispute, of the six changes in working practices which he had laid down in 1981 Bob had achieved all that he wanted. What was left was not worth fighting for. Remarkably, disputes over working conditions would cease for thirty years. There were other strikes, but over different things.

19 PERSONALITIES

BOB'S PERSONALITY

By now, in mid-1985, Bob's achievements were clear for all to see. For the government, he was creating the kind of railway they wanted. For journalists, he was a discovery, someone different and interesting, someone to write about. There comes across a sense of relief, joy even, that a chairman had been found for a nationalised industry, the railway no less, who could successfully deliver change.

In the June Birthday Honours he was knighted, becoming Sir Robert Reid, along with other greats of British industry: Walter Marshall of the Central Electricity Generating Board, John Harvey-Jones of ICI, Martin Jacomb of Kleinwort Benson and the British Telecom flotation – and David Attenborough.

He dined at Windsor Castle, not a Tier One dinner perhaps as it was held for the Ambassador of the Socialist Republic of Romania, but Windsor Castle nonetheless.

Newspapers, instead of castigating the railway, could be found writing it up in complimentary terms. In Scotland, Chris Green, 'the man behind ScotRail with its new image, and new business', was weaving his magic. The *Edinburgh Evening News*, under the headline 'DEFINITELY GETTING THERE', complimented the redevelopment of Waverley Station and added more broadly, 'The much-needed Bathgate service is also making progress and, of course, the whole of the exciting prospect of electrification between Edinburgh and London is underway.'

The *Scotsman* wrote:

> Meanwhile rail is showing that it is capable of bursting out of the marginalised, miniaturised role assigned to it by the present government. Will it be allowed to? Dyce station near Aberdeen reopened with 14 trains a day and now has 24; South Gyle near Edinburgh is a new station and far busier than expected; eight

> other new stations have appeared from nowhere, along with new business on the once doomed Fort William and North Berwick lines. There are packed 125 trains from Inverness, and the promise of more business on the modernised Strathclyde network, with electrification of the Ayr/Largs route boosting revenue from 57% to 93% of costs.[92]

Such praise would soon propel Chris Green to London, where he would be given the job of creating Network SouthEast.

The entire railway came in for praise. The *Observer* wrote:

> Since 1980 Britain has actually developed the most cost-effective railway network in Western Europe, far more so than France, Italy or West Germany. As many as 27% of the industry's workers have gone over the past five years and a further net saving of 15,000 staff is expected by 1987, with cuts in the managerial grades in particular. At the same time, we have not seen any dramatic axing of branch lines, and the fears of a Beeching-style closure operation following the Serpell report of January 1983 have proved groundless. In the past, Mrs Thatcher may have felt BR was a bottomless pit of wasteful public expenditure. Now, in the language of Chancellor Nigel Lawson, it is beginning to look like a good investment.[93]

Heady stuff indeed!

With such success – or at least promises of success – there was much interest in Bob Reid the man. Who is this person, what is he like?

Amongst all the words printed, the description 'he is the iron fist in Parker's velvet glove' best sums him up. All agreed that the Parker–Reid partnership had been a productive one, but the two people were very different.

The following is taken from various newspaper articles.

> Bob Reid looks like an underfed but unusually cheerful Scottish divine'. Skipping over the word 'cheerful', Bob replied that his 'spare, rugged, starved appearance' was down to his Presbyterian background. 'It didn't stop sin, just stopped you enjoying it.[94]

Another journalist writes:

> He was forged in a hard school. As a young man, he was a prisoner of war for almost four years. Perhaps what he learnt in the camps, in Italy and Nazi Germany, is still reflected in his management style today. 'You learn a great deal about human nature and human weakness,' he said reflectively, 'and you learn self-control and patience. You also recognise how important it is to adopt certain codes of practice. You must be honest. And you must stand by what you are asked to do. If you do not, the whole group falls apart.[95]

What does this mean? In the camps, some prisoners share what they have and look out for you; others are deceitful, promise to help but let you down; while others brazenly look out for themselves. To survive in this dangerous hurly-burly, you must hold your own and know who you are dealing with. If there is a task to be done, you choose people you can trust, and once they've agreed to do something, keep a watch for the guard while others steal food, they must do it. The group depends on it.

Life on the run is different. You are on your own, in the mountains, sheltered by farmers or herdsman. Such a life is wholly dependent on the bravery and intelligence of others. A farmhand might be asked to take a message, a warning possibly, over hills, through villages, past German soldiers hunting for partisans, for no reward, but facing capture or worse if caught. They must do it. If a woodsman gives you shelter, relying on you to keep out of sight, you must do it.

It is best summed up in the phrase 'right behaviour'. Right behaviour sums up the standard he set himself and what he expected from others. There is right behaviour and there is behaviour that is not right. Such will not be tolerated.

A consistent theme brought out by everyone with a description of working for Bob is that he would leave you, trust you, to carry out your job as you saw fit, would support you in facing real difficulties, but was quite ruthless if you let him down. That was his management style. Some interviews record what he said himself about his management style. These are strung together below, keeping his own words and phraseology.

> Bob: A leader must be fair and just and have integrity. Must be open and honest in how he faces up to problems. One must listen and talk through problems with the management team, so everyone understands and is a party to the result. But you have got to finish up with a decision and make sure everyone gets on with it.[96]
> : You must delegate so you can pin individual managers to success or failure.[97]
> : There is now a greater sense of cohesion to British Rail's senior management. For many years the industry was having its success undermined because of divisions internally. That does not happen now. Semi-autonomous empires [referring to how the regions used to be managed] are not tolerated.[98]
> : I don't, I'm afraid, have a consensus style of running the industry.[99]
> : As chairman of a nationalised industry, you have to be very determined about your responsibilities and how you want them to be discharged. These responsibilities are now of the strictly commercial variety: satisfying the customer and behaving like any other business manager.[100]
> : British Rail used to be not so much a management but a vast administrative machine. Profit was not a dirty word, it was a word that didn't exist.[101]

He had a profound sense that the railway should be commercial. It was more than an intellectual conviction. He felt it in his bones. It was a matter of honour. Seeking to end a year declaring a profit, with passenger numbers on the rise was an honourable endeavour. You could be proud of such success. In his words:

> Bob: You mustn't think about railways, you must think about transport. Britain has some of the best motorways in the world, highly efficient road hauliers, and very intensive air services.

> We are not a monopoly. The acid test of customer satisfaction, therefore, as in any other business, is whether he comes back for more. With the abundance of alternative transport, it may be that the customer is better satisfied elsewhere. If so, and we fail, why should the government bail us out?[102]
>
> : There is a realisation by myself and my colleagues that the railways have no right to survive unless they are competitive. None of us thinks we can defy public wishes just because we have a historic position. I think this is what marks the change of view that has taken place over the last few years.

This comment confirms how different Bob's beliefs were from those of Peter Parker, who had talked of 'a manifest destiny for the railways in this country'.

Bob was not political. 'I flop around from right of centre to left of centre.' He explained his cordiality with the present government by pointing out that it set objectives he could meet, and that he happened to like Nicholas Ridley as a man. Someone said of him that:

> It is almost as if he had an understanding with ministers – though even that is putting it too strongly – that he will stay off their patch if they do not interfere with the way he runs the rail business. He is very loyal to ministers – not in any party-political sense – and they seem to respect him for that. I think that is one of the reasons why the government has been generous in approving his investment plans.[103]

Bob knew, and said, that it was more effective to work with government than be in conflict with it.

What Bob would not do was lobby for more money. That is what 'keeping off their turf' meant. The quantity of money was a government decision; how it was spent was his.

He did ruthless things, but he was not a ruthless person. They are different.

While he knew when managers needed to be moved, he was not in fact comfortable with the actual process. Some bosses are able to talk to the person, have a conversation, acknowledge the human concerns. But there are two or three instances of Bob moving people on in peremptory ways. Frank Paterson, known to be sceptical of sectorisation, had had a visit from Bob and a long conversation only a week or two before receiving a letter proposing his early retirement. 'Why didn't he talk to me about this when we met?' Frank asks.

Leslie Lloyd, then general manager of the Western Region, had failed, by mistake or otherwise, to do something important during the ASLEF strike. The following day he received by motorcycle messenger a letter on Bob Reid's personal notepaper asking him to confirm by return his retirement from British Rail. He left the office by lunchtime, never to return. He had been, not so long before, a 'vocal critic' of sectorisation.[104]

Regional general managers were powerful people. With support from their regional boards and with some support on the top board, they could have made difficulties for the next stage of sectorisation. The alternative they might have favoured was 'regional railway companies' an idea supported by, for example, Simon Jenkins on the Board and would be in the mind of John Major in 1994, and as contemplated by some now.

There had been an article in *Railnews* at the end of 1984 which seems to hint at such a thing. It began, 'Three Eastern Region area managers have been given complete freedom in the planning and marketing of their local passenger services for an indefinite trial period.' But this was the very task of the sectors. Was the Region working to be independent of the sectors? Thoughts pointing towards regional companies, were definitely alive. Bob had to head it off.

Bob Reid's knowledge of the railway can be taken for granted. He had been in it for thirty years. But he had not become part of the railway. Its culture was not his culture. He was in-the-railway but not of-the-railway. The values he held came from elsewhere; from within himself of course, but also from his upbringing and his experiences. He was, after all, the son of a Governor of Assam and Bengal. In thinking about the railway, he could be quite detached. Because other people thought in one way did not mean he should, and he did not.

A patrician is a good description. What does this mean? In his case, dignity, self-worth and a sense of duty.

A good deal of the commentary in the press concerns the struggle with the unions, but that must not be seen as the defining feature of his time in office.

His real achievements were twofold.

First was sectorisation. But to describe it with this single word is to underrate its significance. It was, as Gordon Pettitt says, 'a fundamental change in the direction of the railway towards being business-led, towards putting the passengers first. While before it was operator-led, or production-led, or cost-cutting led.'

Second was inspiration to managers. Through the debates he encouraged on his tours, his refusal to tell managers what to do and the certainty people felt that you did not let him down, a sense of freedom was felt. Managers were able to get on and do what they saw was right – it was most uplifting.

He was, as someone said, 'a very skilful manager and very imaginative and forward-thinking in his own quiet way.' Much of his skill was about people, not simply as a judge of character, but as a judge of how to get the right people into the right positions, how to build a team, and how to let them get on with their jobs. He was not a chief executive, as some are, who know what each manager should be doing and tells them. His was a higher skill, or at least the particular skill required in the railway. He knew what he wanted done and was able to put people in place who would make it happen, but in their own way.

Anton Buckoke told a story. He had been pointing out to Bob the failings of a particular manager. Anton remembers Bob's reply, 'Ah, yes, but you appoint someone for their strengths, not their weaknesses.' There is a good example later.

People often say, with a laugh, that when the first sector directors were appointed, they were given no instructions, or even a desk to sit at. They were told the purpose of their job in a few words, and that was that. How to achieve it, they had to work out for themselves.

Change management is something much talked about. In terminology used today, Bob's policy would be called 'Emergent Change', the opposite being 'Unfreeze-Change-Refreeze'. The latter involves a high degree of pre-planning. You plan the changes you want, you unfreeze the organisation, you make the changes, and then freeze the organisation again. It is a perfectly respectable course of action, but it was not the way Bob worked.

He knew that with an industry of the size and complexity of the railway, the head office could not sensibly direct matters on the ground. For decades, this had been attempted. It was the nagging instructions from the Board to Gerard Fiennes when he was a general manager that so enraged him and caused him to write the book that got him the sack. It was the idea that lay behind the Field Organisation.

Bob wanted to see change but wanted it to emerge through the initiative of people in the organisation with a proper, local knowledge of what was happening.

Bob had a clear sense of the dynamics of the railway. He understood the pace at which it was sensible to make things change. The railway, so large and integrated, with each piece relying on another piece, can only change over time. Attempts to cut corners, to press down bravely on the accelerator, are soon followed by cost overruns and projects abandoned halfway through – as we have seen! Bob was quite cautious. Some say that he could have moved more quickly to the later organisational structure, OfQ, described later, but that was not his style.

He knew the kind of people he wanted. The first directors for the three passenger sectors, Welsby, Bleasdale and Kirby, were all from outside the traditional career path. They did their work well.

His later appointments as chief operating officers while he was stepping back as chairman – first Myers and then Kirby – did not work out. You might wonder if Bob made it difficult for them. A chief executive remaining in the business as executive chairman is said to be a source of trouble. Possibly, with Bob being so engaged in the business, Myers then Kirby could not make it 'their railway'. There is a story that at a meeting with senior managers addressed by Myers, after he had been put in charge of the railway, some of the managers voiced objections to something Myers was saying. Myers hummed and hawed and Bob, who should not have been there at all, stood up, interrupted and said something like, 'Come on Myers, you're not going to put up with this.' Someone who remembers that meeting could see, or certainly thought, that in his interruption Bob was undermining Myers. In this case, it did not matter for, as Chris Stokes said, 'Myers was no shrinking violet'.

Unfortunately, Myers had to retired after eighteen months for family reasons. He could have been a good chief executive.

More seriously, and much later, when Kirby had been managing the day-to-day railway for some years, he and Bob fell out over the conduct of a dispute with the NUR. The circumstances are certainly strange. Possibly, with Bob in the background, Kirby did not properly own the whole picture, and therefore went along, mistakenly, with the dogmatic and disastrous view, held by the head of HR, as to how the dispute should be handled; and was required to resign almost immediately.

In placing people in position, Bob was aware of the conflicts he might be setting up. Indeed, he positively wanted to see a degree of tension. He understood that some grit should be in the mix. He had a book, which Frank Paterson remembers, about conflict and how it can be used to good ends. Teams need more than Kumbaya round the campfire. Groupthink and complacency are dangers which a measure of tension avoids. The team mattered. 'A great industry like ours,' Bob said, 'does not depend on a single figure. It depends on a group of senior managers.' But it does not need to be a cosy team. Some have said that Bob had no close friends in the railway – 'kings have no friends, only subjects and enemies'. But he did, out of sight, kept below the parapet.

Finally, Bob had some skill for surviving in the world of politics. In the words of another journalist:

> Running the railways was a political job..... Treading on eggshells between the government, opposition, unions, customers and competitors is not for a man without some kind of political nous. Reid seems to have picked up the skills without pushing any strong political convictions. He was a Tory voter, but probably more in the Whitelaw than the Thatcher mould.[105]

Management training manuals talk of 'competencies', of things which can be written down and taught, one by one. Perhaps they can. But in its leader, a great enterprise requires a spirit and skill which is not often found and cannot be taught. It should be no surprise. Great artists are rare beasts. Art schools train plenty of students, but Picassos are not often found. The same with great managers. The judgements they require about people, events and the capability of their own industry, the personality they require to lead and dominate, the spirit running through it all, are not often found together.

BOB SCHOLEY

For all his talents, it is hard not to regard Bob Reid's knowledge of the railway as fundamental to his success. He has been compared to Bob Scholey chairman of British Steel. Scholey's career in steel matched that of Bob in the railway. A captain during the war, like Bob, he joined United Steel in 1947 and retired as chairman of British Steel 45 years later, just a couple of years after Bob retired from British Rail.

Scholey, as Bob, drove his business to be amongst the most efficient in the world. He took it back to the basics – making quality steel more efficiently – and brought it into profitability after years of terrible losses. Both knew their industries from the bottom up. They had joined as young men and spent their careers in them.

Though Reid and Scholey were equally successful, their temperaments and talents were different. Bob Reid's essential skill was to establish the team and have them change the railway. Bob Scholey, on the other hand, knew the details of what had to be done and made it happen. Fortunately, their skills matched their industries. A railway, in its great variety, spread out across the country, cannot be directed from the centre. A steel industry, concentrated in a few vast plants, can. Bob Reid was a quiet, soft-spoken, 'working in the background' person, respectful of politicians. Bob Scholey, quite the opposite; he 'called an ingot an ingot' and was happy to be in conflict with the government.

PETER PARKER

If Bob was the iron fist, what of the velvet glove? It is easy to be dismissive of Peter Parker. In one journalist's words:

> The consensus man made flesh..... Essentially a performer, charming, extrovert, one of the best dinner hosts in London, an ardent admirer of the poet Blake, a maker of phrases which he

> deployed relentlessly and, occasionally, *ad nauseam*.
>
> He had much to do with the union leaders, met them socially, took them into his confidence. He believed that if you treated the chaps decently, they would respond in kind.

Bob Reid watched the theory fall apart. 'Peter felt you could persuade them by personal charm,' he said, 'and they dropped him right in the mire. We all learnt a lot from that.'

David Howell, who would have known Peter Parker well, as he had been Secretary of State for the two most fraught years of 1981 and 1982, saw Parker quite differently and had this to say when he retired in 1983.

> Obviously there is much more to be achieved, as many rail travellers will testify. But obviously, too, the corner really has been turned for Britain's railway system. It is now better placed to give efficient and comfortable service, and to modernise its facilities and embrace new transport technologies than at any time since the war.
>
> When the history of the period comes to be written it will be seen that the successful handling and outcome of the railway's industrial strife of 1982 marked a major turning point not just on the railways themselves but in public services, industrial relations and work attitudes generally.
>
> It was never my job to agree with the railway's managers at every turn, but I do not believe that Sir Peter has yet to be given the credit for what has been done recently to carry forward the railway reform. In fact, he has been the target of much ill-informed and prejudiced criticism.
>
> But the way is now truly open towards the better railway, the first part of the efficient, customer-oriented public transport system the nation requires. And Peter Parker has played a mighty part in bringing this about.

David Howell was right. The velvet glove had been part of the solution. Peter believed in 'the railway family', and spent much time and charm talking to the union leaders. As Bob said, they turned round and dropped him in the mire, but that didn't mean the effort was wasted. Parker communicated the direction of travel to the 150,000 employees. When it came to the crunch, when ASLEF refused to agree flexible rostering, he did not waver or back down. He supported the message that drivers who did not turn up for work would be sacked. He provided the air cover for Bob to get the work done on the ground.

20 THE GOLDEN YEARS (1986–88)

NEW PEOPLE

It is now 1986. The sky is clear, the task is known, all is excitement: the start of a golden age, if not entirely for passengers very much so for managers.

Strike threats had receded; there were plans, there was money, there was Nicholas Ridley at the Department, encouraging not sniping, there was a chairman, standing back but willing you to do your best. What more could you want?

'Bliss was it in that dawn to be alive, but to be a manager on the railway was very heaven.'

The advertising slogan 'We're getting there' caught the public's imagination. People laughed, 'Forty years late!' But they could see that it was true.

The government extended Bob Reid's contract to April 1990. New people would come onto the Board; there would be new sector directors and new general managers.

In Railnews, 'Board chairman, Sir Robert Reid, has reshuffled his top-level management team to take BR into the New Year.'

Bob was stepping back – not far, but back. There would remain a triumvirate at the top. David Kirby joined the group.

The triumvirate from January 1986 became:

- Geoffrey Myers – responsible for 'the total management of the railway'.
- Jim O'Brien – as before, responsible for 'business direction'.
- David Kirby – 'current operations and engineering' (i.e. most things).

OPPOSITE: *Bob smiling happily on the footplate and looking down at David Lindesay-Bethune, the owner of the train which he renamed The Great Marquess* [106]

It was certainly intended that Myers should remain in the business and become chief executive when Bob retired. Bob believed that in appointing him he had got the succession planning done, but family reasons required that Myers retire early – he left for Malta – and in October 1987 David Kirby took over the 'total management of the railway'.

When Myers left, David Rayner, then general manager of the Eastern Region, joined the Board with his place at Eastern taken by John Nelson.

The triumvirate from October 1987 became:

- David Kirby – the total management of the railway.
- Jim O'Brien – business direction.
- David Rayner – engineering.

Neither Geoffrey Myers nor later David Kirby, though responsible for 'the total management of the railway', could properly be called the chief executive. They were the chief operating officer. They chaired the big management group meetings and made the machinery work. But Bob

still ran the railway, though from a slight distance. Chairman's group meetings, just a small number of people, were held 10 a.m. every morning without fail. When Bob was away, they were chaired by Simon Jenkins. Bob, gently, kept his fingers on the business. His PA, then Jim Collins, read the daily log and made sure he knew anything important. Bob met senior people one-to-one, not often but enough, and continued his tours around the regions, which he loved, twice a year to each region: one tour every month, with comments and action points to the general manager the following day.

Jim was Bob's lightning conductor, on the phone to managers at Euston, Liverpool Street, King's Cross or wherever, checking the mood on the ground, and feeding what he learnt to Bob, who would use it well.

MUSCLING UP THE SUB-SECTORS

The sector directors were very much in the driving seat. They had been in place for four years, and in 1986 it was time for change. It was time, too, to muscle up their organisation. The three new passenger sector Directors were:

- **L&SE.** Chris Green came down from Scotland where he had been general manager to take over from David Kirby. He was followed at L&SE. by John Nelson (1992–94).
- **InterCity.** John Prideaux, from the policy unit, took over from Cyril Bleasdale who moved to become general manager of London Midland. Prideaux was followed by Chris Green (1992–94).
- **Provincial.** John Edmonds. Sometime earlier, in 1984, he had taken over from John Welsby who had moved up to headquarters. Edmonds was followed by Sidney Newey (1987–90) and Gordon Pettitt (1990–92).

In Freight, Colin Driver took Henry Sanderson's place, and in Parcels Brian Burdsall took over, with John Nelson as his National Business Manager. Burdsall was followed by Adrian Shooter (1989–91) and

Glyn Williams (1991–94).

Putting the sectors further in charge was seen as the right way to go, but to be fully effective they had to evolve and become more substantial, more muscular organisations. They had to be able to carry out the detailed work in planning and marketing their services, but the people doing such detailed work were still in the regions. They had to be moved up into the sectors. Rolling stock allocation was within the regions and that too had to be moved up to the sectors, called 'resource dedication'. In turn, the sectors, with the greater resources within them, organised themselves according to their sub-sectors.

In the case of InterCity, for example, there were five sub-sectors: IC West Coast, IC East Coast, IC Cross Country, IC Midland Main Line and IC Great Western. Across the whole country, there were twenty-three in all, each of them reflecting a particular market, a natural grouping of routes and traffic flows.

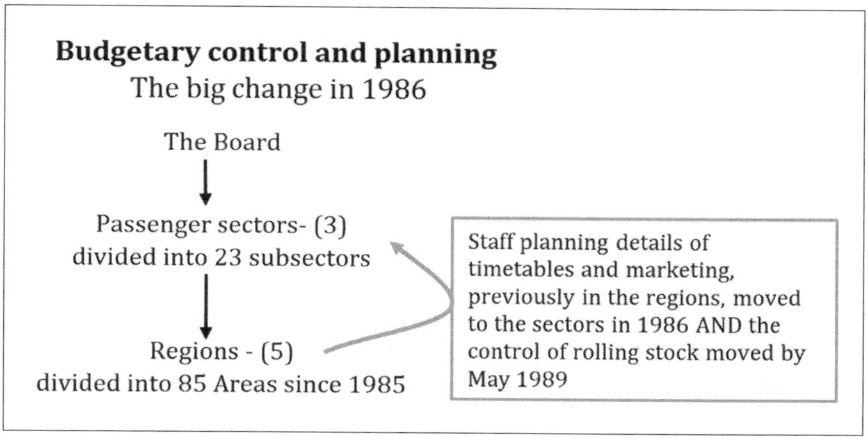

It is the development of the sub-sectors of the passenger railway which forms the next stage in sectorisation.

The development was first pressed forward by John Edmonds somewhat earlier than 1986 when he took over as Provincial Sector Director in 1984/5. John, as Chris Stokes, who would work for him, says 'had an incredibly powerful intellect, incredible determination and believed what he believed. I had a lot of time for him.'

John Edmonds, in charge of budgets and plans for his sector, had business managers for the different parts of his sector, with the staff doing the detailed planning of the timetable and marketing still in the regions. Edmonds, however, says Chris Stokes, was 'thick as thieves' with Jim O'Brien, the general manager of London Midland. They agreed together that in O'Brien's region these people, led by Chris Stokes, though nominally under O'Brien, would instead report to Edmonds.

It was, therefore, Chris Stokes who became the first sub-sector director. From then on he would agree budgets and plans with the region: 'inevitably sometimes a fraught process'.

What John Edmonds and Jim O'Brien initiated at London Midland in 1984/5 was a precursor to what would happen across the country: the creation of fully staffed sub-sectors. The new arrangement was announced in January 1986.

> Railnews: At the moment, sub-sector business managers report jointly to the regional general managers and sector directors. Under the new proposals they will respond only to the sector directors while taking on increased responsibilities for the generation of new revenue, marketing and the management of resources, such as rolling stock.
>
> Essentially this restructuring is about strengthening the sub-sector business managers. It will give them a lot more autonomy and power in the marketplace.

The muscling up of the sub-sectors began. The organisation chart of Network SouthEast, for example, would soon show over fifty people across its six sub-sectors (Network North; Anglia; South Eastern; South Central; South Western; and Thames and Chiltern).

From 1986, sectors and sub-sectors, fully resourced to control the planning and marketing of their services and the authority to allocate rolling stock, could be held responsible for the profitability of their business. They still, of course, had to work through the general managers to have their plans implemented. Drivers, engineers, signalmen, the vast bulk of the railway, continued to report to the general managers.

The high-level objective for these new people was set out in the corporate plan at the end of 1985. The modest investment in the previous plan was greatly enlarged. Expectations of financial success grew. The December 1985 front page of *Railnews* proclaimed:

BR SET TO CUT GOVERNMENT AID BY 25%
Massive investment and better service in new 5-year plan

The target, after a later adjustment, was to reduce government support, already 25 per cent less than it was in 1983, down to £555 in 1989/90. 'Demanding but achievable,' said Bob Reid. InterCity, however, was still falling short of its profit plans and there was much for all the sectors to do.

But, taken altogether, it was an exciting plan.

The new spirit was exemplified in a conversation that took place at the Longsight engineering depot in Manchester. One of the shift leaders, Richard Lockett, remembers it well. The depot looked after trains for IC West Coast. The sub-sector manager, Richard Brown, came along one day. 'Good morning,' he said, 'half the air-conditioning units aren't working.' The traditional reply would have been, 'Can't be helped, defective design, cost too much to rectify.' But this was not said, for the engineers knew that maintenance was the problem. As there had never been any money for maintenance, it was safer to blame the design. The director went on, as managers never had before: 'Passengers are paying for nine coaches: five standard-class, three first-class and a functioning restaurant car, with air conditioning in all of them. If it's a question of money, make a case and I'll get it for you.' The engineers were delighted, we have a proper job to do, they thought, wonderful.

There are excellent books about each of the sectors, but the following gives some flavour of what was happening.

PROVINCIAL SECTOR: CHRIS STOKES AND JOHN EDMONDS

Chris Stokes, then a director working for John Edmonds in the Provincial sector, describes the arrival of some new trains, not great now, but immensely better than what went before.

Fifty new Pacers and fifty new Sprinters were arriving. Edmonds set up a competition between the managers of his three sub-sectors. Who could come up with the best use of the new trains? Chris won. He won all the Sprinters and half the Pacers.

The two routes crossing the Pennines were run on a line-of-route basis. Birmingham–Leicester–Peterborough was in Chris's sub-sector. The service on that route had been just six trains a day, loco-hauled, old Mark 1 coaches. Chris proposed an hourly service using two-car diesel Sprinters. It would be enormously cheaper to run and would earn more revenue. John Edmonds chose it. Chris had been innovative in the train service structure and the train maintenance schedule, which was what John was wanting: obvious now but not obvious then, and no one knew what the Board would think of such a large increase in train miles. In reality, faster journey times, quicker turnaround at each end, lower maintenance costs would greatly improve the economics.

Chris had seen the service in the round and looked to the real effect on the bottom line, something which would have been difficult before. The plan was approved.

Chris, talking in general, explains what Edmonds did.

Chris: John wanted to see fast and frequent services established between provincial cities. Before, services had been spasmodic and badly planned.

: He drove business thinking into the Provincial sector through the sub-sectors. We looked at driver costs, we got rid of loco-haulage on Trans-Pennine, we developed increasingly better specified diesel trains and increased the frequency, introduced new routes with the new 158 Express Sprinter units. We spent time with the civil engineers who were very helpful. There was investment in dynamic track stabilisers so that after track work, the route could be opened at 125mph on Monday morning instead of having a week-long 25mph speed restriction.

: John transformed the Provincial sector.

ANGLIA AND PETER FIELD

Turning south, Peter Field, a new person in this story, describes how he became a sub-sector director within Network SouthEast. The Gordon he refers to is Gordon Pettitt.

> Field: God bless Gordon. He says 'come', and I cometh. I started life up in the Midlands but moved south and found myself, for my first real job, as Assistant Station Manager at Liverpool Street. I was on shift, there were three of us, round the clock. I must have done something right for Gordon, the divisional manager, promoted me to Area Operations Manager at Broxbourne, and then to Southend and then to Stratford.
>
> : When Gordon moved to Southern as general manager of the region, he again said 'come' and I was made Area Manager London Bridge within Gordon's region.
>
> : I'll tell you a Gordon story. It was about 1985. My drivers at Charing Cross decided to go on strike, happened all too often, usually over nothing at all. If they go on strike in the morning, it is not too bad, people can rearrange their day, but my guys decided to go on strike in the afternoon, so all the commuters were in London. They could not get home; they were extremely fed up and creating quite a rumpus. So I did an off-the-cuff deal with the drivers, quite beyond my authority, to get them working again. Alec, my boss, walked into my office and sacked me on the spot. But his boss was Gordon. Ten minutes later I had a phone call and I was back in my job.

Alec was old school. Managers could be quite aloof in those days and he was following policy, which was that you do not give in to strikes: a policy which clearly did not work. It was a style both hard edged and weak, at the same time. Gordon and Peter had quite different ideas. They would lose the odd battle but, by engaging with the drivers and guards, would win the war: flexible, but much stronger.

Peter Field goes on with a colourful description of what after the great change in 1986. He was not the only vigorous manager, but he tells the story well.

> Field: When Chris Green came down from Scotland in 1986 to set up Network SouthEast he asked me to move from the region into the sector and I became one of his sub-sector directors, the one covering the services into Essex and beyond, in the Eastern Region. But that region was managed far, far away in York and we were getting a pretty raw deal. We pressed to have Anglia carved out and set up as a region of its own.

John Edmonds was appointed to do that in October 1987 and became the Anglia general manager when the new region went live in April 1988.

> Field: I spotted something a little before the separation that made me livid. I knew the area intimately, so I could see that the best modern tamping equipment was mysteriously migrating north from Anglia. We were going to lose it. I kicked up a stink. Fortunately, the general manager at York stepped in and sorted it out.
> : That was David Rayner. He was super. New up there, new ideas and very supportive of the carved-out Anglia Region.

With forceful managers in the sectors, the tension likely to arise between them and the regions is obvious, in this case between Peter Field and John Edmonds.

> Field: We rowed a lot. He would not give in and I would not give in; I suppose we were both strong-minded.
> : Edmonds did not change things much, he couldn't. Performance did not improve. He couldn't wave a magic wand; there were too many deep-rooted problems, too many flat junctions, too many old trains, too much old signalling. He couldn't get the improvements he wanted. The rest of the SouthEast was pretty good, well built, particularly South West, with all these flyover junctions, but there was just one in the Anglia Region at Ilford, maybe a couple more,

> they just did not exist, so there were all manners of delays and cascades and cumulative delays when things went wrong. It was really, really bad.
>
> : Edmonds had quite a small team – top people, but small – so he was a bit hamstrung. The sector was better placed. It had, for example, Ernst Birchler, supremo of all things train, a Swiss guy; no one knew more than he did. Anybody who tried to get past Ernst would get nowhere. He had a direct line to Chris Green, he was that good. He bypassed me, but I did not care. We were pretty heavy-hitting. He could mobilise the fleet engineering capacity in the region and the Board.
>
> : We could make plans, do the numbers and be pretty persuasive. We had schemes oven-ready and on the shelf.
>
> : Increasing revenue and cutting operating costs was a huge driver to get things done and done quickly. In those days if you didn't spend your money in the year, it disappeared. Chris Green would go to the Board and say, 'Great Western is underspending by £50 million this year and I could spend it in the next two weeks.' We did spend it, or made it seem that we did, though how would not pass muster with the accountants now.

Chris Green confirmed, 'Peter Field was very good at spending money effectively.'

> Field: There was a lot we could do. We had money, quite a lot. We could do big schemes, handle big opportunities. It was a heyday for managers. The rest of SouthEast was in a reasonable shape, so it was difficult for them to make improvements. But, so long as you have the money, it is easy in a region that was, frankly, terrible to make things better.
>
> : The stations had not been looked after, all the money had gone up north. We ripped out the dirty old sodium lights and put in white lights which immediately looked brighter – we knew people would notice the difference – and we painted everything NSE red, as you know. We bought a load of red seats and things like that; it was very cosmetic. But passengers liked it.

: Operating costs were not my business, that was Edmonds' job, but revenue was. Anglia had old tamping machines. After relaying track you had to wait at least a week with 20mph speed restrictions until the track bedded down, which hit our income. But we had seen that the Eastern Region and the Great Western had these brand-new machines, dynamic track stabilisers, massive vibrators that go over the track with two passes. With them, you can open up at line speed. We went to the area's civil engineers, just bypassing the region, John Edmonds and Co., and said we have the money and will buy these for you.
: We got problems removed like the old signalling, which had been a big cause of delay. We got all the old telephone exchanges stripped out, every single one, they were based on an old Strowger design. We were the first of all the regions to have fibre optics, the new signalling needed it. It saved costs and we could sell the extra capacity to the private sector. We bought new trains. Network SouthEast had the money to buy trains.
: We got electrification done, we got Royston–Cambridge done and we got Bishop's Stortford to Stansted Airport done. Don Heath, the master of electrification, was brilliant at getting things done to a budget; he had management skills in construction and infrastructure. I got Bishop's Stortford through to King's Lynn done – that's a story.
: The MP for King's Lynn, Sir Henry Bellingham, was getting an awful press in his constituency for it was discovered that there was a high-class call girl operating in the House of Commons and this lady had managed to get her security pass from him. Well, he thought that if he could get the government to find the money to improve the railway to his constituency, he might become a hero instead of a villain.
: And that, with one thing and another, is just what happened.
: As I said, for all the talk, John did not change the organisation much. It was pretty silo-ish but we cut across them.
: The idea of cross-functional teams was very embryonic, very, very embryonic. It came in a bit, but not nearly as fast as it did from '92 onwards, when OfQ came in. In the sector it was different. Each

> of the route managers – I had four under me, Trevor Hill, Charles Devereux, Peter Newbold and John Wilson, all excellent, went on to bigger things – looked over everything, developed a strategic plan for their route with an investment plan. Very multifunctional.
> : It was not my job to manage performance – that was John's job – but I was pretty interested in it, and we chided the region if they were not delivering. If it was really bad, if I thought one of his people was not trying as hard as he should, I might have words with John Edmonds. But he was fiercely protective of his staff and it always ended with a row.

John, someone else has said, hated his job at Anglia. He was not an operator.

After two or three years, Peter Field left Network SouthEast. But in 1989, a year after the Clapham accident, Gordon again said 'come'. He wanted Peter to become the chief operating manager of the Southern Region. 'Gordon was magnificent,' said Peter. The region was shaken to the core by that accident and Gordon helped it to recover.

At that time, the Southern Region, a very big region, was divided into Areas. Peter had twenty area operating managers reporting to him: he had an impossible job, and he told Gordon so. The solution came with OfQ, which led to the region being separated into three: South Eastern, South Central and South Western. Peter became manager of the then vertically integrated South Western. Later still, it would be renamed South West Trains and be the first train operating company to be privatised.

EASTERN AND JOHN NELSON

John Nelson was appointed general manager of Eastern in November 1987. It was at the same time that John Edmonds had been nominated to be the general manager of the Anglia Region when it was set up in April following year. Nelson was the youngest ever to be made a general manager, just 40, and in his first week the chairman arrived for a tour of inspection. John describes these tours.

> Nelson: When I came here as general manager, which I did only a few years after I'd worked for him, he did a tour in my very first week. The tours were so that he could meet and talk to the managers and meet staff on the ground. He used these very effectively.
> : The form was always the same. He'd arrive in the evening. There would be a dinner that evening and my whole management team would be there; and the people from the sector would be there, the sub-sector manager for the IC East Coast would be there for example.

Note: the Eastern Region served all five sectors: InterCity, Provincial, Network SouthEast, Freight and Parcels. They all used Eastern.

> Nelson: Bob, over dinner, would, as he always did, at first hold forth and then pick a subject and most probably pick a fight with someone, deliberately. Now, it always seemed to be me. Happily, I came to realise that he only picked an argument with people he had confidence in, and it was in order to make a point to everybody else. He used any meeting with a group of managers as a means of making a point, possibly several points, about the importance of sectors for example.

John goes on to describe the changes he wanted.

> Nelson: I wanted to take sector management to the next level. I was very much an advocate of integrating the production side of the railway with the commercial side. I still am; it is the biggest lost opportunity since privatisation.
> : My views were well known so my appointment to Eastern, along with Edmonds to Anglia, was emblematic to people who worked in these places. These appointments were saying, 'Things are going to change. This is a new regime.'
> : I was asked by the Board to do a report on how I thought the production side should be organised. I can remember putting my proposal to David Kirby; he was then chief executive and my

> boss. He read the paper and said, 'Basically you are proposing the abolition of the regions.' He was gobsmacked. And I said, 'Well, yes, I suppose I am.' He could not get his mind round that.

Technically, what John proposed would not abolish the regions, but it was intended to have the same effect.

> Nelson: There was then a period of about eighteen months with a lot of tension between the sectors and the regions, a power struggle, and a philosophical discussion about what should happen. Sometimes the tension could be constructive, but it could get to the point when it was no longer constructive, quite the opposite.

As you saw from Peter Field's description.

> Nelson: Bob interested himself in this totally, whether we should continue with the matrix organisation or have something more integrated. It was what he wanted to talk about, he wanted your views on it; when he met people he would ask them what they thought.

John goes on to describe how he reorganised the region.

> Nelson: Anyway, on the Eastern Region, with the Board's blessing, I completely restructured the production side. When I arrived the area civil engineers were all 'area'-based. The area civil engineer at Doncaster, for example, covered part of the East Coast Main Line as well as the other lines radiating out of Doncaster.
> : I changed these areas to make them route-based. The routes radiating out of Doncaster would have their own engineer and the East Coast Main Line its own engineers based at Peterborough, Doncaster or Newcastle. Sounds obvious, but it was a huge innovation.
> : At this stage they all reported to me but in terms of their role they were no longer to talk to me and say, 'We want to do x, y and

z,' and argue about their budget. Instead, they were to go to the sectors and say, 'If I do x, y and z, I can make the business better, will you pay for it?'

INTERCITY AND JOHN PRIDEAUX

In his last month in charge of InterCity, December 1985, Cyril Bleasdale wrote about his plans in *Railnews*. There was some way to go to make a profit, but he was proud of what he had done: 'The business is on course to better its promise that it would stand alone commercially by 1988/89. Of the £103 million turnaround originally required, £33 million is already achieved and there are firm plans for the remainder.'

The task, as Cyril said, was to trim at one end and grow at the other. Trimming is the easy bit; you can bite off bits one at a time. Growing at the other is much harder, for if everything is not right, nothing is right; you must inch forward on all fronts.

Refurbished trains had moved the service upmarket with clean interiors and better catering. Pullman-branded trains had been launched, or relaunched, 'with spectacular success'. As for savings, there were plans to make trains longer but run fewer of them. Some trains were poorly loaded: 'If they do not pay then they need to come off. We have some poor earners, particularly on the cross-country routes.'

The marketing department of British Rail loved speed records in those days. A press preview run took place to launch the Tyne–Tees Pullman, 'a celebration of 50 years' luxury high-speed travel on the East Coast Main Line'. With everything cleared out of the way, with 'special, top-secret timings and working instructions issued', an HST train loaded with journalists set off from Newcastle to London. The speed achieved is quite extraordinary, an average of 140.1mph over an eighteen-mile stretch just north of Peterborough. That is getting up towards the speed of electric-powered European high-speed trains.

'Says a lot for the HSTs and their Paxman engines,' said Cyril.

A serious problem was punctuality, generating a lot of complaints on the West Coast Main Line. There was overhead wire damage caused by faulty pantographs, there were unreliable hot axle box detectors causing false alarms, the switch diamond crossings failed in hot weather, there was failure of twenty-year-old track circuits between Rugby and Euston. The list goes on. It is all very familiar, the everyday life of the railway – but bad. Trains got stuck so often there had to be 'specially trained boarding parties' to go to the aid of the stranded passengers. Cyril would move to the region, becoming general manager of London Midland, so it became his problem to fix.

John Prideaux took over InterCity. Except for the unreliability, he was lucky with what he got. He asked Chris Stokes to move and join him as the InterCity Resources and Planning Manager. The sectors were being beefed up considerably.

> Stokes: We had more in the engine room than Cyril, so we could do more. We cleaned up the act and the resources. We took out chunks of essentially loss-making services like Euston to Blackpool, like Euston to Shrewsbury. We rationalised maintenance depots. There were lots of things the sector could get its hands on which previously the regions kept their arms around.
>
> : John Prideaux was very hard-nosed. In planning ahead for the future service once the East Coast Main Line electrification was complete, he contemplated taking trains off the West Coast Main Line north of Preston or Carlisle altogether and running them all to Glasgow via Edinburgh. There is little difference in the journey time, but a lot in symbolism and a very dubious proposition, thought the Board.
>
> : We pushed progressive market pricing. We were carrying a lot of commuters from places like Peterborough and Rugby to London. The traditional season ticket fare structure had an enormous taper. It wasn't unprofitable, but it would bear extra pricing. John pushed prices up on these flows like it was going out of fashion. There was some price elasticity, so passenger numbers stopped growing but, what the hell, we were getting a lot more revenue than when we started.

And a profit? When the year 1988/9 arrived, Cyril's and John's work had paid off. In its first year without government grant, InterCity turned in a £57 million profit: revenue up 10 per cent on the previous year and volume up 4 per cent.

There were a few accounting changes affecting the result. Is it fair to say that Prideaux made InterCity profitable? Stokes: 'Yes, it is. He was helped by the strong economy, but yes, he did make a profit.'

NETWORK SOUTHEAST AND CHRIS GREEN

We must come back to Network SouthEast, for it was the arrival of Chris Green in the South that enabled Peter Field, and so many others, to stretch themselves and have the best years possible as railway managers. He was a person, using Bob Reid's words, 'appointed for his strengths, not his weaknesses'. If times had been hard, Chris might not have been ideal but, as it happened, he more than anyone embodied the vision Bob Reid had for how the railway should be managed. They go together. Bob Reid led to Chris Green. Chris Green brought to life what Bob Reid wanted the railway to be.

> Chris Green: When I went up to Scotland in '79 as chief operations manager. I was shocked at what I found. The whole of the previous ten years had been spent cutting costs; everything was grey and dingy and dirty with trains cancelled because of the vacancy gap. It was so bad we feared Strathclyde Council might close the railway altogether and rely on buses. It took from '79 to '86 to get it to something we could be proud of.
> : I had been promoted to deputy general manager in '84 and then general manager. Scotland was within Provincial so John Welsby was the sector director. Technically, it was he who planned what should be done but he was quite happy with what we were doing and left us alone. I was, in effect, both general manager and sector director.
> : To earn money to invest we invented the ScotRail brand. It was a public statement that we were going to be different and independent, which went down well with the Scots.
> : Somehow, we had a little more money than in England and we went our own way. Bob knew we were doing things differently, and

Railnews

No 303
Newspaper of British Rail
MAY 1988

Snow drama as mid-May deadline nears

SUMMER is just around the corner.

Try telling that to these ScotRail S&T men shovelling snow on the summit of the White Corries mountain, 3,636ft up in Glencoe.

Buffeted by howling winds and horizontal hail, they're valiantly trying to dig down to a radio station buried in 18ft deep drifts.

The snowbound station, out of use for several months, is the missing link in a chain of six needed to bring radio electronic token block signalling to the West Highland line between Fort William and Tyndrum Upper.

The site was chosen for the vast coverage it offers. But the mountain is fickle.

Arctic conditions and winds of 130 mph can cut off the peak within minutes. That's why the radio station hut is equipped with a supply of survival rations.

As Railnews goes to press ScotRail engineers John Sandiland, Ronnie Meek and Harvey Irving with chairlifts manager Bruce Forbes face a fierce battle with the elements to dig the radio station out of the snow and get RETB working before a mid-May deadline.

● *Engineers get ski lessons Page 3, and Railwayman Eddie Tod is invited to a summit conference Page 7*

New Network trains give fastest-ever journeys to coast

3 SPEED RECORDS IN 48 hrs

THREE non-stop high-speed runs within 48 hours have swept Southern Region into the record books.

First of the record making runs came when one of the new flagship Wessex Electric trains sped between London's Waterloo and Weymouth in just a few seconds under two hours to give the fastest-ever time on the 142 mile route.

● *Bournemouth drivers Jack Gardiner and Alan Condon took it all in their stride at Weymouth after notching up two non-stop high-speed records in a new class 442 Wessex Electric. "It makes a big change," said Jack.*

... Weymouth station — exactly 142 miles 64 chains from the Waterloo buffer stops — official timekeeper Peter Semmens went ...

New pay offer

THE Board has announced a revised pay offer for rail staff.

FINAL OFFER story — Page Two.

PROPOSED new rates — Page 16.

Railnews

No 304
Newspaper of British Rail
JUNE 1988

£120m order takes freight well into the 21st century

Artist's view of one of the new Class 60 locomotives to be built for Railfreight

By PAUL WHITING

100 NEW LOCOS

RAILFREIGHT has been given the Whitehall green light to build 100 new generation heavy locomotives at a cost of around £120 million and each with a life span of 40 years.

The new diesel fleet of class 60s represents the biggest Railfreight investment ... built by Brush Electric Machines of Loughborough and will meet Railfreight's traction requirement well into the next century.

The super locomotives with their 3,100 hp motors will be capable of hauling between 2,000 and 4,000 ton trains, mirroring the success of the powerful privately owned and American built class 59 diesels.

... new locomotive will begin in ... Brush building up to a rate of three to four locos a week. All should be in service by the end of 1991.

The hauling power of the locomotives — they will be able to haul double the trailing weight of a class 47 diesel — means that Railfreight will be able to scrap some 240 existing locos which are more than 25 years old and are costly on maintenance and repairs.

Their increased productivity will eliminate the need to use two locomotives to haul some trains. They will have 100 kilometres an hour capability and their 40 year life span will allow for half life rebuilding.

The new fleet will be used to haul heavy freight trains for Railfreight's core business — coal, construction materials, metals and petroleum.

Current size of the diesel fleet is 980.

The go-ahead to build came from Transport Secretary Paul Channon.

American, British and European manufacturers were invited to tender to build the locos and the three bids each came from UK companies — GEC, MetCam and Brush.

Railfreight director Colin Driver said: "This investment, more than any other, shows the confidence we have in the future of our business.

"These new locomotives will give us the scope to sustain and develop our business profitably, by employing ever larger trains to service the heavy end of the UK industry."

PRIVATISATION AND BR — Sir Bob Reid writes on Page Two

Railnews

No 305
Newspaper of British Rail
JULY 1988

'A very successful year by any standards' — BOB REID

BEST-EVER RESULTS!

INSIDE
- The Bob Reid Column
- Results in detail
- The next 5 years

BRITISH RAIL's group profits rocketed to £291 million in a record breaking year which saw passenger volume at its highest for 27 years.

At the same time the railway operating profit of £109 million before interest was the best result recorded in the 25 years history of the British Railways Board.

The record figures contained in the 1987/88 annual report and accounts compare with a previous year's £2.4 million profit and show that BR is on target to cut its need for Government grant by 25 per cent to £605 million by March 1989.

On all fronts the year's results smashed records.

● Passenger volume soared by over eight per cent to 20.6 billion passenger miles, the highest since 1961.

● Passenger earnings at £1,662 million were the highest in real terms since 1948.

● The group surplus of £291 million after interest was the highest ever achieved.

● Railfreight had its best result for a decade with an operating surplus of £43.6 million.

● The seven per cent growth in InterCity earnings was the highest since the services were introduced 22 years ago.

● Network SouthEast increased earnings by a record 8.5 per cent to gross £804 million. Commuting in the sector has increased by a staggering 15 per cent in the last three years.

● Provincial earnings grew by a record seven per cent to gross £247.2 million.

● Investment of £543 million in railway renewal and expansion was the highest ever — and BR paid for it from its own resources without any long-term borrowing.

● Property sales at £180 million was the highest ever recorded and income from lettings rose by more than nine per cent.

● Station trading income increased by 12.5 per cent to over £15 million.

● Travellers Fare increased its operating surplus by 36 per cent to £7.5 million.

● Freightliners container traffic was up nearly seven per cent on target.

● BR Engineering Ltd won orders worth £180 million in competitive tendering.

Chairman Sir Robert Reid welcomed the results but again called for an all out effort to improve service quality.

He said: "By any standards it was a very successful year, but we do not yet produce a uniformly improved quality of service so that all our customers share the fruits of our improved financial position.

"We are determined to reduce the variability of our performance."

Signs of a new high-speed era

spending whatever extra money we could find, but he was very supportive. We overspent one year by £10 million and expected a kicking, but not a bit of it. Silence from the top, so we carried on.
: We did a huge clean-up, we opened new stations and reopened the Bathgate to Edinburgh line. What really wowed Bob was when he stepped off the train in the cleaned-up Glasgow Central station and saw the gleaming white floor with bands playing and bright, clean lighting where before it was dingy, grey tarmac and dim lights. By 1986 we had most of the main stations looking like that; it would have been hard to find a bad one.
: So, I was called to go down to London when all the sector changes happened in January 1986. Bob simply said, 'I want you to do a ScotRail in the south.' It was such a good remit because I knew exactly what he meant. I took over from David Kirby. He had had the worst of it. When he went to the London and South-East sector, he had to make spectacular savings, run the same railway with £126 million less money, one-third less, which he did. What thanks did he get from the politicians? None – they hated what they saw, and so did the media.
: Nicholas Ridley had said to Bob Reid, 'Why is the condition of the railway so terrible?' Months later I was moved from ScotRail. I think there was a link.
: I was a Londoner so I knew exactly what I was taking on, but I was still amazed at the difference with ScotRail where you would have struggled to find such dingy stations and trains. I travelled around and could see that quality was on its knees with late trains, cancelled services, dirty trains, grey stations. Demoralised staff were grimly keeping services running, and no one felt pride. There were vacancies in all grades. The railway hadn't done this; it was the government. You can't live with cancelling 10 per cent of your commuter trains because you have not got the money for enough guards.
: I knew what to do: it was a cut-and-paste job from ScotRail. Everyone was with me. Even the government had changed its tune. They wanted a railway that the public would like. The stars were all in alignment.

: By then, Gordon Pettitt had been made general manager of the Southern Region, so I worked with him, and with the three, soon to be four, other general managers whose territory stretched down from the North or West into London. We were all new in the job and keen, so we got on and worked things out.

In Chris Green's first year in the south, there followed a programme so large, so fast, and so effective that has become an icon of the best of British Rail. His programme turned around public attitudes and delivered much of substance in this huge London-based railway in just twelve months.

Chris Green: In April, I announced Operation Pride. I wanted a rebranding, but you absolutely cannot do that unless you first improve the product. The marketing agency, J. Walter Thompson, said they wouldn't take on the job unless we did. Somehow, we were able to do things very quickly. Operation Pride meant recruiting 1,700 new staff: guards, ticket office staff, train cleaning staff, station cleaning staff.

: We held back the launch of the new brand till we had done enough for passengers to know that things had been improved.

: We trained more ticket office staff so people would not have to wait more than three minutes to buy a ticket. That kind of thing, people notice.

: Staff were central to what we were doing. A lot of Operation Pride was about staff. We got advice from Marks & Spencer's. How do you create customer service? The answer: 'Look after your staff and they will look after the customers.' Richard Branson did the same ten years later.

: For the first three months, we did nothing but Operation Pride. On 10 June we were ready to launch. It was a big public event. We got all the media, the TV, the minister, everything we could and issued a public manifesto pamphlet. We had to make what we were doing unstoppable in case the budget ran out. We burnt our bridges behind us. It had to happen.

: There had been a lot of planning, a station modernising group, a training group, a marketing group, but all in the background until 10 June. Then flat out.

: The new livery started to appear on trains. We had chosen bright, garish colours to get away from a dull, grey railway: deliberately red, white and blue, the colour of the Union Jack. Newly painted trains were not released back into service until they had had a deep clean inside. When you hit the seats, clouds of dust would rise up and that could not be allowed. A train with the new brand on the outside had to be clean on the inside.

: We were painting the trains, cleaning the stations and painting staff restrooms as fast as we could, but it would take time.

: There was one thing we could do quickly. It became our iconic symbol. The red lamp post. Every lamp post in a huge circle from Brighton in the south to Peterborough in the north was to be painted NSE red. The instruction went out, 'All lamp posts to be painted red within six weeks – how you do it is up to you – but just do it.' Painters were pulled in from all over the south. If you went to a station and it had not been done, the staff would say, 'When are our lamp posts going to be painted?' There was a lot of enthusiasm.

: The cost of what we were doing was well more than our budget so we had to take a gamble on extra revenue. It was quite against the rules, but Bob knew what we were doing and didn't say anything.

: We didn't really want more commuters; the morning peak was already too high, where would we put them? We wanted more off-peak revenue, passengers in the empty trains.

: The branding helped, clean stations and clean trains helped, enthusiastic staff helped. But what really helped was the off-peak ticket, the One-Day Travelcard. The first one of its kind. You bought one ticket which gave you any amount of travel after 9:30 a.m. It was better value than buying individual tickets and hugely more convenient. Months later, we introduced something people remember even more, the Network Card. It wasn't a ticket: it was a loyalty card, giving discounts on off-peak tickets. And, what people loved, free car parking after 10:30.

: All this was heavily marketed. It was very successful. Revenue

shot up 25 per cent and covered the cost of what we'd done.
: Performance had to improve, so the yellow peril league table got issued. We measured punctuality and other things for all the routes and circulated the paper, very publicly, every month to all the managers. You didn't want to be at the bottom.

Quarterly passenger satisfaction surveys began. Questions about punctuality, information at stations and the ease of buying tickets were the most important, but the cleanliness of toilets also mattered (at first, only 39 per cent of passengers rated them good or adequate). Punctuality had of course been measured for years, but simple numerical standards were developed for the other elements of the service. Most importantly, these were published and available to the passengers every six months in *Network News*: both the numerical standards for punctuality, train cleaning, etc. and the results of the passenger satisfaction surveys.

Things improved. Train cleaning improved, in part because staff became motivated but more fundamentally because money was found to recruit enough people to do the job. A direct link became established between service standards and the budget. Peter Parker's

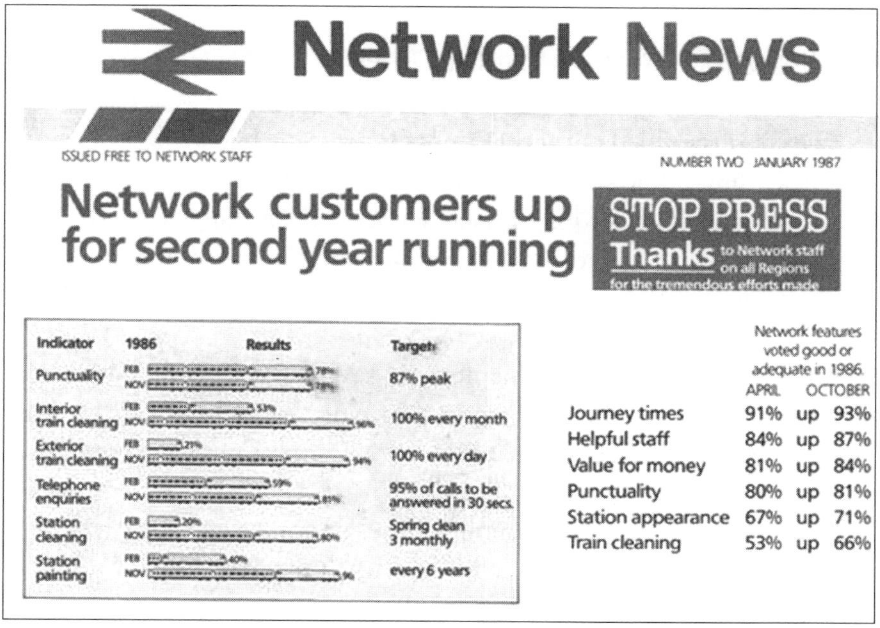
Network News

ISSUED FREE TO NETWORK STAFF

NUMBER TWO JANUARY 1987

Network customers up for second year running

STOP PRESS
Thanks to Network staff on all Regions for the tremendous efforts made

Indicator	1986	Results	Target
Punctuality	FEB	[illegible]	87% peak
	NOV	[illegible]	
Interior train cleaning	FEB	53%	100% every month
	NOV	96%	
Exterior train cleaning	FEB	21%	100% every day
	NOV	94%	
Telephone enquiries	FEB	59%	95% of calls to be answered in 30 secs.
	NOV	81%	
Station cleaning	FEB	20%	Spring clean 3 monthly
	NOV	80%	
Station painting	FEB	40%	every 6 years
	NOV	[illegible]	

Network features voted good or adequate in 1986	APRIL		OCTOBER
Journey times	91%	up	93%
Helpful staff	84%	up	87%
Value for money	81%	up	84%
Punctuality	80%	up	81%
Station appearance	67%	up	71%
Train cleaning	53%	up	66%

speeches about the 'crumbling edge of quality' (or, as some described it, the 'bleeding stump') were no longer needed. If the government wanted satisfied passengers, people who vote!, then the money had to be found.

These standards, developed and rolled forward and made binding in contracts with train operators, became a legacy of the Bob Reid railway.

Gordon Pettitt, by then general manager in the Southern Region, is proud of what got done. Even in the straitened times before 1986, by 'pushing a bit here and pushing a bit there', he had electrified two routes, got the large, most urgent Waterloo resignalling started, and slimmed overheads by cutting out the divisions which stood between him and the twelve or so areas where the work really happened.

It was a constructive time for all the routes. Things got done: sixteen electrification schemes done, the 'Total Route Modernisation' of the Chiltern line got done. These managers understood that piecemeal modernisation gave poor returns, and only Total Route Modernisation gave value for money. Thameslink 2000 got planned and so did Crossrail.

> Chris Green: We found on lines north of the Thames, that our trains were on the slow lines and InterCity on the fast, that they had continuous welded rail and 125mph line speed while we had jointed track, 75mph line speed and speed restrictions. General managers saw no profit or kudos in local services. Everything was for the InterCity. That had to change. We paid the regions to upgrade the slow lines for 100mph running.

Jim Collins, then running Thameslink, says his local civil engineer at Bedford was quite shocked when told what he wanted on the slow lines. 'I had 100mph trains running on a 75mph railway.' That had to change.

> Chris Green: We were running thousands of slam-door trains, the last railway to do so. That had to change too. There was a problem: £600 million. We put a huge effort into preparing the

business case for what would become the new Networker fleet. It had to show a financial benefit compared with keeping the slam-door trains. Bob had a dinner with the team to challenge the case: tore us to pieces, pretty aggressively. You know how he could be when he had a drink in the evening. Well this was one of the worst. But he called up the next morning to apologise, in a roundabout way. He did that.

: The economy was booming, business was good. Bob Reid got the Networker fleet through the Board – some were against, but he was totally on our side, he wanted to grow the railway – the government loved it, Cecil Parkinson loved it and Margaret Thatcher was pro-rail enough for a day for the order to go through. 'Spend it quickly,' said Cecil Parkinson. The contract was signed on 31 August 1989. Thank goodness it was. Weeks later the sky fell in: financial crisis, political crisis. I think Cecil had a hunch about this which is why he hurried it along. Days later all investment got switched off. But the Networkers could not be cancelled, and they started arriving in 1991, even in the middle of the 90s slump.

: All this time, the unions were quite cooperative. We got driver-only trains – including the Networker fleet – introduced everywhere except on the lines out of Euston and Waterloo where the sectional councils turned it down: pure ideology. And that's really where we are today on these routes.

: We didn't have that much to do with headquarters. First Myers then Kirby ran the MD's Executive Meeting. These were huge, twenty or thirty people, the full matrix, the sector directors, the general managers, the functional heads, lots of people. They were quite unmemorable. Then there was the investment committee which did matter. It was chaired by the deputy chairman, Derek Fowler. He was very good, we had something at his meeting every month. Almost everything got through after the ritual scolding.

: You must remember that Network SouthEast was a very big business: £1 billion turnover, nine train operating companies, as they would now be called, and all of them with good people running them. We got the budget approved, and then got on with it.

Chris was well supported. Indeed, the entire railway at that time seems to have been lucky with its people: Prideaux, Edmonds, Green, Nelson, Pettitt, Bleasdale, all the people mentioned in this book. Chris's deputy was at first Richard Edgeley, on whom he relied greatly. But one day in a lift Bob just said, 'You've lost Richard.' That was all, no explanation. 'Typical Bob,' said Chris. He was free to choose the replacement and found the equally experienced Chris Stokes. His finance manager was Richard Norton.

> Chris Green: When I first came down, Myers was head of the railway but Bob was very much involved and he wanted to mentor me. Quite paternal really as I was only forty. We would occasionally meet privately. He encouraged me and asked how things were going, but never told me what to do. That was not his style. Later on, this would become more formal; we would have quarterly one-to-one meetings. The only frustration was that he would not tell you if you were doing the right thing. He wanted you to keep going unless you were told to stop, and if you were, it would be serious.

There is a railway saying which used to be heard: 'There's no trouble you can get into which I can't dig you out of, except doing nothing.' That was Bob's style. And one much better known: 'Always remember it's easier to get forgiveness than permission.' It probably goes back to the Romans, *Memento semper est facilius quam ut veniam veniam* – the Romans had seen it all.

Managers under Bob had a can-do attitude, but in the knowledge they had to get it right. It was one of Bob's legacies.

In truth, as Jim Collins, Bob's PA, explains, Chris was shrewd in handling Bob. Chris would mention things he planned to do to Jim Collins, knowing that Jim would let Bob know. Chris was adventurous, always pushing boundaries and Bob liked that, provided he was warned. John Prideaux did not warn Bob and had a more difficult time. Chris was even forgiven a most expensive event when, on one route, though new equipment to allow driver-only-operation was installed, guards had to be kept on. The same equipment had been acceptable elsewhere, but on this route, for some reason, it was not.

> Chris Green: Bob never talked about himself, except once. I remember we were walking across London together, back from a meeting, and he opened up quite a lot about how different it was being a chairman and not an operator. But added, 'I couldn't go back, I'd be bored.' How different it was, he said, dealing with politicians and civil servants. Politicians make quick decisions; civil servants want you to go away and do another study. You had to deal with both.

The early 90s recession was severe for the whole country. Investment was turned off and the budget cut. Suddenly, from being a revenue-led business it became a cost-driven grind. Chris was told he could not paint the Aylesbury station. He cheated and got it done. He tried to prevent quality being sacrificed – the new Networker trains, at least, could not be cancelled so they started arriving – but great damage was done in the three or four years the recession lasted. Plans for improvement were put on hold.

The success of Chris Green, John Prideaux and others in cutting the need for government support had one unfortunate consequence: it allowed Cecil Parkinson, the Secretary of State, to dream for a while the impossible dream, that a no-subsidy railway was in his grasp, and cut Government support sharply.

John Nelson, who took over in 1992, when Chris moved to InterCity, had therefore no money, but he did what he could, quite a lot in the circumstances: resignalling the London, Tilbury and Southend line, finishing the modernisation of the Thames and Chiltern lines into Paddington and Marylebone, taking delivery of the Networkers, and improving punctuality.

But below the surface, the state of the assets slipped backwards.

21 THE REVOLUTION RECOGNISED

By the mid-1980s, the great cost of the large European railways and their failure to deliver what passengers wanted had become a major concern. Deutsche Bundesbahn had become unaffordable, with Chancellor Helmut Schmidt admitting 'we can afford the railway or the armed forces but not both'. The Japanese National Railway suffered from 'intractable problems of excess labour, bloated size and flabby management'.[107]

More generally, according to a World Bank paper:

> In many countries, the mismatch between what the railways offer and what customers want has caused both pronounced economic inefficiencies and severe financial strains for the railways and their government owners. In much of the world, the railway's losses of market share, burgeoning deficits, and mushrooming demands for state funding had led to enormous pressures on governments to affect a fundamental restructuring of the railway entity itself, and of its relationship with the state.[108]

The exception to this bleak picture was British Rail: 'A useful first step in bringing the market to the railway is a transition to some form of lines-of-business strategy' as done by British Rail.[109]

After recognising the complexity of the BR sector–region relationship, the report continues:

> Whatever its drawbacks, BR's reorganisation of the 1980s seemingly achieved, without undue disruption or start-up costs, an opportunity to give commercial sectors a realistic profitability goal, and incentives to 'non-commercial' lines of business to reduce their losses. Having met its financial objective is the 1980s, BR reports that 'the railway now costs the taxpayer 51% less in real times then in 1982.[110]

There was therefore great interest in what Bob Reid had achieved and how.

Central to the new British Rail was focus on the passenger. Lines-of-business, to succeed, require satisfied customers. Their views matter. Possibly uniquely amongst the world's railways, British Rail published its performance measures and the results of passenger satisfaction surveys. In Germany by contrast, punctuality figures for Deutsche Bahn were not available even twenty years later.

The information published by Network SouthEast led not to an easy ride but often to howls of rage from the Transport Users' Committees. The information empowered passengers and drove expectations, but that was the point: a dialogue with passengers. Out of that dialogue came the improvements. The budget was able to be allocated in a rational way – money spent on things which measurably mattered to passengers.

Nonetheless, things were not easy. Passenger growth lead to overcrowding and complaints, approval for new investment was always touch and go, relations with government always fragile, and privatisation with the possible break-up of the railway looming ever larger in the background.

There was therefore much to discuss with other railways. In the case of European railways, they discussed their dealings with the European Union. Bob led the discussions as the first chairman of the CER, the Community of European Railways, a grouping of the European railway companies within Europe. They were 'Close allies in saying 'no' in unison to Brussels, but with 14 shades of opinion on what to propose together in return,' explained Leo Ploeger of Dutch railways.[111]

The entire subject was of concern to the World Bank. Borrowers in developing countries sought loans to develop their railways but often in ways likely to deliver poor value for money. The Bank therefore appointed a railway adviser, an American, Lou Thompson. Talking to him recently about Bob Reid, this is what he said:

> Lou: I couldn't say that I was a friend of his, though I met him a number of times. My first encounter was when I worked for the Federal Railroad Administration, managing the upgrade of

the Boston–New York–Washington Railroad and before I went as Railways Adviser to the World Bank in 1987. The Northeast Corridor Improvement Project made extensive use of BR experience.

: After a business meeting in London, he arranged for me to take a ride in the cab of the HST from London to Cardiff, after which I was finally convinced that what we were trying to do in the NECIP would be possible (albeit painful).

: As Railways Adviser at the World Bank, we had many occasions to ask for help from BR and he was always willing to assist. I can well remember a briefing he gave to Bank staff on the BR reform process after which we spent a full evening at the sumptuous restaurant in the newly rebuilt Union Station in Washington, DC. He was absolutely first-class, highly intelligent, and the people with him, very good, knew just what they were doing.

: What Bob Reid had done was innovative within Europe. He had shown how monolithic railways could be run more like a business, especially using the line of business concept that was, incidentally, carried over nearly unchanged into the later privatisation structure. He showed how it could be done. British Rail was then one of the most efficiently run state railways, anywhere.

: For a number of years, the World Bank sponsored an annual Railway Roundtable in Vienna where we invited groups of railways from the Bank's regions to meet to discuss issues in railway reform. Sir Bob was a regular at these meetings, with the BR approach forming part of the basis for Bank lending for rail reform in Latin America and Eastern Europe. His presentations were always impressive and exactly on point. Better yet, the meetings always included other managers from elsewhere in Europe and the debates about railway management philosophy were a real pleasure.

: Probably the most memorable encounter was in New Delhi, where the UIC sponsored a discussion with senior Indian Railways officials and with senior government and private sector officials about the problems of Indian Railways. This meeting included Stig Larsson of Swedish Railways and Reiner Gohlke of DB. I have never seen a better set of presentations of the European approach to rail structural evolution as opposed to the frozen and internally focused status of Indian Railways. A truly memorable highlight of the trip was a dinner involving only Sir Bob, Stig Larsson, Reiner Gohlke, Jean Boulet and me. I wish I could have recorded it. The next day, the lowlight of the trip came in the summing up meeting with Indian officials in which the message was that while the discussions were interesting and thank you for your time, nothing would change.

: Sir Bob was, I believe, a seminal figure in breaking the shell around the traditional monolith that operated a railway, maintained the track, served the interests of the staff, and viewed shippers and passengers as an incidental result. He understood that the railway was there to serve markets and that there should be a linkage between revenues and costs at a level below that of the chairman. It was an unsettling concept that is still working its way through many EU railways.

Bob Reid's reputation had begun to spread abroad rather earlier than this, before he became chairman, when he was then president of the Chartered Institute of Transport. It was in this capacity that he and Anton Buckoke began to work together and become friends.

Anton had briefly worked in the mainstream railway but had left and joined the consultancy Transmark, the British Rail transport consultancy offering advice overseas. Anton tells the story of his engagement with Bob Reid in ways that show the deep impression Bob could make with people.

Buckoke: I'd worked in Africa so I became Mr Africa for Transmark. I could even speak an African language. That's how I met Bob. When he became president of the Chartered Institute of Transport, he was expected to visit the membership which was all over the world. His predecessors had been to Canada, Australia and New Zealand and South Africa, places like that. No one had been to Africa proper. So Bob said, 'I'm going to Africa.' And he asked me to join him.

: That tells you a huge amount about Bob Reid. He wasn't looking for creature comforts or lovely holidays, he wanted to contribute – however hard it was.

This was in 1983. The changes made in British Rail were being noticed and Bob and Anton were well received wherever they went.

A long conversation with Anton gives a good flavour for their trips together.

They were there to give help and advice and possibly get business for Transmark, but in those days things were very difficult in Africa. When they arrived in the VIP lounge in Ghana only one light bulb was working, dangling from a wire. Nothing worked. Cars were running on the cord lining of their tyres. Bob and Anton were nearly caught breaking the midnight curfew but, with a few minutes to spare, got back to the family where they'd been having supper and shared a room for the night.

Such experience lets people get to know each other, and they became friends. 'You couldn't help making friends with him. He was perfectly relaxed.'

Their hosts in these countries wanted to learn from the British experience, they wanted to improve their railways, but they faced deep and difficult problems. The things you would do to improve the railway in Britain, Canada or Australia simply weren't going to work. There was so much their hosts had to think about, way beyond the experience of Western consultants.

But Bob was not a consultant. He was more than that. He could not solve the problems, but he could listen and talk. This is what impressed Anton. It would be wrong to say that Bob understood, for he did not pretend to understand, but he could feel for the enormity of the issues the African leaders faced. Someone with a sense of entitlement would have said, 'This is not for me, I am required in New York.' But Bob had experienced hard times and knew that good people could be swamped by problems. He had the humility to know that he was not above his hosts. Bob's style, as Anton insisted in a long conversation, was to listen.

Anton: He could listen, but not with his ears. He could feel behind people's minds and grasp the problems they faced, as they saw them. Humility and integrity. These are the two words I would like you to take away.

They went together three times to Africa. The first to Ghana and Nigeria, pretty rough, pretty rough. And later to Kenya and Zimbabwe and Tanzania.

The second visit to Kenya was for the start-up of a large contract which Transmark had won. The head of the railway, Julius Nimani, was a bit of a rogue, but he had worked in British Rail workshops and knew BR. He wanted done in Kenya what had been done in Britain: define business sectors, delegate responsibility, all that Bob had instituted. It was a big consultancy job, about ten consultants. But it ended badly: ran into political problems, cut across vested interests, and ground to a halt.

Anton met Bob again in very different circumstances. It was 1989.

Anton: I was the first person Bob met after he had been to see the minister to be told the conclusions of the Anthony Hidden report into the Clapham accident. We were at Heathrow Airport going to Washington. He said, 'It was as much my fault as anyone else's. I put pressure on people. Perhaps I overdo it. You can't just point the finger at this guy, because I'm involved. I took the decisions which led to him being under pressure and I have to be careful.

: That was a man. No wriggling, no wriggling at all.

They continued to be friends. After he retired Bob visited Anton and his family at his home. The children liked him a lot and he helped with their donkeys.

Anton: When he retired, Bob was asked to be chairman of the West Lambeth Health Authority at St Thomas's Hospital. They had decided he was a man who could really help them, but it was soon after that he developed cancer and he didn't live very long after that.

: I have one regret in my life, and I'll never let it happen again. He lived over in Suffolk and I knew he was unwell, and I should have gone to talk to him, and remind him of his value. But I didn't.

Finally, Anton had this to say: On a personal note, let me say, Sir Bob Reid was a man of great spiritual stature who has contributed positively, not only to my life, but to many others, for which I will always be very grateful.

Later, Anton wrote this.

'Bob Reid spent almost the entire period of WW2 as a prisoner, first in Italy and then in Germany. Between the two, he had three months relative freedom shielded, together with two other British Officers, by the Gaustis, a farming family. They left their sanctuary because, amongst other things, their responsibility for the likely outcome of discovery for the family was unbearable. On his return home after the war Bob said that he was a changed man. I suggest that the outstanding experience, which changed him was this three months with the Gaustis. It was so important to him that he subsequently returned to visit them; on his own; then with his wife on their honeymoon; and then with his children, Janet and Bob.

'I also suggest that what he saw, understood and became his Principle when with the Gaustis, using Jesus' words, was and is: "Thou shalt love thy neighbour as thyself"; "Suffer it to be so now, for thus it becometh us to fulfil all righteousness"; and "It is the spirit that quickeneth, the flesh profiteth nothing". All these imperatives apply absolutely to the Principle that governed the Gausti family, whose only human reward would have been death. On the basis of the similar wartime experiences of Brigadier Hackett, Eric Newby, and Corrie Ten Boom, the Gausti's actions were totally without fear, confirming St John's words, "Perfect love casteth out fear.

'I am absolutely clear that it was this Principle that lay behind the Railway Revolution that Bob fathered. He probably would not have used the specific words, but he certainly lived them and would have recognised them - they were his Life, Truth and Love'.

22 THE LAST YEAR IN CHARGE

SAFETY BEFORE CLAPHAM

Safety, of course, was always a concern, but the thinking was that it was under control. True, some accidents happened – passengers were injured and sometimes killed – but that, it was thought, was inevitable with speeding machinery and humans so close together.

This diagram, taken from the work of Professor Andrew Evans, tells the story.

It is a graph of the number of accidents per billion train-kilometres. The points on the graph are the average for successive five-year periods. An accident is defined as an incident involving a moving train which kills or injures either passengers or workers. It does not, therefore, include injuries to track workers not involving a moving train (eg falling of a ladder), and suicides are excluded.

You can see that there has been a massive improvement over the years. In the first period, 1967–1971, the accident rate was very high:

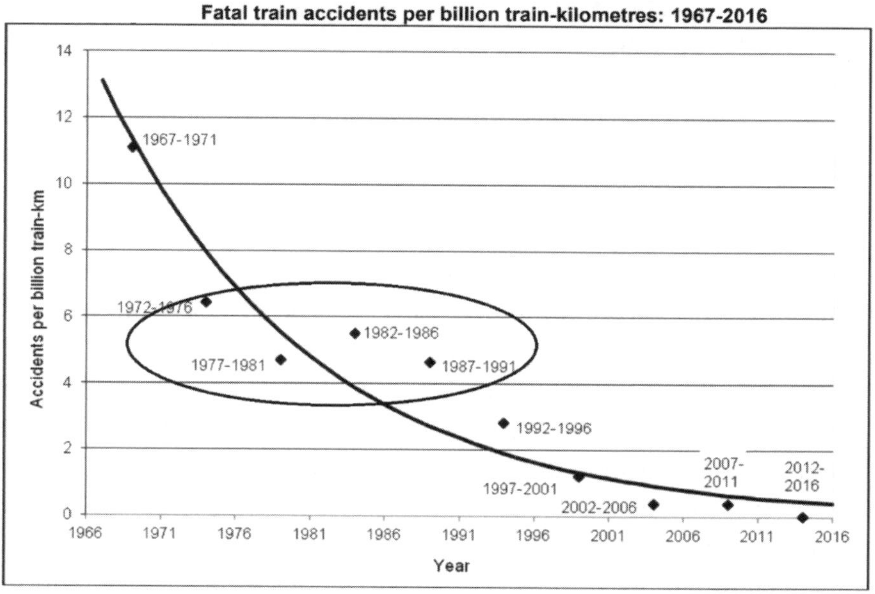

eleven accidents per billion train-kilometres.

There was then a marked improvement. Many improvements in the management of the railway began during the Barbara Castle transition and under the management of Johnson and Bowick, the 1970s. Perhaps these account for the improvement in safety. The accident rate fell to half the previous rate. But for the next twenty years, all through the 70s and 80s (four data points on the graph), there was no improvement. It remained on a plateau of between 4.3 and 6.2 accidents per billion train-kilometres. Bob's management saw no improvement in safety. Given all the other problems the railway faced, this may be understandable, but compared with current accident rates, safety was not good. The accident rate was five times higher than it is today.

Fairly typical of the times was an accident at Methley in December 1987 killing four track workers. A gang had been working on the track at Methley Junction, near Leeds, using Kango hammers on an active line. Kango hammers are noisy, and a strict system is required – and did exist – to give warnings to the workers to get out of the way when a train was approaching.

In principle, it was a good system. Two lookouts were posted, one nearby and one in the distance, equipped with a switch to turn off the power to the hammers when a train was sighted. But a practice had grown whereby after the first warning, the hammers were switched on again – 'for the men like to get a last shovel in' – until a second warning, when the hammers were again switched off and the men left the track quickly.

On the day in question, as the gang was a man short, the nearby lookout was required as an extra duty to step on to the track and remove some piece of equipment once the men had stopped working. But on one occasion during that day, after the distance lookout had seen a train approaching and given the first warning, he turned round and, seeing the first lookout moving on to the track, assumed that the men had stopped working. 'I did not give the second warning,' he said at the inquiry, 'because he seemed to have it covered.'

But the men had not stopped working. With their backs to the oncoming train, hunched over their hammers with ears covered by padded mufflers, they carried on. The driver of the train blew his horn, braked hard but could not stop in time. The train ran through the gang, killing four men.

This was no isolated incident and it was obvious that things were not right. Sixteen track workers were killed in 1987/8, the year of the Methley accident, and in the first six months of the following year, nine more lost their lives. In response, a panicky 'short, sharp, track safety campaign' was kicked off in September 1988.

Railnews

No 307 Newspaper of British Rail SEPTEMBER 1988

Board alarm as track death figures mount

MAJOR DRIVE TO CUT LINE ACCIDENTS

By EDDIE TOAL

SIXTEEN RAILWAYMEN DIED ON BR LAST YEAR.

They waved goodbye to families, went whistling off for another day's work, and never came back.

Sixteen families devastated by tragedy on a scale that we – the lucky ones – can only begin to imagine.

And still it goes on. Already in 1988 nine more have lost their lives in accidents that could have been avoided.

[illegible] 83 rail workers killed on duty since January [illegible] more than half have been struck by trains [illegible] crossing, walking or working on the line.

In the bland jargon of statistics each of these tragedies is listed as a "movement fatality".

Now the latest figures indicate a disturbing trend – movement fatalities are on the increase.

Concerned by this development senior Board executives have called for a "short, sharp, track safety campaign" targeted at those most at risk.

Thousands of civil engineering, S&T and mechanical engineering employees will be asked to take part in the campaign, titled "Your Life On The Line", which begins this month.

"Statistically, only a tiny fraction of the numbers of people working around the tracks every day become involved in incidents leading to injury or death," said David Rayner, BRB joint managing director (railways).

"Nevertheless, we are appalled at the tragic loss of life and injury that there is. Very often the difference between a major injury and death can be less than half an inch. Figures in both categories are creeping upwards. That's why it's time to issue a personal reminder to those whose job takes them around the running railway that it is a potentially dangerous environment – whether you are working in a yard or out on the main line.

"We have very adequate rules and safety practices but, in the end, everything boils down to individuals observing them sensibly, to the letter, for their own safety and that of their colleagues.

"It's as simple as that."

- *BOB REID: 'We must act NOW' Page 2*
- *Check safety hazards appeal: Page 3*

Making

Railnews quoted David Rayner, the Joint Managing Director (Railways): 'We have very adequate rules and safety practices but, in the end, everything boils down to individuals observing them sensibly, to the letter, for their own safety and for that of their colleagues.' And, he adds, in a somewhat facile manner, 'It's as simple as that.'

But it is not as simple as that. David Rayner was quite wrong. His well-meaning campaign was bound to be ineffective.

A thoughtful letter in *Railnews* from the NUR safety officer explains why. 'Many trackside workers, although having seen the leaflets, have received no word from their supervisors or managers which would denote local involvement. There have been very few formal or informal meetings.' Another letter claimed that safety briefings generally consisted of a manager reading the rules out loud to the staff to an apathetic audience with no explanation or discussion.

A much deeper understanding of how safety must be driven into a business was needed, but that would have to wait for the horrors of the Clapham accident and advice from DuPont.

THE CLAPHAM ACCIDENT

What happened at Clapham Junction on the terrible day of Monday 12 December 1988 – just eight weeks after the launch of David Rayner's safety campaign – brought out the strengths and weaknesses of Bob Reid's railway. The strengths were many, particularly the response to the accident; the weakness, that unsafe practices had been allowed to continue.

The cause of the accident lay some weeks before the event. The signals controlling the routes into Clapham went back fifty years. They were 1936 vintage. There was a growing failure rate, and the integrity of the system was at risk. Approval had been given to resignal the area. One small element of the project was the abolition of a particular signal on the route into Clapham from the west and its replacement by a new four-aspect signal, WF 138. The work to do this would necessitate rewiring relays in the Clapham Junction A relay room.

Part of the work was carried out on Sunday 27 November. The technician, Mr Hemingway, was required to disconnect a particular wire which ran between a relay and a fuse. Instead of removing the entire wire, or at least taping it safe, he simply disconnected one end of the wire from the relay end and tucked it out of the way.

All went well for two weeks. Then, on the night of Sunday 11 December, two weeks later, more work was done in the relay room, this time on the relay adjacent to the one previously worked on. It is supposed, though no one can be sure, that it was that work which dislodged the wire so that it swung loose and was able to make contact, at least

Accident outside Clapham Junction station. The undamaged train to the left is the empty train coming from Clapham. The train by the bank to the right is the stationary Basingstoke train. The train by the bank to the left is the Poole train, which had struck the back of the stationary train throwing its rear carriage up the bank. (Alamy)

intermittently, with its previous point of connection. Should it make such contact, a false feed of electric current would flow, preventing the proper functioning of the new signal.

As the track approaches Clapham from the west, it curves round to the left. A driver coming round the bend would see a bank on the left, with trees on top, and then a straight stretch with two or three signals, including WF 138, and the Clapham Junction station beyond. WF 138 controlled the track on the inside of this bend on which trains travelling towards Clapham would run.

The following morning, a Monday morning, a number of trains passed the signal safely. The driver of one of them saw a strange flicker in one of the signal lights but carried on and arrived safely at Clapham.

The next train coming around the bend was from Basingstoke. It was a long, twelve-car train, made up of three four-car units carrying possibly about 900 people. After stopping at Woking, it was full and standing, carrying well more than its nominal capacity. As it came around the bend approaching Clapham, WF 138 showed green. But just before it reached that signal, the driver saw it turn from green to red, which should not have happened. Acting correctly, the driver slowed his train and stopped at the next signal to report the incident by trackside telephone.

He got out of his cab on to the track, climbed a ladder to a platform, found a phone, rang through to the Clapham signal box and spoke to the signalman. The signalman said he could not explain what had happened. He had not changed the signals and there was nothing wrong with them. The driver therefore returned down the ladder and headed back to his cab. But while he was on the telephone, coming up behind his train was one from Poole, carrying over 400 passengers. The inquiry report suggests about 1,500 people were in the two trains.

With the first train stationary on the track, the signalling system should have caused the signal behind it, WF 138, to show red and the one behind that yellow, thereby warning the second train to stop. But they did not. The signals were green.

The Poole train was travelling at about 40mph when the driver saw the stationary train ahead. He slammed on his brakes but, being only 300 yards away, a collision was inevitable. By this time, the Basingstoke driver was heading back to his cab. 'There was an almighty crash,' he said at the inquiry. 'I knew immediately what had happened. My train had been shoved forward four, five, six feet, something like that. I had tears in my eyes at the time. I went back to my cab..... I told people not to get off the train because I was not certain the juice was off.'

The impact of the Poole train hitting the back of the Basingstoke train was so great the Basingstoke train's rear carriages were hurled sideways up the bank to the left and its front carriages skewed together, forcing them sideways, to the right, on to the adjacent track.

At this moment, a third train coming in the opposite direction from Clapham, fortunately empty, was passing on that adjacent track and it too was derailed.

The front carriages of the Poole train were completely destroyed. They were forced between the Basingstoke train and the derailed train from Clapham. A tangled, twisted mass of steel and human bodies filled the narrow gap.

The trains were made up of slam-door 1965 Mark 1 coaches. Though an old design, 'Mark 1 vehicles have good ride qualities, and are not intrinsically lacking in collision resistance.'[112] But the frames were prone to concertina in serious crashes in such a way that the metal skin was torn into ragged pieces.

In all, twenty-nine people died in this first carriage, including the driver, while sixteen were injured. In the second carriage, a crowded buffet car, six people died, with many more injured. In the stationary Basingstoke train, none were killed, though many were injured.

The debris on the track caused circuit breakers to cut off the juice, the traction current along the line. This system worked properly and allowed a fourth train to brake and stop just 20 yards short.

Amongst the first to arrive at the scene were masters and boys from the nearby Emmanuel School, who helped free trapped and injured passengers. The emergency services responded quickly. Soon, scores of people were on site helping the injured, many trapped in the wreckage and in great pain.

Those on the bridge over the track could hear their cries. Michael Portillo, the transport minister, knowing that he would have to answer questions in Parliament, asked how many people had died. He was told they did not yet know as they had not yet joined up the legs and arms and bodies.

Bob Reid, mortified, for he had been informed of the cause of the accident, arrived at the scene, stayed a while and then went back to his office. Jim Collins got to the office at about 12:30 and asked Bob's secretary, who was sitting 'ashen-faced', if anybody had been in to speak with the chairman. 'No,' she said, 'nobody has wanted to go in, but I think he'd like to see a friendly face so put your head round the door.'

> Collins: I knocked and quietly went in. He half-smiled and was clearly pleased to see me. I sat down at his desk and asked if he was all right as he was clearly shaken. He seemed to gather his thoughts quickly as he went through what he had seen. He told me that the S&T engineers on site were already certain of

the cause. He said he planned to go to the press and TV that evening and explain what had happened and accept full liability. He then called Derek Fowler to tell him the plan. There was some pushback from Derek and the lawyers, but Bob had made up his mind. He said, 'If we explain how this accident has happened, we can move on and we can begin to help the families and all our people who are a much more important priority just now.

Cutting equipment and cranes were brought to the site ready to move wreckage, but first the emergency services had to complete the task of ensuring that all the injured had been located and taken to hospital, and that dead bodies had been moved to a temporary mortuary. That done, the heavy equipment moved in and cleared the site.

The immediate cause of the accident was obvious to the signal engineers who checked the relay room and found the loose wire. It had clearly been dislodged from wherever it had been tucked and had been able to short circuit the proper operation of the signals. The press got hold of Mr Hemingway's name and where he lived, so he and his family had to be moved to somewhere safe.

Two days later, Paul Channon announced a public inquiry, to be chaired by Anthony Hidden QC. On the first day of this enquiry, Bob Reid accepted, without equivocation, full 'responsibility and liability' for the deaths.

More important than the immediate cause, the loose wire, was the need to understand why it had been allowed to be there.

The following soon emerged. The technician carrying out the work had been working long hours, too long: eleven-hour days. The team was short-staffed and had been under pressure to finish the job.

This should not have mattered as there was a requirement for a system to check that the work was done properly, but it was not in place. Proper practice was to remove unnecessary wires completely or, at the very least, cut them short and secure them out of the way with insulating tape. It might be presumed that the failure to do this was a one-off lapse caused by pressure of work. But, on the witness stand, the technician said that what he did was his normal practice. He had not taken short cuts because of pressure of work.

The inquiry accepted his statement, and it was said therefore on behalf of the Board:

> I make it quite plain to you that in relation to all those matters we recognise that those are not satisfactory and indeed bad practices but that the blame for that does not lie with you, it lies with British Rail. Either it should never have been allowed in the first place, or once it had happened and the practice had become your practice and indeed was commonplace, it should have become stopped because the matter should have been monitored. So, there is no criticism of you for those failings which we recognise our failings and not yours…[113]

The inquiry soon heard, *The Times* reported[114], that more than twenty other loose signal wires were found within two miles of Clapham, some of which had not been cut back or made safe with tape. The record showed fifteen wrong side signal failures from 1985 to 1988 in the Southern Region.[115] This being the case, the inquiry turned to the broader question of why such unsafe working practices had come into being and been allowed to persist.

Departmental instructions had been issued detailing safe working practices and requiring adequate training in the standards. There should, for example, have been a count of the wires removed. But managers had not ensured that the instructions were followed. Indeed, the most recent instructions had not been received by Hemingway, the technician.

There is some similarity here with the Methley Junction accident the year before. In both, an unsafe working practice had been allowed to persist until one day, triggered by something unexpected, it caused an accident.

But there was another, deeper, cause: money. Bob's weekly Chairman's Group meetings, again and again, sought to dig down to understand why things had gone so wrong. Jim Collins remembers these meetings.

> Collins: It was a really difficult time. I remember Ken Burrage, the Deputy S&T Director, coming to a meeting. Very nervous, got his

words muddled up, but the chairman helped him through.

: For everyone, it was a shock to face up to what we feared: what Peter Parker had called the 'crumbling edge of quality', the consequence of the relentless saving of money.

: It was heart-wrenching, the admission that resources were too thinly spread, too much overtime worked to make up a salary, shortages of staff.

: People were very good, very clever at running things on a shoestring without compromising safety, or not much, but I would never go back to how it was.

Out of these meetings came the decision to appoint DuPont, described later.

With the inquiry underway, the spring and summer were difficult for the Board. When sorrows come, they come not as single spies but in battalions.

The Clapham accident was followed by two other railway accidents. In March, a train on the fast line through Purley station, having gone through a red light, hit a train ahead which was pulling out from a platform stop. Five people were killed and eighty injured. Two days later, at Bellgrove in Glasgow, a train passed a signal at danger on pulling out of the station and ran into the path of a train coming towards it, killing two people and injuring fifty. In both cases, the cause was accepted to be human error.

The Purley accident was traumatic for another reason. It was a Saturday and Bob had flown back from Italy that morning. He was met at Gatwick Airport and driven, not to the accident site, the boss can do nothing, but to his home. There, up the hill above Purley town centre, Bob could see from the back of his house, over trees and housetops, the wreckage of the carriages forced off the track and on to the embankment. Jim Collins remembers how Bob had been steadfast after the Clapham accident and all that followed, but Purley shook him up. That accident, visible from the rear of his house, seemed to lead to his health beginning to go downhill.

As Anton Buckoke suggested, such accidents were felt to be a personal failure. Accidents and the failure of managers to prevent them were then very much in people's minds. Nine days after the Clapham accident, Pan Am Flight 103, flying from Heathrow to Detroit, had been destroyed by a Semtex bomb which had been smuggled on to the flight. It crashed close by the town of Lockerbie in the Scottish Borders, killing all 243 passengers and sixteen crew. What failure in security had allowed a bomb to be smuggled on to the plane?

The inquiry into the terrible King's Cross fire on the underground had been reported only a month earlier. Old rags and grease under an escalator had caught fire and a great tongue of flame had swept up the escalator, killing thirty-one people. What failure of management had allowed inflammable material to be left lying around? In that case, the managers, Transport for London managers, prevaricated and made excuses for the failure.

Yet another example which people would have remembered: the car ferry, the *Herald of Free Enterprise*, which had capsized outside the Belgian port of Zeebrugge in 1987, drowning 193 passengers and crew. What failure of management had allowed its bow doors to remain open as the ship left the harbour? In that case, the enquiry found such a 'disease of sloppiness' that seven people were charged with gross negligence manslaughter and the company with corporate manslaughter.

With these accidents in people's minds, the mood of the country was highly sensitive to the competence of managers. For British Rail, therefore, it was a dreadful time.

On top of everything, a difficult and dangerous dispute with the unions was gathering pace.

JIMMY KNAPP STANDS FIRM

For some years, as Paul Watkinson explained, the aim had been to transfer the negotiation of pay and conditions down to local areas in the hope that this would lead to greater flexibility, and to pay and conditions reflecting local circumstances.

In the late 80s, a raft of disputes in other large, long established industries arose over attempts to become more flexible, more local. There were disputes in the docks, in the electricity supply industry, within universities, in the Post Office, the health service, the Ford Motor Company and P&O cross-channel ferries over broadly similar things.

The railway sought the same, more flexible, more local. In the previous year, 1988, the Board had put to unions 'radical proposals for a major streamlining of negotiating machinery', declaring it a 'quantum leap forward, the biggest alteration in negotiating practice since 1956'. Quite obviously, nothing could have been more calculated to put the unions on the defensive. Leaps forward and changes to negotiating machinery were what Jimmy Knapp had been fighting all his life.

The objective – pay and job flexibility – was contentious enough, but the method of getting there – the end of centralised bargaining – was the reddest of red lines. Centralised bargaining was what union officials lived for. The Board rubbed it in: 'Local decision making at local level is the cornerstone of the new proposals.' Out would go the 'seven-tier' machinery of the 1956 Agreement; in would come new simplified arrangements – as *Railnews* covered it.

Paul Watkinson declared: 'There is no reason in the world why issues should take months to resolve as they do currently.'

Railnews

No 300
Newspaper of British Rail
FEBRUARY 1988

Staff win praise as landslip threatens line

WHILE Whitehall continued to grapple with the fate of the closure-threatened Settle and Carlisle line BR's engineers in the North West were battling to keep its trains running.

Nearly 50ft of embankment at remote Mallerstang, near Kirkby Stephen, was washed away by torrential rain which hit many parts of Britain during January.

The up line became impassable and trains had to use single line for 18 miles between Kirkby Stephen and Blea Moor. The risk of further damage meant that the loco-hauled service had to be replaced by lighter DMUs until repairs were completed.

"It was a major slip which virtually undermined the up line for over 40ft," said Preston area civil

"Over a 52-hour weekend possession engineers and operating staff braved foul weather at the remote site to make good the damage.

"We cleared out the dirt and slurry from the hole left by the slip and replaced it with a new embankment formed of 3,500 tonnes of rock brought in by train."

HURRICANE HEROES REWARDED: Page 31

Mr Duncan paid tribute to local staff who had to walk a quarter of a mile over fields to reach the isolated scene.

"All local staff gave maximum co-operation," he said. "They put up with horrible conditions and worked far beyond their normal

BR MOVE TO STREAMLINE 'MACHINERY'

RADICAL proposals for a major streamlining of British Rail's negotiating machinery are being put to the railway trade unions.

The main thrust of the far-reaching changes proposed centres on what is seen as an urgent need to devolve decisions on many employee relations issues to area management level.

rangements as an important part of the process of encouraging greater involvement of all employees in the business.

"The proposals represent a significant and radical step forward and are of real importance in under-

Negotiations on the matter, when they began in June 1989, became tangled up immediately with a pay dispute. The pay issue could have been handled in a peaceful way, as there was only a couple of percentage points' difference between the sides, but the BR negotiating team, with David Kirby in charge and Trevor Toolan as head of HR, seemed for mysterious reasons to have been determined to provoke a strike. Perhaps they imagined a great victory over the unions; Toolan certainly wished to marginalise the unions and end their involvement in operational matters. He might have thought this could be achieved if the unions called a strike and 'lost' (whatever that means). If this was his plan, it had no support from Bob Reid.

Every stage of the negotiation, which ground on for weeks, was in the public eye. Jimmy Knapp made sure the press could see the aggressive tactics adopted by the BR negotiating team. The dispute escalated, strikes took place, passengers suffered, and in a public and humiliating way, the Board, fronted by Bob Reid, had to back down.

Bob was not a public figure who people would recognise in the street. Jim Collins remembers one day that he put on a raincoat, walked out of Euston House, round the corner and up Eversholt Street to the picket line outside the Euston train crew depot, just as if he was a passing member of the public, and began chatting to the drivers picketing the depot – 'What are you doing, what's this all about?' he asked, that sort of thing – and came back to the management meetings with some interesting insights. No one else could do that. They would not know how.

> Collins: He was good like that. He had a lot of empathy with people on the ground, with what they were doing and with what they had to put up with. Once he got over his shyness, he was a naturally shy man, he could talk to people for they soon realised he knew what he is talking about and was listening, taking in what they said.

Negotiations recommenced. But again, against Board instructions and with a solution within grasp, 'the grotesque aggression', in the words of the *Evening Standard*, of the negotiating team threw the opportunity away. British Rail seemed to be bringing the problem on its own head. Again, Bob had to step in and back down over restructuring in order to restore peace. An argument over small differences with a pay claim ended up with abandonment of the bigger prize, decentralising pay negotiations. It looked very bad.

Bob Reid felt let down by David Kirby's poor judgement. He had to go. With his leaving and Bob soon retiring, John Welsby was called onto the Board to become chief executive. Welsby was a very different person; as clever as Kirby, but with his own mind and not afraid to challenge Bob. John Edmonds also joined the Board at this time.

Out on the railway, the service, though hugely improved, was still very fragile. Bob agreed that the Fenchurch Street to Southend line had slipped 'to a wholly unacceptable level'. Its Total Route Modernisation had been cancelled for lack of money. Commuters were right to complain of 'delays, cancellations, filthy and freezing carriages of indeterminate age and dangerous to woman at night'.

PRIVATISATION

Yet another difficult issue came to test the Board. Major utilities such as gas and electricity were already privatised, and the privatisation of British Rail was on the cards. Were it to happen, what form should it take? Should it be a single entity or be broken up in some way?

Although banks were retained by the government to study the issue, the Thatcher government was winding down, an election was due within two years, and the Prime Minister's authority was on the wane. She felt it was not the time to start another privatisation. Margaret Thatcher could be quite cautious, and the whole issue was put on the backburner.

THE CLAPHAM REPORT

Later in the year, but just months after the ignominious end to the dispute with Jimmy Knapp, Anthony Hidden QC presented his report on the Clapham accident.

The signalling technician who did the work was taken to task for his poor working practices, but was not to take the blame for the accident. Eleven people senior to him, who had allowed the unsafe practices to continue, were named.

The most senior, Clifford Hale, the Regional Signalling and Telecommunications Engineer, resigned. He was by no means the most negligent. Nonetheless, as the report said, 'Having identified the problem and arrived at solutions, he then turned his attention to other things, and made the dangerous assumption that the problem would go away.'[116]

When asked if he should have resigned, Bob, who was clearly distressed, replied, 'Every man must make up his own mind.'

Criticism of the S&T department was most harsh. It had been subject to four reorganisations in recent years, which had not helped morale, but the standards and attitudes within it were most unsatisfactory. Fortunately, other departments were in better shape.

Also criticised were the unions: 'The unions too must bear their share of responsibility for attitudes of entrenched resistance to change which are out of place in a modern world.'[117]

Most significant was criticism of British Rail's higher-level management. The enquiry accepted the 'total sincerity on the part of all who spoke', but 'the concern for safety was permitted to coexist with working practices which we have seen were positively dangerous. This unhappy coexistence was never detected by management and so the bad practices were never eradicated.'[118]

Amongst the many recommendations was that safety equipment, Automatic Train Protection (ATP), should be fully implemented within five years once the specific type had been selected. Prototype systems were installed on the Great Western Main Line and the Chiltern line, but they were never seen as realistic propositions for the entire railway. Eventually, after the Ladbroke Grove accident ten years later, a more simple system, the Train Protection and Warning System (TPWS), was adopted and rapidly rolled out to protect every signal on every running line.

The report demanded that 'the concept of absolute safety must be a gospel spread across the entire workforce and be paramount in the minds of management'.

To this end, over the summer, the board appointed DuPont to review and advise on safety matters. This chemical business had learnt some fundamental truths. A quite different approach to the establishment of a safety culture was required, quite different from David Rayner's airy remark that 'There are perfectly good safety standards, it's just that people don't follow them.'

Their advice was followed and over the years safety improved greatly. The graph at the beginning of this chapter tells the story. The accident rate would halve and halve again.

Years later, Justice Hidden's recommendations and DuPont's advice were still referred to with respect.

Though the report concluded that 'Weakness at the top was the underlying fault', there was fair sympathy for Bob, even admiration for the honesty and purposefulness of his response. Nonetheless, the *Evening Standard* called on him to resign. The *Daily Mail* was offensive, *The Times* less harsh. Bob's retirement must have seemed a welcome prospect. All in all, it was not a good year.

Commenting later on this period, Peter Parker wrote:

> He was the most private of public men. Yet when public pressure was on him cruelly in the last years of his chairmanship, with massive concern in strikes and accidents, he responded characteristically. His reaction to the Clapham disaster was memorable, old-fashioned when I think of some of the ways other chairmen respond to disasters on this scale. He went to the scene at once, took total charge and responsibility. The clarity of his public demeanour steadied a tragic scene and restored to the railways a dignity amidst all the traumatic difficulties – now there was a man, a delightful, demanding leader with the primary qualities of courage and honour so strong in him.[119]

In fronting for the railway and carrying the blame on his shoulders for the faults disclosed, Bob Reid served the railway well. The new managers could face the future without distraction.

For managers, the railway's future looked good. Passenger volumes were up and the Board had again made a substantial profit in 1988/89: an operating surplus of £107 million (after a reduced government subsidy of £549 million). Railfreight was profitable, without subsidy. The first InterCity 225 trains entered service in October pulled by the new Class 91 locomotive (a test train reached 162 mph). It promised more speed and comfort for InterCity travel. Cecil Parkinson approved the first order of 400 Networker coaches to replace the slam door trains in north Kent and south-east London. The Carlisle-Settle line was reprieved. And plans were announced for what would become Crossrail. As for safety, a realistic programme to get on top of the problem was taking shape.

SAFETY MOVES CENTRE STAGE

Immediately after the Clapham accident, David Rayner asked David Maidment to establish a group to coordinate the evidence for the judicial inquiry and look into the state of safety management across the company. Maidment was quickly able to report that, like many traditional industries, it was reactive. One waited for an accident to happen, and then tried to put right what caused it. New industries, like nuclear or chemical, acted differently; they knew that the consequences of one of their accidents were so horrendous that they must be prevented from happening at all. They were proactive. The railway should be the same.

DuPont was appointed in the autumn of 1989 to review safety on the West Coast Main Line and to report with recommendations to the board.

The insights they brought were: (i) that safe methods of working had to be developed by those doing the work so they became owned by, for example, those with the Kanga hammers at Methley, and became self-policing; (ii) that small infringements of the rules had to be stamped on immediately – prevent the small accidents and the big ones become less likely to happen – and (iii) that risks should be identified in advance and the cost of preventing them calculated. Fundamentally, safety had to become as prominent in management thinking as finance or punctuality.

These insights, says David Maidment, the Board took on board wholeheartedly. In 1991, 800 senior managers were trained in safety over three days and examined at the end; the Board too.

Managers were required to conduct safety inspections, to observe and record any infringement on the ground. Departments received a sum of money to enable the niggly safety problems which everybody knew about to be removed. Shift leaders were trained to deliver short safety briefings before any task began where there was risk.

Risk assessment and cost analysis was carried out on 300 projects to address 700 identified risks. Where the cost of rectification per life saved was assessed as falling below £1 million, the rectification was carried out. Where it was between £1 million and £2 million, it was further examined and possibly carried out. If over £2 million, it was kept under review.

One of the earliest rectifications was aimed at preventing people falling out of trains. About twenty people a year had fallen out of a train in the previous decade. The cost of central door locking, the measure required to prevent this, was estimated to cost £300,000 per life saved – a low figure – and the project was carried out.

Most troubling to justify were new in-cab signalling systems. They would prevent accidents, but at vast cost, about £14 million per life saved. The frequency, however, of drivers passing signals at danger was quite high – 'SPADS' they are called – about a thousand incidents every year, of which a hundred were potentially serious, and some, as at Purley and Bellgrove, disastrous. Development therefore proceeded on a more affordable and reasonably effective system to prevent SPADS, the TPWS at a cost of about £5 million per life saved. It was eventually rolled out, but not until after the dreadful Ladbroke Grove accident in 1999.

David Maidment set up meetings with his opposite numbers in the European railways. They discussed accidents, and numbers, and what they had learnt, and shared their research. British Rail was far in advance, says David, in the proactive measures taken and in the Board's commitment to pursue safety. It was ground-breaking. In Europe, only the Dutch were close to thinking along the same lines, and some were still sceptical, even hostile.

The result of this work is evident in Professor Evans's graph shown earlier. The accident rate halved from 1990/91 and would halve again. For two years, David proudly says, not a single track-worker's life was lost.

23 WELSBY TAKES OVER AND BOB RETIRES

ORGANISATION FOR QUALITY

'Did you know,' I asked John Welsby, 'when you were appointed chief executive that you would be presiding over the end of the regions?'

'Oh yes. Oh yes. No question, the regions were gone.'

John had been handling difficult problems for years. Though Bob had shouted that he was 'Thatcher's lackey', the privatisation of BREL had gone well. He had then been given the job of promoting BR's badly conceived plan for the Channel Tunnel rail link: 'Oh dear me, the most traumatic thing I've ever done.' Much of Kent was in an uproar over the supposed ruination of their lovely countryside. He had been summoned to Downing Street. Margaret Thatcher marched into the room at the head of a phalanx with arms outstretched stating, 'So you are the man that's going to lose me the Kent elections.' After a lengthy exposition, he was given permission to proceed.

Welsby had been in hospital during the rail strikes of 1989 so had not been drawn into that fiasco. When he returned to the office, with Kirby gone and the Board in need of new leadership, he discovered that he was to be the next chief executive. He started in January 1990.

The last story to be told in any detail, therefore, is how the regions came to an end, to be replaced by the structure called Organising for Quality, or OfQ. It was the final flowering of Bob Reid's vision for a business-led railway.

Until now, the day-to-day running of the railway had been in the hands of the six general managers who ran the regions, with planning and financial control in the hands of the sector directors, both having to answer to the functional heads of engineering in the centre. But it was described by Welsby, towards the end, as an 'appallingly complex matrix' of internal contracts between the people specifying the service and those providing them. 'We are spending an ever-increasing portion of our time chasing this internal a matrix around rather than the addressing our attention where it should really be – to the needs of our passenger and freight customers.'[120]

It was obvious, if it could be achieved, that the business of the regions should be moved under the sector directors. But how?

The decline of freight made things easier. Freight traffic crosses boundaries. But passenger traffic tends to flow on reasonably coherent groups of lines, the lines which made up the sub-sectors. In the passenger railway, there were nine such sub-sectors in Network SouthEast, five in InterCity and five in Provincial. The six freight sub-sections would buy track space from the passenger sub-sectors.

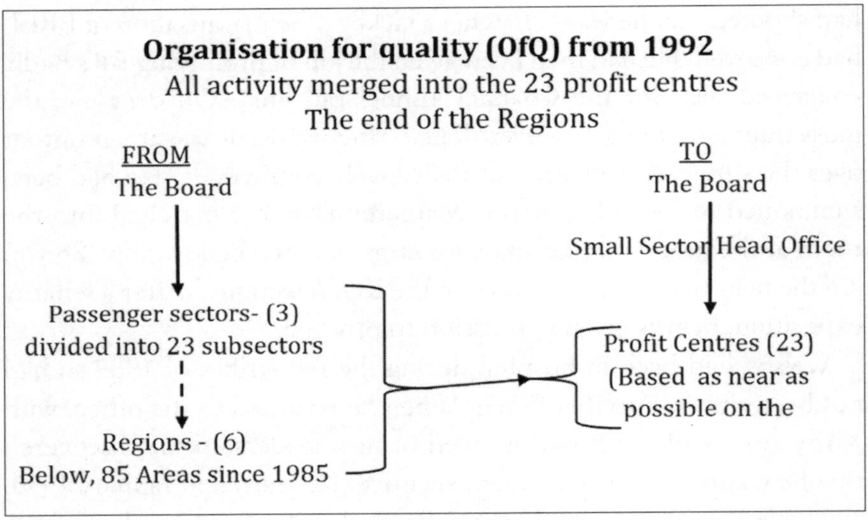

These sub-sectors would become the core operating units of the passenger railway. It was a simple arrangement. The manager of each sub-sector would, to a substantial extent, have control over every aspect of the railway within his or her patch, from the guards on the trains to the gangs on the track with Kango hammers, and could be held responsible for its financial performance. They were 'profit centres' and renamed as such.

Some tasks were reserved for higher up the chain, at the sector director level, and some for the functional heads of engineering at the centre. But the aim was to reduce to a minimum direction from the centre. Under OfQ, for the first time since 1948, cost and revenue came together on the desk of a person with a realistic ability to manage what he or she saw.

The plan was agreed at the Board, of course, but its outline, as Jim Collins explains, was first roughed out on bits of paper at Bob's favourite Italian restaurant by Russell Square. 'What you doing for lunch?' he asked. So off Bob and Jim went to the Trattoria Bardigiana. The idea was simple enough: break up the six regions and put the bits into whichever of the twenty sub-sectors they most obviously served. Teams looking after the East Coast Main Line would, for example, go into IC East Coast. Many details are not so obvious.

Every depot, every station, every piece of rolling stock and equipment had to be 'owned' and controlled by a single entity: shared control never works. Others, if they need it, would have right of use. So, who, for example, should 'own' Birmingham New Street Signal Box, York station or Neville Hill Depot? On the West Coast Main Line, who can put their trains on the graph first? Whose train can leave King's Cross exactly on the hour, at 08:00? What capacity should the sub-sectors have for carrying out capital projects and how should a headquarters project team, for the larger works, be established?

Bob was not trying to answer these questions. He was looking across the whole country and making sure, in his mind, that they could be answered.

John Edmonds was given the task of putting this arrangement into place. Edmonds had an acute aversion to the present structure and was the ideal person to oversee the new organisation. He called in Richard Goldson, whom we have mentioned before, and asked him to assemble and manage the working team to deliver the new structure. 'Richard,' Edmonds said to Goldson, 'you have access to every person in the railway, the general managers, even the Department but you may not speak to the chairman. If he calls, prevaricate, and tell me. I, only, speak to the chairman.'

It was Richard's clear impression that Edmonds had received very precise instructions from the chairman as to what was required, and would react badly if he learnt, in the wrong way, that anything different was being done. Edmonds was a good person to work for, but could be rude and bullying. There were those he liked and those, more numerous, whom he did not. All engineers, he thought, defended their patch and made things that cost too much. The least disliked, as Richard Goldson tells it, were the mechanical engineers, then the civil engineers, and finally, in the far reaches of his dislike, the S&T engineers, for whom he had the deepest aversion, suspecting they would scupper his plans, that they would argue that signalling was different and had to be kept out of the new arrangement. All, doubtless, unfair.

BR Regions to be axed

The British Railways Board announced on June 29 a series of structure changes that will eliminate the existing Regional based Sectors and functions. These changes will be implemented over the next two years, on a progressive basis.

The revised management structure will transform BR into a totally business-led railway which is able to respond more efficiently to the needs of each particular function. However, this could result in the death knell of the corporate railway.

The historic railway administration centres, such as Birmingham, York and Swindon, may not survive in their present form. The new business profit centres, as they will be known, may wish to locate to a more central point in the areas they cover.

The new 'business sectors' will have responsibility for all aspects of railway operation, right down to drivers, guards and signalmen - who currently respond directly to the various Area Managers. At the present time the 'sectors' are essentially a marketing tool, with day to day operation being dealt with at area level.

Sector name change predicted by *RAIL*

The Board has also decided to rename its Provincial Sector. Regional Railways, the name chosen, was one of the suggestions made in the editorial of *RAIL* No. 110. The new name has been chosen to better reflect the role of the Sector, whilst making it more recognisable to the travelling public. The change will be effected later this year, probably from October 1 when the winter timetable is introduced.

Whilst the Sector will be known as Regional Railways, the business, that is the face presented to the public, will remain as present - with services continuing to be marketed under the Midline, Network NorthWest, Express etc. branding.

Parcel sector to be abolished

The Parcel Sector is also set to be abolished as a stand-alone organisation. It will be replaced by a Parcels Group which will be responsible for Post Office and other parcels traffic, but will respond jointly to the three passenger businesses.

The new look for BR

Senior management appointments have already been announced for the new structure as follows:

InterCity

Managing Director: J C D A Prideaux.
There will be five Route Directors for the main InterCity business and the appointments for these posts include the present General Managers of the Eastern, Western and London Midland Regions:
East Coast Main Line: J G Nelson.
West Coast Main Line: I W Warburton.
Great Western Main Line: B D Scott.
Cross Country and Midland Main Line: R H Brown.
Anglia and Gatwick Express: A J Cooper.

Network SouthEast

Managing Director: C E W Green.
Reporting to Mr Green will be nine Divisional Managers, responsible for broadly the present sub-sector areas.
South Western: P Field.
South East: G Harrison-Mee.
South Central: C Jago.
North (Euston): E Cameron.
Thames & Chiltern: A R Fearn.
Great Eastern: I Dobbs.
West Anglia: R Breakwell.
London Tilbury and Southend: K Bird.
Thameslink: J Collins.

Regional Railways

Managing Director: G C Pettitt.
The new Regional Railways sector will have five areas each with its own director.
ScotRail: C Bleasdale.
North East: D K Wharton-Street.
Central: M J Causebrook.
North West: C R Leah.
South Wales and West: T L T Steel.

Railfreight

Mr Colin Driver will retain overall responsibility for the freight business. and will be responsible for two separate businesses Trainload and Distribution.
Trainload
Managing Director: L W Smith.
Director Coal: K A R Jordan.
Director Steel: J K Worth.
Director Construction: J P Bates.
Director Petroleum: K C Hasted.
Distribution
Managing Director: I A Brown.
Director European: P O'Donnell.
Director United Kingdom: T J Hansford. ■

BR in surplus but strikes take toll

In 1989/90 British Rail had a group surplus of

the effects of falling disposable income had

posed problems.
Sir Bob Reid had no

Networker Turbos for Waterloo-Exeter

The work took two years and the resulting plan was announced in April 1991 by John Welsby. One of the first OfQ units to go live was the East Coast Main Line. John Nelson was made its manager.

It brought many advantages, as John Nelson explained in a newspaper interview at the time:

> At present, the main identification of the track workers, supervisors and management is with civil engineering, not with

> a business. In fact, there is a sense in which they would see civil engineering as the business.
>
> Once you have got an identity with the business, the civil engineer can see the contribution he or she can make to the success of the business in a way that is not really possible now, and I think that will bring tremendous benefits.

It was the direct opposite of the functional/silo organisation Cyril Hurcomb imposed through the Railway Executive forty years before.

There were some downsides to the new structure. The greatest financial risk the managers faced involved infrastructure. As a consequence, simple matters like painting the passengers' waiting room could too readily be pushed down the list of priorities. Nonetheless, those who knew it usually say that it was the best management structure they have ever worked in. Though it was launched by John Welsby, it was the fruit of Bob Reid's vision and was planned at his instruction while he was still chairman.

Bob's replacement, also called, to much hilarity, Bob Reid, came on to the Board in January 1990. He had run Shell's African operation, so was quite new to the railway and a very different person, outgoing, genial and wise in his own way. He was a good chairman and did much to restore confidence and morale after the difficult year that had just concluded. What he did not do, which Bob did, was keep the Department properly informed. Coming from the outside, he could not see the need. Bob could, and had, every week, called on the permanent secretary to tell him what was going well, what going wrong and what the Secretary of State needed to know.

Two things were left for Bob to do before he retired. The first, deliver a speech. It would be a very positive speech. It was a positive time. 'The railway is really going places,' Jim Collins thought: ThamesLink finished, electrification schemes, East Coast Main Line soon to be completed, new 125mph trains, Networkers coming in. It was a good time.

The speech was roughed out 30 December 1989 on a journey back from Holyhead: hours late, train broke down twice. Bob pushed his notes across to Jim Collins. 'Work it up, get it typed, and we will go over it again.' The speech became the first of the annual Robert Reid Lectures. It is set out in full in Appendix II. The Lessons Learnt begin: 'Be absolutely solid about the main framework.' Which is exactly what Bob Reid was.

The second thing, one of the happiest, certainly the jolliest, was dinner at the Gay Hussar. The three unions invited him and there was much hilarity and joking around. They had been through a lot together and by now respected and liked one another. And so he retired, on 1 April 1990.

24 RETIREMENT (1990)

After he retired, Bob kept a place in London but moved his home from Purley to a house at East Bergholt in Suffolk, not far from where he had grown up and from where his father had lived on returning from India. He had not been well, and one might have supposed, would have planned a quiet retirement. But not so. Peter Lazarus explains:

> Over the last few years since he retired from the railways, he served as chairman of St Thomas' Hospital. He was not an obvious choice and I'm not sure how much he knew about hospitals before he arrived. But in a remarkably short time he convinced them all that he was an ideal candidate, wise, effective, courteous and firm, and an excellent man to take charge during a period of great problems and dangers for the hospital. He led them out of a period of financial difficulty through to a period of stability and success.
>
> His great love of the railways helped them to understand the very strong feelings that so many who work there have for their hospitals. He foresaw the joint future of St Thomas' and Guy's as a united trust with great enthusiasm, and they will remember him as a man who did more than any other, in recent years, to restore their sense of pride and self-confidence as a great teaching hospital. He was very greatly loved and much missed, and this last chapter in his working life, although brief, was of quite enormous and lasting value to all.[121]

From Peter Parker, a moving sentence:

> He wrote to me a note not so long ago after a luncheon. He was frail and, in his words, 'fighting the demons'; in it he said: 'I reckon we had the best years, didn't we?'[122]

It is a happy man who can say that.

There had been many 'good years together', but it is probably the first few, when facing disaster on every side, that he was referring to.

There were struggles, defeats, victories; times which required patience, and times which required hot-blooded activity. It is what you look back on most fondly at the end of your days.

These were followed by the three golden years. He saw Network SouthEast, InterCity and Provincial become successful business-led railways, and he could declare that he met the commitment he had made to Government.

The doctors diagnosed cancer in the summer of 1992 and said he would probably make that Christmas but maybe not the next – and he did not.

He died three years after leaving his beloved railway, on 17 December 1993.

At his memorial service Sir Peter Lazarus went on to say:

> I have known all those who have led the railways since nationalisation of the industry in 1948. I'm in no doubt that, amongst many men of talent and ability, Bob was in very many ways the best.
>
> What were his personal qualities? I suppose, above all, that he was such a nice man, without a touch of self-importance. He was, of course, tough. He needed to be. Life had not been easy. He lost his wife in 1975 and was always a rather lonely figure after that. But he had a wry sense of humour, real modesty, he kept the steel well hidden beneath high-quality silk. It was there for those who took liberties. But his kindness was so practical that those who went to him for help were never disappointed. His personal staff on the railways were so devoted to him that they continued to see him regularly, and indeed went to his home to eat with him only a few weeks before he died.
>
> He was extremely wise; he was extremely effective in conceiving, negotiating and implementing policy change in all his various fields of endeavour. He was also one of the straightest, kindest and most human men I have ever had the good fortune to meet. He is greatly missed not only by his son and daughter, but by all his friends and the countless more who worked with him. It was our good fortune to have known him.

Leo Ploeger, President of the Dutch railways, praised what Bob had done to aid the railways of Europe and ended simply, 'We lost a great man.'

PART FOUR
POSTSCRIPT

It is easy to see the story of the thirty years since Bob retired as being about privatisation, but that is only half the story. The other half is the explosion in passenger demand and the massive effort to cater for that demand and to renew, again, almost every item of equipment.

So much has happened that only a brief summary is possible.

Railway assets were being improved right up until the end of Bob Reid's time, but the early 90s recession cut back the money that might have been available. Six years went by in the lead up to privatisation in 1996, with the least possible being spent. While the human capital was in good spirits – managers foresaw freedom to make their mark – the physical capital was in a fragile state, notwithstanding the great skill of British Rail managers in keeping in good order the things that mattered most.

The position is well summarised in a report, European Railway Comparisons, by the Institute of Transport Studies at Leeds University in 1994 – the time we are talking about.

> The overall impression is that BR's commercial performance is mixed, its operational performance is medium to good and its financial performance is good to excellent. The general impression that emerges is that BR is one of the most consistently good performers in our sample along with the Swedish, Netherlands and Swiss railways.[123]

On the surface, therefore, things seemed in good shape. BR was one of the best railways in Europe. But below the surface there were serious problems with a backlog of maintenance and renewal – the extent can be debated – which would have to be dealt with.

Maybe, as many argue, the future railway could have been built with less disruption and at less cost had British Rail been allowed to continue – but that was not to be.

In August 1993, Sir Robert, Bob Reid 2, was summoned to see the Transport Secretary, Malcolm Rifkind. 'We are going to announce,' Rifkind told Sir Robert, 'the privatisation of the railway in the forthcoming Conservative party conference – there's nothing you can do to stop this or alter how we intend to do it.' Or words to that effect.

Needless to say, Sir Robert and John Welsby had given thought to the matter and had, as you would expect, decided that if the railway was to be privatised, it should be as a single unit. In other words, no change. They underestimated the government's conviction that change was needed. The railway was going to be broken up. One view, in the mind of John Major, was that it should be divided into regions similar to the Big Four, with each sold to the private sector, in other words 'horizontal separation'. Many officials were in favour, but the Treasury was not. Intent on the virtues of competition, it insisted on 'vertical separation'; the separation of the track from the train, as we have it now.

In the view of John Welsby and most railwaymen, the separation of track from train was a mistake. Quite the wrong way to do it. But it became government policy and, to his credit, Welsby and his people set about putting it into practice. There followed an extraordinary twenty-four months of work.

As an entity, British Rail continued to exist. John Welsby remained its chairman, but its discrete activities were established as separate companies with appropriate rights and obligations spelt out in legal documents. The largest, the operation of the network became Railtrack on 1 April 1994, with John Edmonds appointed its first chief executive and Sir Robert Horton its first chairman. It was floated on the stock exchange in May 1996.

Amongst the business packaged and sold was track maintenance. So much else was well conceived, but this was not. It was a fatal mistake, indeed the first of two great mistakes. On its flotation, Railtrack had thirty-six contracts with seven infrastructure management companies (IMCs), each subject to penalties for track failure in their particular area. It seemed such a sensible arrangement but, besides being an attempt to outsource a problem, which should never be done, it was implemented in a most extreme form. Railtrack, determined to prevent its own staff suffocating the new companies required that its procedures for keeping a handle on track condition be passed over to the IMCs. From then on, Railtrack had no means of knowing how safe the track was upon which the trains were running.

The baleful consequence was inevitable. It is not that the IMCs took their responsibilities lightly, they did not, but the arrangement was not suitable for the railway. Some years went by till, on 17 October 2000, a dangerously cracked section of track on the East Coast Main Line collapsed under an express train at Hatfield killing four people and injuring seventy. Crippling speed restrictions followed for months on end while the whole network was properly inspected.

The second great mistake concerned the upgrading of the West Coast Main Line and the commitment to use, the flotation prospectus said, 'a transmission-based train control system to replace existing lineside signalling'.[124] Beneath these ten innocuous words lay a plan to use the newest, most sophisticated train control system from Europe, in its most advanced form – 'moving block signalling' – and the promise that it would save costs, increase capacity and enable line-speeds of 125mph (later increased to 145mph).

Who could say 'no'?

Thus were lit two fuses, snaking away to barrels of gunpowder, not in a cellar but out in plain view, ready to explode and blow up the company.

Other parts of the railway were packaged to create the twenty-five separate passenger train operating companies. These were, essentially, the sub-sectors which had been created in Bob Reid's time, though some were split. Under OfQ they ran the track and the trains, but this the privatisation process undid. The train operators would run the trains, while Railtrack would manage the track. (The structure was in fact reminiscent of that which had existed for six years prior to OfQ.)

The franchise agreements contained obligations of various kinds, certain basic standards to be met – a standard for punctuality, a minimum timetable, a limit on how crowded trains could be, for example – but otherwise train operators had considerable discretion as to what service to run and what staff and what trains were needed to serve their market and meet their financial requirements.

What was lost was a single place within the industry where costs and revenue came together. They came together only on the desk of the Secretary of State, and it seemed sometimes that they did not meet even there.

Rolling stock was transferred into the three rolling stock leasing companies, and numerous other companies created doing different bits of railway work. *Railnews* was taken over by Cyril Bleasdale.

A new organisation was established, the Association of Train Operating Companies (ATOC). It was both a service company, running the large central computer systems required by train operators and a trade association representing their interests. I was its Director-General from 1999 to 2008.

The first privately operated train ran without incident on 4 February 1996 from Twickenham to Waterloo. Stagecoach, under its chief executive Brian Souter, had won the franchise for South Western Trains. Two months later, South Eastern went live – shortly afterwards I was appointed its managing director (1997–1998) – and the others followed, all twenty-five.

The intention of the new owners was entirely positive. They had high aspirations. They wanted to run a good railway.

But almost immediately, crises and disasters with only the occasional success tumbled after each other without pause. Criticism in the newspapers was unrelenting. The entire basis of what was being done was constantly under attack. Every commentator had an opinion, most that the separation of track from train was wrong, that private train companies were deluded and incompetent, and that the years of British Rail had been a golden age. On and on it went. European railways, when approached for a view, were scathing in their smug comments. And smug they were, for gradually what was put in place became again one of the best in Europe.

My own personal and most partial observations on these events is offered below.

HOPE MEETS REALITY

The Office For Passenger Franchising (OPRAF), the body responsible for franchising, understood its task and did what was required quickly and efficiently. The contractual structure worked. Franchising obligations were clearly understood. Passengers expected an improved service, or at the very least cleaner trains, and they were made cleaner, frontline management was far more demanding than in the past, and the service did improve. But there were limits. The train washing machinery in a location in Kent was fifty years old, and its rotating brushes so worn they did not reach the surface of the train.

Train cleaners with long-handled scrubbing brushes – 'carriage bashing' it was called – worked through the night in the bitter winter wind off the North Sea at Ramsgate without shelter. They did, as it happens, work most diligently, a most admirable team, but a thirty-year old train cannot readily become clean in this way. The glass roof of the maintenance shed at the same place had so many broken panes that rainwater dripped on to the floor of beaten earth. To inspect under a train, engineers might have to crawl over mud.

Within months, outrage, stoked by those who objected in principle to privatisation, swept through the press. Journalists competed with each other to find the most offensive words – 'I'd rather sit in a skip' was the kind of thing written.

Making good the infrastructure would take twenty years. The first attempts were often ludicrous failures for it was a pivotal time in the technological cycle. New equipment was far more sophisticated than what it replaced. There was enthusiasm to bring it in. 'Work out of the box' was the cry. But new trains required months, years even, of tender care before they could be relied upon. New computer systems, driver scheduling software, timetable software, passenger information systems, promised much but delivered mostly frustration before, often, being abandoned. Some skills seem to have disappeared altogether, the elusive, high art of train planning for example or the instinct for 'unknown unknowns' in the management of projects.

A more experienced person took over my position at South Eastern, and I moved to head the trade association, ATOC.

PASSENGERS MATTER

A small but telling incident occurred soon after I arrived. ATOC ran the very large call centres which provided information to the public about train times. We knew that at busy times, a certain percentage of callers could not get through – greatly inconveniencing the caller. The regulator had set a standard for the call centre service: 90 per cent of calls should be answered within thirty seconds. ATOC was in breach of that standard, not greatly, but in breach. It had calculated that the cost of the extra staff needed to meet the standard would not be justified by the revenue lost through unsold tickets. Callers had nowhere else to go and would probably make the journey anyway. Nonetheless, as fines were imposed for the breach – £350,000 was paid in fines in 1998 – an attempt was made to meet the standard, but it was not met. Then, suddenly one day, in December 1998, the regulator informed ATOC that from then on for every month the standard was not met the fine would be £500,000. A truly huge sum. Every month! We huffed and we puffed – unreasonable, outrageous – but we got the message. They were serious. The passengers' convenience matters. More staff were hired, and the calls were answered.

Which introduces a fundamental feature of privatisation – one of the most important. For the first time, passengers through their representative, the government and its appointed regulator, had clout and used it. Railway managers were required to think not 'what is a good railway?' or 'what makes commercial sense?' but 'what am I obliged to do to please the passenger?' Chris Green is right in saying that his managers did not want to appear at the bottom of his NSE yellow peril league table, but 'not wanting to' is not the same as suffering a £500,000 penalty.

Across the railway, large fines were threatened and imposed for poor service – late trains, cancelled trains, late completed infrastructure work, call centres not answering calls – with little or no regard for excuses. Spending by the industry was forced therefore on to areas which mattered to passengers but had previously been neglected.

In these years, 1996 to 1999, passenger numbers grew but many, many things went wrong. Matters came to a head in October 1998. Labour Party delegates to its annual conference in Blackpool had been held up for hours by train failures, some forced to clamber out of their stalled train and trudge along the track to safety. John Prescott, the Secretary of State overseeing transport, fulminated to a cheering audience at the conference about the 'national disgrace'. But, out on the railway, people were already pushing, shoving, pounding and sweating to get work done.

The task, the difficulty, the cost of delivering a reliable, high-intensity railway – passenger numbers were growing strongly – was very much greater than anyone had foreseen.

Railway leaders, about twenty key people in all, began to meet in private every month in the Railtrack boardroom to discuss with entire candour what was going wrong and how to fix it. I was joint secretary of the meeting. It was obvious that the industry could not continue without a body authorised to formulate railway strategy. OPRAF was replaced by the Strategic Rail Authority.

John Prescott tried to help. He summoned a National Rail Summit for February 1999, with hundreds of people talking together in Queen Elizabeth Hall. Memorable, though nothing to do with punctuality, was what Jimmy Knapp wanted to say. Declaring from the platform in his strong Ayrshire accent that he had no fancy slides just a scruffy piece of paper with a few notes between him and the audience, he said, with great feeling, almost with tears in his eyes, 'for 40 years I have been struggling to halt decline and the loss of jobs on the railway but now, for the first time in my life, I can see a growing railway and a good life for the people in it.' It was an emotional moment.

Gradually, things got better. Effort was paying off. Punctuality was at a respectable level. Passenger numbers grew. Then, in October 1999, disaster struck.

TWO TERRIBLE YEARS

That month saw the first of a series of terrible events, spanning two dreadful years.

In these two years the railway saw the Ladbroke Grove accident (October 1999), the abandonment on Black Diamond Day of the notorious moving-block resignalling plan for the West Coast Main Line (December 1999), the Hatfield accident caused by cracks in the steel rail (October 2000), crippling speed restrictions while the whole network was inspected, meaning that on some days nearly half the trains in the country were cancelled or running late (October 2000–December 2001), and finally the insolvency of Railtrack (October 2001).

The atmosphere of crisis and despair throughout the industry is hard to exaggerate. Things had to change, and they did.

Railtrack emerged from administration in October 2002 as Network Rail, with a new, most vigorous, management team: Roundheads replaced the Cavaliers.

2004 – THE YEAR OF REFORM

The government introduced a series of reform outlined in the 2004 White Paper 'The Future of Rail'.

The Railway Inspectorate, responsible for overseeing safety, was moved to be under the Rail Regulator.

The functions of the Strategic Rail Authority were moved up into the Department of Transport, which thus became directly responsible for strategy – something it should never have given up – and franchising. Notable in that diagram is the strange way Network Rail is shown, stretching across the diagram and seeming to loom over the train

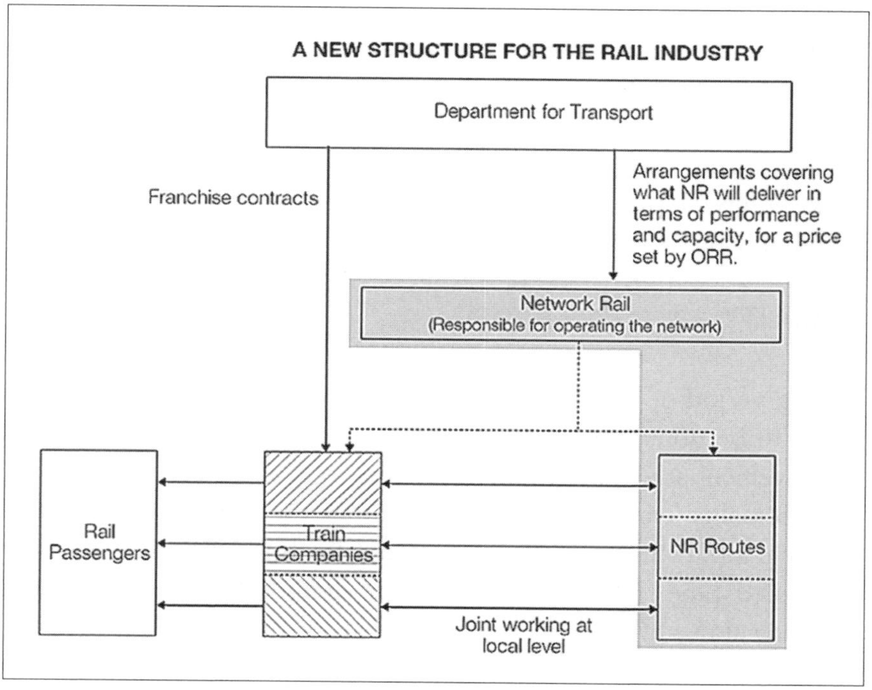

operators. Alistair Darling, then Secretary of State for Transport, would have much preferred to get the Department out of any management function for the railway and put Network Rail in charge of everything, track and train, but doubts as to its abilities prevent that happening, but it was invited to play a 'leadership' role.

By then, franchise contracts had become highly prescriptive. No longer were train operators expected to develop the timetable which best suited their market or to choose their rolling stock – to be funded and owned by leasing companies – or decide on station staffing. All that became the job of a team within the Department for Transport. The train operators were to deliver the contract: to manage the staff, the IT, the operating procedures, safety, relations with Network Rail, the entire package that got the trains running.

A system for the setting of five-yearly strategic plans, with funding, was established. The first such five-yearly period, called mysteriously Control Period 4, began in April 2009. That the date was some years after the White Paper showed that, for once, someone had understood the amount of work involved in developing realistic plans for the railway.

One might regret some of the changes made, but it was a coherent system for managing a growing railway. Travellers were seeing the railway as an attractive alternative to congested roads and passenger numbers were very likely to continue their strong growth. To handle these numbers, prodigious sums of money would be required, which could only be decided upon by government.

STABILITY

A long period of reasonable stability followed from 2002. There was much to be done but no crises damaging enough to disrupt gradual improvement across the country.

Punctuality climbed. This graph shows the percentage of trains arriving within five minutes (ten minutes for InterCity trains) of their scheduled time. For a good railway it should be 90 per cent, but anything above 85 per cent is adequate, just.

More and more passengers flooded on to the railway. The numbers

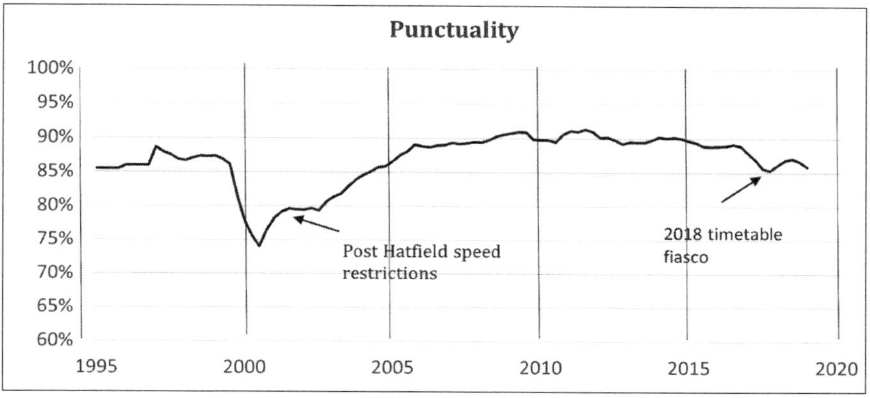

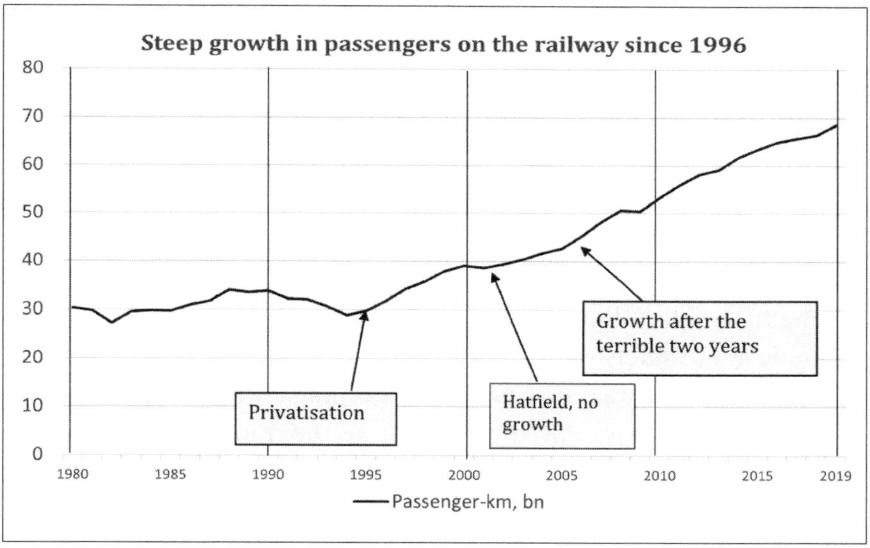

were a revelation. The rapid recovery in ridership after the Hatfield accident shocked the government and drove its willingness to properly fund railway investment. Now, in 2019, ridership is more than double that at the time of privatisation. Handling such growth, maintaining passenger satisfaction, with rail fares far from cheap, has been a notable achievement.

PASSENGER SATISFACTION

In about 2006, still enduring abuse in the press, I was asked on to

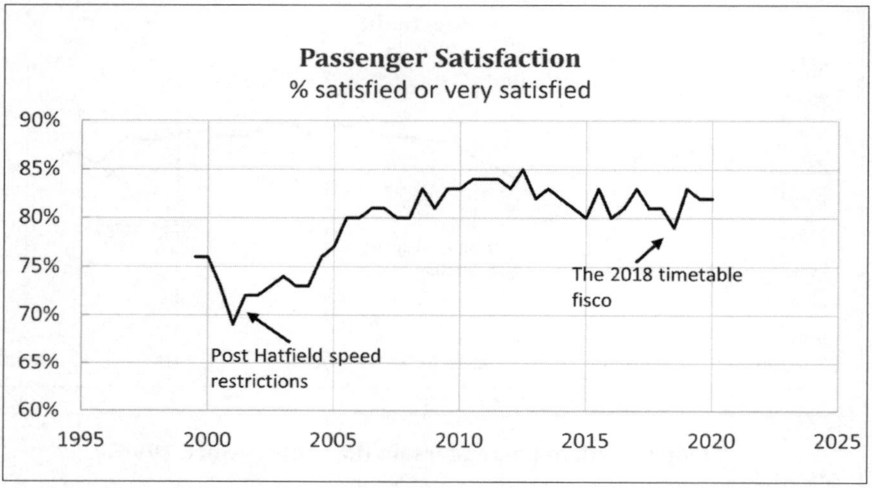

a radio phone-in programme to respond to listeners' telephone calls. Christian Wolmar, a leading railway commentator and critic, would also be answering the phone calls. Steeling myself for the expected complaints, I sat down in the studio, put on the headphones, and waited.

The first caller: 'I'm a passenger in (let us say Reading), and I want to know about safety on the railway.'

The question was directed to Christian, who answered it in straightforward way. All quite dull, so the radio host asked the questioner, 'What do you think of your local train operator?' I think they expected a lively response. The caller replied: 'Well, I quite like them. They're pretty good. They try hard.'

And another caller. After some to-ing and fro-ing: 'My train company? They're good.' And so it went on. About ten callers and, I think, only one criticising their train company. So, it struck: we are not bad. It is a good service out there, and passengers can see it.

The passenger representative body, Passenger Focus, continued to survey passenger satisfaction, as Network SouthEast had done. The dire consequences of the post-Hatfield speed restrictions are evident in the figures. Satisfaction in that year fell below 70 per cent. But with perseverance, things improved; satisfaction rose steadily, reaching 83 per cent or 84 per cent for some years. Over 80 per cent is good for a railway.

Since then it has slipped somewhat for the railway has become very busy, very crowded. There is one noticeably bad figure, that for 2018, a consequence of a timetable fiasco.

Similar satisfaction surveys have been carried out by European Commission across all twenty-six member states. The EU's overall measure for satisfaction with rail travel for 2013 is shown in the illustration. Finland is ranked first and the United Kingdom second. The other large railways: France sixth, Spain seventh, Germany sixteenth and Italy twenty-fourth.

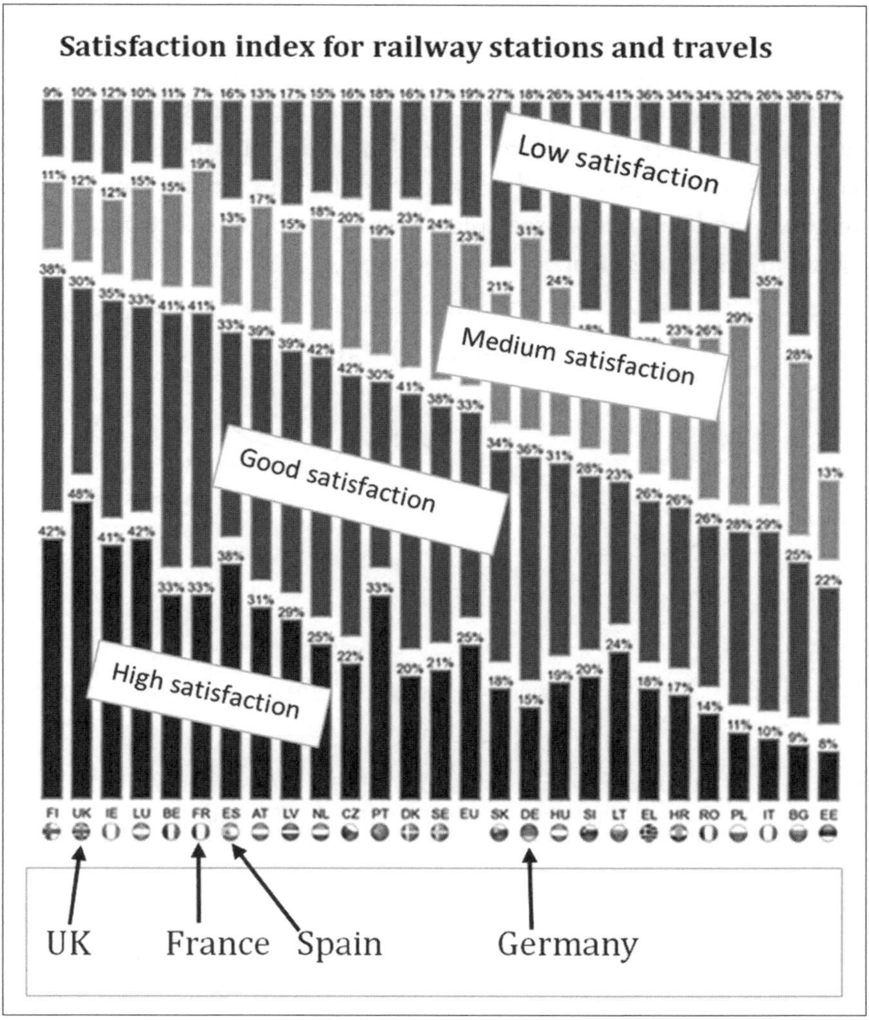

Two other EU surveys, in 2011 and 2018, show the United Kingdom's railways in a similarly favourable light, ranking well ahead of France, Germany and Italy. The railway in Spain shows up well, though not ahead of that in Britain.

There are other measures which also show the UK railway in a favourable light: safety and the growth in passenger numbers for example. Britain's good safety record, in comparison with other European railways, was built on the work initiated in Bob's last year in charge. In truth, most railways are now operated in the safe way, but that was not the case fifteen years ago.

Freight did not disappear – far from it. The private freight companies have increased the amount carried by rail since 1996. Coal has gone, almost entirely in the last year or two, marshalling yards have gone and wagonload freight, never profitable, has gone, but there has been a good business in specialised container traffic, in carrying construction material, and in other large-volume heavy products. Freight on the railway is highly efficient.

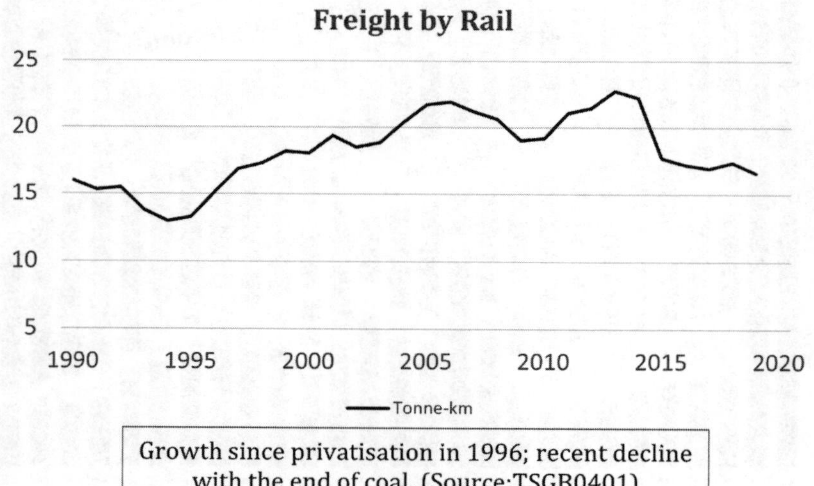

Growth since privatisation in 1996; recent decline with the end of coal. (Source:TSGB0401)

May 2018 should have been a moment of triumph. It was the completion of the Thameslink project, largely on-time, largely on budget and largely doing what it had promised: new journey opportunities from the north to the south of London, with many more trains. It saw instead a fiasco over the new timetable intended to deliver these services. The mess got tidied up but that it happened showed the extraordinary difficulty of running a railway, or at least the many opportunities to make mistakes. There is an army tag, 'No plan survives first contact with the enemy'. There should be a railway one, 'No timetable survives first contact the passengers'. But this was worse than that – very bad indeed.

By far the greatest difficulties lie on the desk of Network Rail. Consider their current workload. It is they who have just completed the upgrade and resignalling of the Great Western Main Line; are now working to complete other large area signalling and traffic management systems; are working on what will be the resignalling of the southern end of the East Coast Main Line with the version of the European traffic management system used in Thameslink; are working on the Northern Hub, on Crossrail, and more. The list is long.

It is at the same time running, with the train operators, the day-to-day railway, and seeking to strike a balance, as has been the case since 1948, between central control and decision-making by its local managers.

It is often train operators who are in the news. I was one of them. Their job is difficult enough, but I look with respect at the scale of work Network Rail has had to do.

REFLECTIONS

The railways in Britain have quite clearly become among the best in Europe. It is confirmed by EU surveys. In truth, most countries have now learnt how to run a good railway. But it was Bob Reid and the people around him who showed them how. The old railway dominated by the professions had to go. The focus had to be on customers, what they wanted and what they would pay for. It had to be a business-led railway, organised according to lines of business.

Bob Reid would not recognise the railway now, but, though it is not how he would have liked, it is a good railway.

Many argue that success would have been achieved with less disruption and at less cost had British Rail been allowed to continue without privatisation. That might be so. What Chris Green achieved with Network SouthEast and John Prideaux with InterCity was impressive and could have been built upon. Certainly, the most egregious errors might have been avoided. But, overall, we will never know.

Cost is the greatest problem. Grotesque, say some. But is it a railway failing or is it the unavoidable consequence of the complexity of any work in this crowded island?The split of commercial from delivery is part of it, but it is not a problem unique to the railway.

Looking back, the changes that have taken place since 1948 – a 70-year period – are quite startling. From being a vast, sprawling freight railway, it is now a passenger railway of the most intensive kind. Passenger numbers are far higher, the distances travelled far greater. The commuter belt is no longer Mitcham to Romford, but now from Southampton to Cambridge, Swindon to Southend; the gardens of London are no longer Hampstead Heath and Richmond Park, but now stretch to the countryside of Somerset. Nine magnificent steam trains each day used to take passengers from London to Edinburgh. Now twenty-eight much larger trains a day are in the timetable.

What has happened reflects both social changes and Britain's strengths and weaknesses. Indeed, looking back, it can seem that what happened, in each instance, was inevitable, was fated to happen. It was inevitable that Robertson's railway would stumble, that a Beeching would arrive when he did and champion the closure of rural lines but be blind to other issues. It was inevitable that Peter Parker in his first few years as chairman would lead a moderately efficient, well-intentioned railway. What was not inevitable was that Parker's choice as chief executive in 1980 would drive the railway in a new direction. It did not happen in other countries.

In the small matter of the railway, Bob Reid changed the direction of history.

APPENDIX I
A BOB REID TIMELINE

Father: Sir Robert Reid, KCSI, KCIE (father)

1883	Born.
	Parents living in Sevenoaks, Kent. Schooling: Malvern College and Brasenose College, Oxford.
1907	Joined Indian Civil Service and left for India.
1909	Married Amy Helen Disney.
1936–1943	Governor of Assam. And on two occasions also Acting Governor of Bengal.
June 1943	Left India for the last time.
1943–1945	Director-General of Post and Telegraph Censorship.
1945	Retired, to Holbrook Lodge, Suffolk.
1964	Died.

Bob Reid – Sir Robert Basil Reid, CBE

7 February 1921	Born.
	Parents' home in England in Sevenoaks, then in Thorpeness, Suffolk then Holbrook, Suffolk.
1934–1939	Malvern College.
1939–1940	Brasenose College, Oxford, reading Modern History.
1940–1941	8th Royal Tank Regiment, captured in Libya shortly before the 15 December 1941.
1941–1945	Prisoner of war, first in Italy then in Germany.
1946–1947	Brasenose College, a wartime degree studying economics.
1947	Joined the railway, LNER.
1947–1950	Banchory and Aberdeen, as a traffic apprentice.
1950–1953	Edinburgh, in the operating superintendent's office, including work on the streamlining of freight traffic following the amalgamation

	of LNER and LMS. And, possibly, Assistant Yardmaster at Portobello.
1951	Married Isobel McLachlan.
1953–1960	York. At first in the general manager's office. In 1957 head of the rates and freight development section in the Divisional Goods Manager's office in Leeds. In March 1958 Goods Agent in York.
1960 March–1968	Glasgow, living in Rutherglen. At first Assistant District Goods Manager. In June 1961, District Passenger Manager, concerned with the introduction of electrified services on the suburban railways north and south of the Clyde. In 1964 Divisional Commercial Manager, concerned with the carriage of motor cars to and from the new Rootes factory at Linwood. In 1967 Regional Planning Manager.
1968 May–1972	Doncaster, as Divisional Manager, then aged 47.
1972 January–1974	York, as Deputy General Manager.
1974 January–1976	General manager, Southern Region. Bought a house in Purley.
1977–1979	On the Board, as Executive Member for Marketing.
1980 March	Chief Executive (Railways). Appointed CBE.
1982–1983	President, Chartered Institute of Transport.
1983 September	Executive Chairman.
1985	Knighted, Sir Robert Reid CBE.
1987–1988	Chairman, Nationalised Industries Chairman's Group.
1988–1989	Chairman, Community of European Railways.
1990 March	Retired. In retirement, moved to East Bergholt, Suffolk.
1990–1993	Chairman of West Lambeth Health Authority.
1993, 17 December	Died.

Preparing British Rail for the 1990s

Sir Robert Reid CBE, FCIT

Chairman, British Railways Board

APPENDIX II
BOB REID'S FINAL SPEECH

Given at the Chartered Institute of Transport.

INTRODUCTION

British Rail has been radically transformed since 1982. The transformation is not yet complete, but the results so far are, I believe, very impressive.

If the results for the financial year 1988/9 are compared with the 1983 financial year:

- **an extra 69 million passengers were carried** (up 10%)
- **an extra 3 billion passenger miles were undertaken** (up nearly 16%) — The highest level since 1960
- **an extra 600 million net tonne miles of freight were carried** (up 5.6%)
- **and productivity has increased sharply on all fronts:**
  train miles per member of staff — up 26% — that's 4% per annum
  train miles per crew member — up 33%
  operating expenses per train mile — down 14%.

As a result of these improvements, in real terms:

InterCity — turned round a loss of £200 million in 1983 to a surplus of £57 million last year.

Network SouthEast — reduced its loss before grant to £138 million in 1988/9, less than half the loss before grant recorded in 1983.

Freight — made an operating surplus of £69.4 million in 1988/9 — the best result for a decade.

Parcels — Red Star revenue has doubled since 1983.

The Public Service Obligation (the Government subsidy) — has been reduced by over 50% in real terms since 1983.

At the same time:

The annual level of investment has doubled in real terms and now runs at £1¼ billion a year (about the maximum rate we can physically manage). There are 72 more passenger stations now than in 1983 and we have introduced over 2000 new carriages and brought into service 110 new locomotives.

Those are a lot of figures, but I hope you have the general message that against the background of a buoyant economy we have expanded and improved our business in every single dimension. The events which began in 1982 and which led to these changes will form the centrepiece of this Address.

But first let me give you some background, starting with managerial and organisational matters within B.R.

HISTORICAL PERSPECTIVES

Organisation

I joined the L.N.E.R. as a graduate trainee in September 1947, just before its nationalisation. My preparation for a business career was 6 years in the army and a degree from Oxford. Nationalisation brought together 650,000 railway staff (now reduced to 128,000).

The railway was then organised and managed in a way which basically remained unchanged until 1982. There were two dominant features which survived throughout these years.

First was the primacy of the Regional General Managers. These were the railway barons exercising great power in the geographical territories which they commanded, and having high status.

Yet the Regions were not separate businesses with profit accountability. Their revenues and costs were only those which originated within the boundaries of their territories. Since many passenger and freight trains moved between Regions there were major discrepancies in revenue and cost attribution.

So while the command structure of the Regional General Manager system was strong, the business basis of their operations was weak. That was a major problem.

The second dominant feature was the railways traditionally strong functional hierarchies. The engineers in particular were powerful people whose word tended to be law. Decisions about infrastructure, rolling stock and locomotives were all seen as being engineering decisions, and they tended to get the blame for high cost, though in truth it was the commercial specifications which were often unrealistic.

The Chief Executive had a difficult time exercising control over these hierarchies, and hence over the railway business. It seemed to me that prior to 1982, perhaps the only person who effectively could take grip of both costs and revenue simultaneously was the Chairman.

There had, of course, been many changes over these years. The Beeching era in the early 1960s was easily the most outstanding.

Dr. Richard Beeching, an ex ICI chairman, provided a great jolt to the system. To the outside observer his Chairmanship marked the demise of the old British Transport Commission, the formation of the British Railways Board and the re-shaping of the network — in particular the emotive axing of many branch lines throughout the country.

To those of us inside the railways his contribution was of a different kind. Under his leadership, for the first time we began to see how to manage the railways in a more businesslike way and how to analyse our situation correctly. He helped us to clarify the role of the railways — "do what you are best at" he said. His strategic thinking about the future of the railways was a revelation. He brought in about 40 people from private industry at a senior level to introduce new ideas and practices. Some attempt was made to focus on marketing but clearly with so many other problems it was not his top priority — Further marketing initiatives were cut short by his departure after only 4 years.

Beeching's management style cut right across our traditions and he gave a number of younger people, especially those like myself who were university trained, rapid promotion. His great skill was in asking the right questions. The trouble was that railway management was still dominated by the traditional notions of being a transport monopoly with common carrier obligations. That is why he took 3 years to formulate his plans for **The Reshaping of the Railways.**

But these 4 hectic years of Beeching — far too short in view of the magnitude of the task — marked a critical stage which looked towards the more thorough transformation of railway management 20 years later. So much for the key features of the environment within British Rail up to 1982.

The Changing External Environment

Externally the most dramatic change for the railways has been the growth in competition.

First came the motorways (map 1958, 1978, 1989) and with them a dramatic growth in car ownership (chart x), in passenger miles by road (chart y, with rail) and in freight miles by road (chart z, also showing rail). Long distance buses also developed, especially after deregulation, offering low cost competition.

Cars and trucks offered door-to-door flexibility for both business and leisure, travelling on an ever expanding road system which in the early years had been provided at far below its full cost to users. One-man truck businesses in particular offered individual services at a price and flexibility which we could not match.

At the same time our Anglo Scottish routes were nibbled at by a significant growth in air services of rapidly improving quality and frequency.

Our own fixed rail system had been laid down before cars or aeroplanes were even invented, and it was designed to serve populations whose distribution has now changed.

Chart x: Car ownership per thousand persons: Great Britain

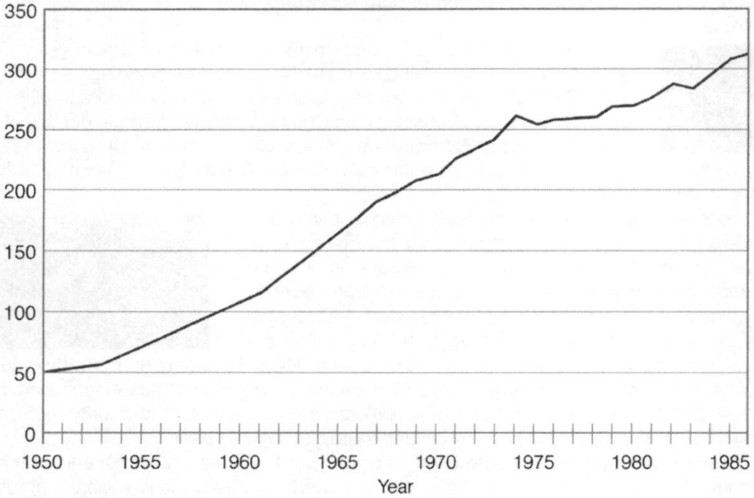

Source: DTp (1989), National Road Traffic Forecasts (Great Britain) 1989.

Chart y: Passenger miles by road
1955 - 1988

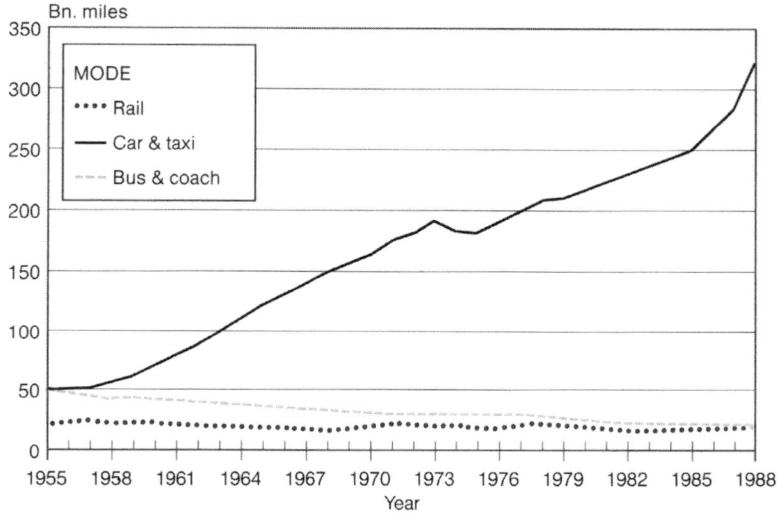

Source: DTp Statistics Bulletin and DTp Transport Statistics Great Britain

Chart z: Road & rail freight transport
(billion tonne miles)

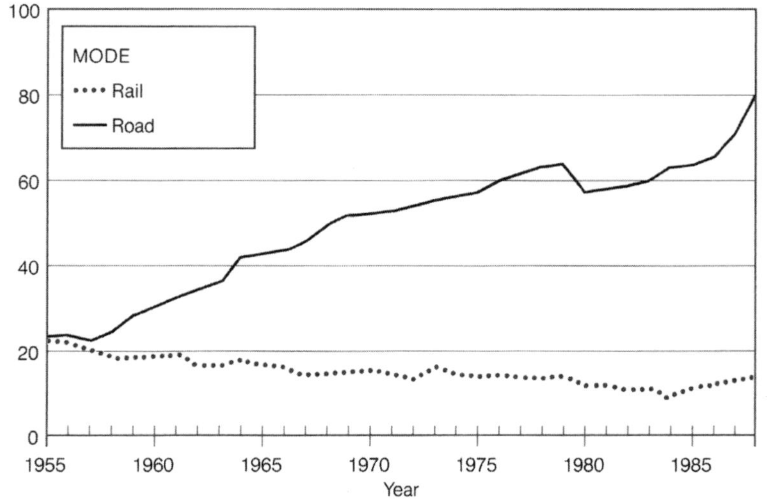

Source: DTp (1989), Transport Statistics Great Britain

4

Motorway map of Great Britain: 1958

5

Motorway map of Great Britain: 1978

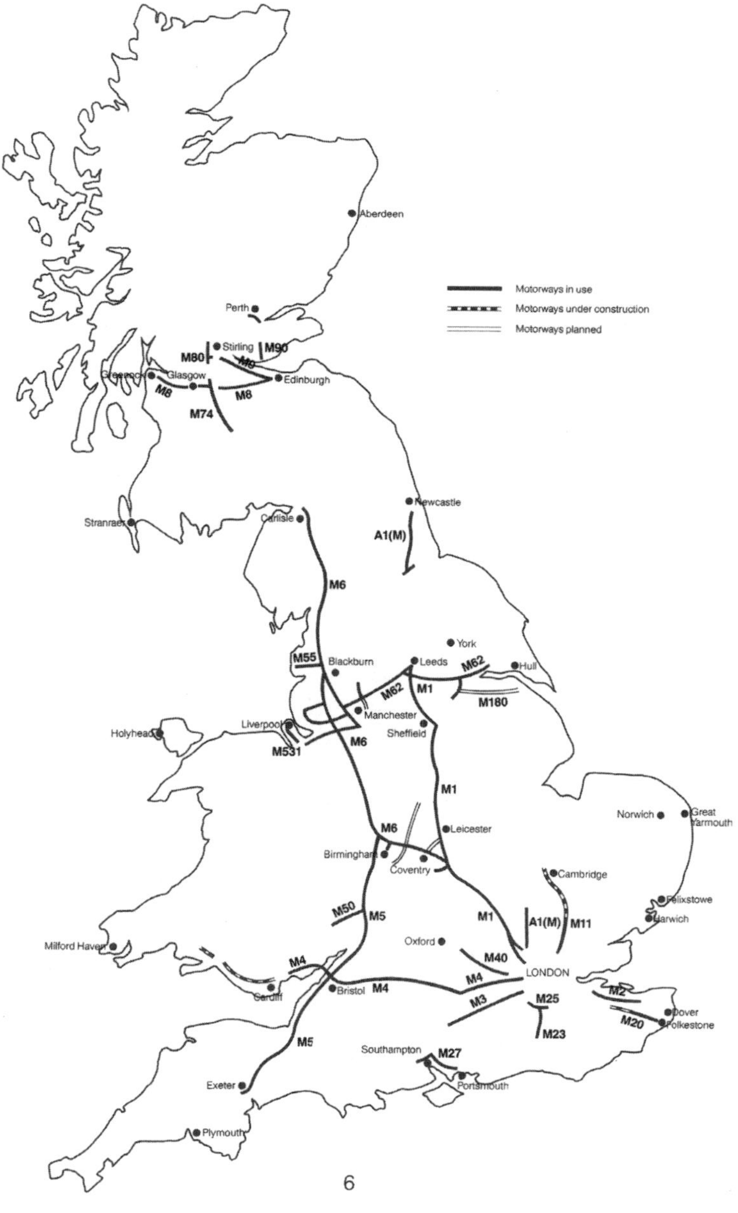

Motorway map of Great Britain: 1989

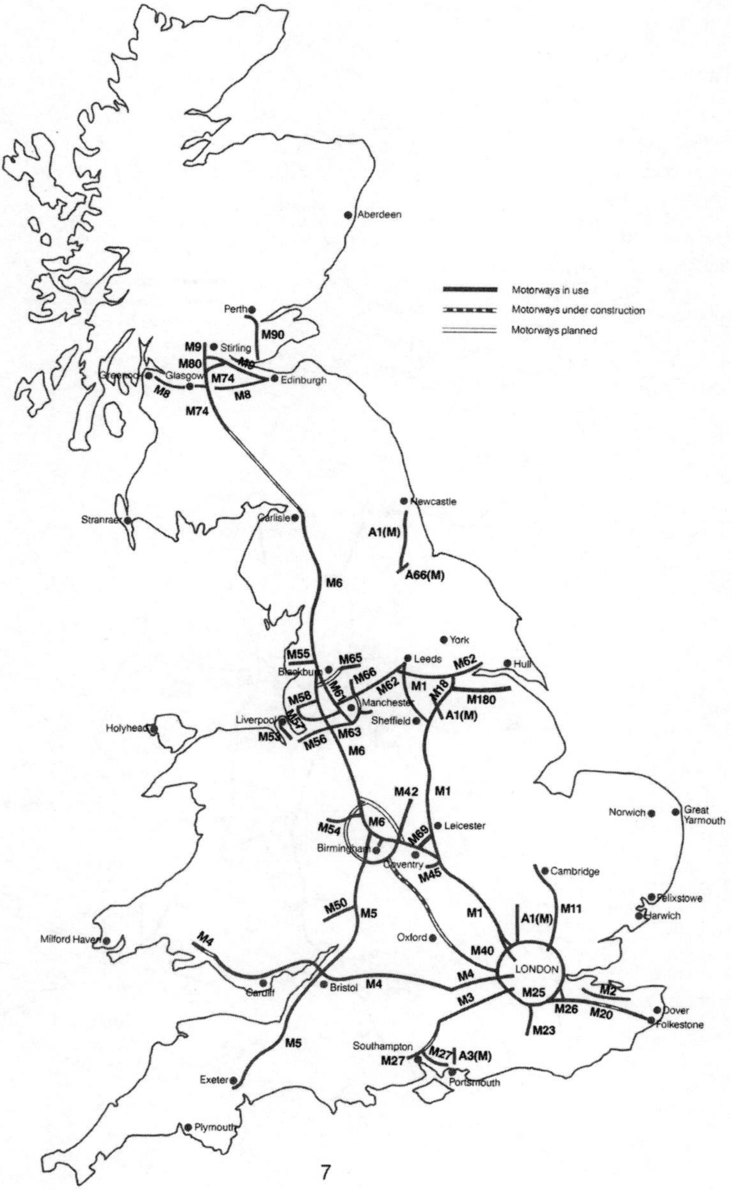

7

Strategy

The other main feature of our external environment was the Government. Our strategy was shaped by Government directives. We had the standard nationalised industry requirement to ensure that our combined revenues were not less than sufficient to meet our combined charges properly chargeable to revenue account "taking one year with another", but there were also some more specific directives.

The most significant was in 1974 following Britain's accession to the EEC. The Public Service Obligation (P.S.O.) system of subsidy (with exclusion of InterCity in 1988) required the Board:

"to operate its railway passenger business so as to provide a public service which is comparable generally with that provided by the Board at present".

While this seemed all right at the time, because it gave us a sense of security, it was very negative. "Stay as you are" it seemed to say. There was no sense of purpose behind it, no focus, no forward looking strategic aim.

And then there were the official Enquiries. We were not short of advice. Especially from people who had never tried to run a railway. Throughout this period there were many official reports and, not to be outdone, we produced a few ourselves!

The only one I will pause over is the December 1982 Report on the "Review of Railway Finances" under the Chairmanship of Sir David Serpell, a distinguished civil servant who had just retired as a part-time member of our Board. It was initiated by the Secretary of State in response to our own 1981 "Rail Policy" report which simply asked for more money. The Secretary of State saw it as important for setting the tasks for whoever was to be the next Chairman. In the event this was me!

The whole report caused an immense rumpus and indeed there was a furious minority report by Alfred Goldstein of Travers Morgan & Partners. There were accusations of the improper selection of consultants and that they spent much time on the wrong things. Cutting costs was all that seemed to matter and the revenue side was virtually ignored. There were newspaper leaks with lurid reports of what was to be recommended, some pretty severe criticisms by the Transport Committee of the House of Commons about what the Committee did say, and a general rubbishing of the report within B.R.

Apart from some of the more outlandish options, like closing down over 80% of the system, it was a matter of fact a rather good report. It should have been — much of the information it contained we ourselves had supplied! On the basis of detailed engineering studies it argued that the system was not running down and that there was not a backlog of track maintenance as we had been claiming. That was what I had believed and this confirmation created the possibility of developing a much more positive and forward thinking approach to our affairs.

When the report was published I was about to become Chairman. One of its results was the letter which followed my initial letter of appointment. For the first time we knew what was expected of us. This second letter gave me well stated objectives and a clear financial remit. In summary these were:

1. To run an efficient railway providing good value for money.
2. To reduce the passenger grant (P.S.O.) by 25% over 3 years.
3. There should be no major route closures.
4. To operate freight and parcels on a commercial basis.
5. To procure rolling stock by competitive tender.
6. To increase private sector participation.

ORGANISATION CHANGE

Sector Management

I described earlier how the railways had always been engineering driven and production led. Striving to maintain our survival, costs were all that seemed to matter (the Serpell Report reflected and reinforced this attitude). But this was wrong thinking for it ignored market opportunities and the possibility of creating our own future in the way we wanted it. Beeching had planted the idea of marketing in our minds but it never took root.

What we did in 1982, just before I became Chairman, was to cut through the old ways of thinking and in a radical reform to set up five businesses, each with responsibility for its own costs and revenues. Each then had a "bottom line" on which their performance could be judged. The five were InterCity, Provincial, London & the South East (later called Network SouthEast), Freight and Parcels.

The heads of these businesses are called Sector Directors, and from the beginning they were marketing orientated. They find out what customers want and what opportunities there are for creating new business. New investment is a large part of their work. They also design our product specifications, decide what services shall be run, where to, at what prices, both this year and well into the future.

A number of shibboleths soon fell to the ground. Our Director, InterCity discovered that rail's competitive position was weak in the London-Glasgow market, though the shorter distance London-Manchester route was ideal for rail. Yet the Advanced Passenger Train, which as a project was engineering driven, had been designed for the Glasgow run. "We have no need for it" he said.

On the occasions when our engineers did deliver the right product, and undoubtedly the most succesful was the High Speed Train, we still failed to get it in all the right markets. That is until the Director, InterCity redeployed some of his very expensive trains to the Midland Main Line — a transfer that would have been unthinkable under the Regional Barons.

But the Sectors did not run the railway day-to-day. That responsibility remained with the Regions, because the assets of the business, all of the depots and most of the staff were out there in the field, countrywide. And we were obsessed with maintaining the integrity of the operational railway while these momentous changes were happening at the top.

We run around 15,000 trains and carry 2 million passengers every weekday, with an operational staff of some 80,000 people. We had to keep that going, constantly striving for improvements, whatever else might be happening.

However, exactly what rail services should be provided, to what standards and at what costs? Sector Directors negotiate with the production side in the Regions and in the next level down in the Areas. Some negotiations are with the Operations people and others are with the Area Engineers (who still report through their professional hierarchy). That is how the matrix of responsibilities and negotiations has developed.

Each sector does its own negotiations for the rail service to be provided. It is quite likely that over the same tracks in an area will be fast passenger trains from InterCity, local stopping passenger trains from the Provincial business, Freight and Parcels trains. It is at the Area level that these requirements are co-ordinated, with clear rules laid down about priorities. There are many genuinely common costs and there have to be clear and simple rules about cross charging. So if a Freight train runs on an InterCity track, Freight will pay the avoidable cost of doing so. To begin with the method was pretty crude, though effective. We are now refining these trading rules.

In spite of such complexities, the focus on the market place for rail services which Sector Management introduced, and their hard-headed planning, quickly brought about a sharp improvement in our affairs. We were determined to beat the competition. Sector Management, combined with fresh thinking on the part of our production managers and their unremitting attention to unit costs, proved to be the turning point in our fortunes.

It was a huge task with a gigantic effort on the part of all our staff, achieved against a background of ever-increasing competition, of constant media criticism and of rising expectations from our customers.

Looked at from the outside, to have restructured the railways into five accountable businesses may sound rather obvious, but for us it was a total revolution. Few had thought it possible. Indeed, we are frequently visited by railway organisations from abroad to see how we did it, and why we are the world leader. But, like all revolutions, it did not settle everything all at once. It started a wave of further changes which continue to this day. It was, however, a watershed in our affairs. There can be no going back.

The financial results can be summarised as follows. In 1979 Government grants as a proportion of railway revenue were on a steeply upward trend — 29% in that year, then 32%, 44%, 53% in successive years — towards an inevitable crisis. In 1982 the railway financial deficit exceeded £1 billion. Then Sector Managers took over. By 1988/89 the proportion was down to 25% and the financial deficit had been halved. InterCity and Freight have turned the corner into profit and now only Provincial and Network SouthEast receive financial support.

Planning

From the mid-1970s we produced annual Corporate Plans. These became increasingly thick with more and more supporting material. They gave our business expectations for 5 years ahead, with the subsidy we would need to "stay alive".

In the early years, however, before our Board Member for Finance and Planning took a grip of them, they had a constant pattern. "This year" was terrible, "next year" would show a marked improvement; "the year after that" we would just break even, and the last two years showed steeply rising profits.

The trouble was that the next year the pattern was repeated — and the next year again. Each time "this year" was terrible, and blue sky was on the horizon. We were, we began to realise, managing the numbers rather than the business.

Until 1984 our planning system was heavily top down. The planning cycle was run from the centre. The Regions were asked for contributions but these plans were not their plans. They did not feel that in any sense they possessed them. To their credit they never really believed them in any operational sense.

Nor did the civil servants really believe them either. A scurrilous document which obtained notoriety amongst our friends in Government described our forecast projections as the "Age of Incredulity". . . . .

It was no way to go on! After 1984 planning was "bottom up" within a broad framework set from the top by the Board; the two met in a plan comprising a series of fully understood and resourced proposals for action.

Origins

Changes as fundamental as this don't just happen. There is always something more behind the scenes. So how did it all start? Now I have to become a bit personal.

Looking back, my first glimpses of what could be done occurred to me when I was a Divisional Manager at Doncaster in the Beeching era of the 1960's. As I've already said, Beeching showed the way, in managing as well as in analysing. He was an inspiration to many of us. I found that giving people real responsibility, communicating with them at all levels, being absolutely clear about what I wanted and expected them to do seemed to work wonders. Why couldn't this be done on a grand scale? It was simple!

So when I was moved up to become Deputy General Manager of Eastern Region at York I tried to take it further. No one wanted to know. I was continually by-passed by the Chief Officers. Deputy General Manager was a grand title, conjuring visions of a great command, but it carried with it little real power. I was continually defeated. Somehow the things I wanted never happened. Meetings began to take place without me. The concensus seemed to be that giving people authority was highly risky — they might make a mistake. Communicating with people might weaken the power base of senior management, and being clear about what we wanted might mean that we could be judged on whether we performed or not. Dangerous ideas!

I moved on. January 1974 and I became Regional General Manager of Southern Region. This was a post of great power. I had my first taste of managing a high level team, and I began to have contacts with the Board. I quickly decided to try to work with the Board rather than to hold it at arms length as seemed to be the habit of the time. Although I myself had now joined the Baronial class, I was determined that when I had the chance I would try to get my fellow Barons under control.

Behind these views was a basic belief that forming a team, giving it enabling power, and then leading it firmly in a direction compatible with Board policy, would be both more effective and more satisfying than the constant internal strife which I saw around me — conflicts which allowed our competitors to take our business and our livelihood.

Then things moved fast. Three events took place which were to be the turning point. First, in 1977 my predecessor, Peter Parker, created a new post, "Board Member for Marketing". This was a most significant event. At that time, as I have said, British Rail was engineering driven and production led in the Regions. There was a strong engineering hierarchy up to Board level, and key decisions were dominated by the engineers. Marketing was neither understood — as being essentially a diagnostic activity with important consequences for the whole development of our businesses — nor properly practiced. Creating a Board Member for Marketing gave the possibility of a totally new balance to our affairs.

The second event was my appointment to that newly created post. The Secretary of State appointed me but it was Peter Parker who did it.

And the third event was Peter Parker's initiative in 1978 in setting up the Strategy Unit. Hitherto there had been nowhere in B.R. where the unthinkable could be thought through with thoroughness; nowhere with the time and expertise to develop options. Peter Parker brought in one of our most experienced and respected Regional General Managers to be in charge (who was later to be Chief Executive), and he brought in an outside consultant from the London Business School. They developed a highly effective team. Ideas flowed. They thought up the new structure of Sector businesses. It fitted with my ideas. The whole plan took over a year to become crystal clear, to create a new vision, and for me to be convinced that this totally new way of organising the business was practical.

When I became Chief Executive in March 1980 the pace hotted up. So many people had to be seen, so much opposition to be overcome. "It won't work" I kept being told. The Strategy Unit became my right hand. Peter Parker kept on giving me his full support through every twist and turn of the argument as it raced through the system.

So I was in a strong position, backed by my Chairman, convinced of the rightness of the plan to take the industry forward and, as a widower being alone, able to devote my whole creative energy to forcing in the changes.

Lessons

In any great endeavour there are always lessons. So let me conclude this bit of our history with what I think we learnt from it. Looking back, the lessons all seem rather obvious and simple, but at the time they were neither of these. Anyway, here is a selection.

Change is continuous. Some are large leaps, others are smaller ripple effects. A large organisation can only absorb large leaps infrequently. We made our last huge leap in 1982.

We are now considering how we can simplify our business organisation so that we are in the best possible shape for the 1990's.

Be absolutely solid about the main framework. This is essential. You must have this clear vision in your mind of what you are trying to create. Conceptual clarity, rooted in a thorough knowledge of the system, is crucial.

When turning an organisation upside down you may have to be quite ruthless in getting your way (and we were). The man at the top has to take this responsibility — it is not something you can delegate.

Be flexible and adaptive about the details lower down. In principle you ought also to get all the details right, but that may be simply too difficult. In B.R. we brought in consultants who did excellent work in sweeping up some of the finer points — but we ourselves did the main framework. Our deliberate policy was **keep it as simple as possible; appoint good senior people — young people with energy, intelligence and revealed talent — and let them work out the details. These first appointments are crucial.** Then monitor what they are doing, find the problems, make adjustments.

You also need a good analytical capability to keep track of what is happening. Our own Policy Unit was nearly always engaged in some internal enquiry and their work constantly helped to shape our responses.

Here I should mention that back in 1971/72 consultants had proposed a radical change in the Regional structure. They worked it out from the beginning, and right down to the very last detail. When this was revealed to our senior management in a highly memorable meeting, to a man they refused to go along with it — with any of it. Not a thing was accepted. A lot of money and years of effort were wasted. It was a long time before we could have another go. That certainly was a lesson to us.

At a point when these organic developments look like becoming too complicated and when there is no simple solution, you have to step in and make another large change. Team spirit was crucial in the years after 1982. But then as complications with matrix management developed, after about 1987 we began to lose that strong sense of unity. The arguments began to be more frequent. There was, however, an emerging view about how to tackle it, and special studies again showed the way.

We deliberately set up a new Region — Anglia — as a test bed for organisational innovation. We needed a new way to organise production which would enable us to simplify the matrix form of management we had adopted in 1982. Anglia has shown the way to handle change. By making the wider team responsible for the detailed management changes there is an in built sense of ownership amongst those who now run it.

You may have to do what you suspect will be wrong in the long term for very sound reasons in the short term. When the divisional structure was eliminated in 1984 it was absolutely essential that the day to day performance of the railway remained unaffected. We needed the Areas because that was where it all happened. We needed the Regions because they would hold the whole thing together while the Sector businesses were being set up and finding their feet; and in any event they were still very powerful and they couldn't be got rid of just like that.

So what we did with the Regional organisations was undoubtedly right in the short term but questionable in the long term. To have made other changes at one time would have been impracticable. Our advisors had suggested it but that would have been simply too much. So with revolutionary change, break it down into manageable chunks.

Next, communication is essential. This works both ways. Listening and telling. In a major change such as we tackled the talking and arguing is endless. But it has to be done. We were able to take most of our managers with us. Some of our older and senior managers, not unexpectedly, did not want to face up to such radical changes after 35, 40 or more years. Generous retirement terms were arranged.

To begin with we needed some intermediate posts at the top — Joint Managing Directors we called them — to help the new organisation to settle down. These two people were between the Production organisation and the Sector businesses on the one hand and the Vice Chairman (Railways) on the other hand, who was effectively the Chief Executive. As soon as the organisation was working well the Sector Directors reported directly to the Vice Chairman (Railways), though we kept the Managing Director in charge of Production.

Consolidate the gains and maintain the momentum. We felt it important not to let up in the long path towards our goal of a modern railway. Having appointed good managers we found that they made the running, which is what I wanted. There was, in practice, no danger of stagnation.

Don't forget that your basic functions — finance, personnel, engineering — also need radical re-thinking. We have probably been rather slow in taking up this challenge. What we saw as an opportunity for the Sector businesses was also a threat to the traditional centrally managed functions. Only gradually did the Sectors acquire their own functional staff as their self-confidence and power increased and as the centre was forced to devolve. The businesses had first to prove their worth.

Slim down your Head Office. I think there should be a minimum number of people in headquarters, say about 150 in our Corporate Office. The rest, I suggest, should be set up as "Self Accounting Units", creating an internal market for activities such as research, information technology, architects, etc. We have now grouped together these services into an organisation we call "Group Services" who compete with external contractors.

As in every transport business,safety must remain top of the railway agenda. There must be no repeat of the Clapham disaster. The only answer is high standards, efficient systems and constant vigilance. "Safety Audit" is now a Corporate level function actively managed from the Board down. Other considerations must not shape our ability to strive for absolute safety.

Training did not play as large a part as you might have expected. Indeed, I think that we came round to it for our top people rather late. But so far, in the context of quality improvement over 800 people have been through a one week experience to get them thinking about their role as managers and about where we are going as a business. This is just the beginning.

Labour relations are not yet right either. We have had our successes — one-man driver operation, the train-crew agreement, the major staff reductions, all without a serious dispute. And the excellent working relations with our staff carried us through the miners' strike. The highly disruptive strikes last year over decentralised wage bargaining and pay taught us a sharp lesson. We did not explain ourselves well either to our staff or to the public generally. Recovery from this will be a long haul. We do not yet have the unions working with us towards shared objectives, which is our goal.

So we need to focus much more on our staff — on whom, of course, our whole future depends. They have already done an enormous job in turning round our performance, as I described at the beginning of this talk. We must take much more care of them and look afresh at how we do so.

Can I now summarise the key points.

Prior to 1982 we were:

— organised as a bureaucracy
— engineering based
— union dominated
— production led.

The customer took a back seat to what was perceived as being of more importance:

— Engineering and operating expediency led priorities — these spending barons produced demands for ever larger subsidy — undermining our credibility amongst those civil servants who governed us.

— In 1983 — our goals were defined — challenging but achievable — we knew we could meet them provided we got rid of the old culture.

— In 1989 we are not completely there and there is much to do. But we are ready for the decade ahead.

PRIORITIES FOR THE FUTURE

The transformation of British Rail that I have described this evening leaves the industry in an unprecedented position of strength — but I will be the first to admit there is so much more to do. Achievement of a further 3 year set of objectives will be the immediate task of my successor, namesake and friend Bob Reid, as he takes hold of the reins of this exciting industry. He may not be quite so fortunate managing an industry so dependent on the general health of the British economy as I have been. One thing he is assured of though, is a firm business base from which to react quickly to outside pressures and influences — something that none of my predecessors have had. There is a well thought out plan, backed by action plans, and a committed management to achieve them. His risks will be in the pace of economic growth and our ability to compete.

We often forget that British Rail in 1990 is very different from the British Rail of 1980. Most if not all of our customers now enjoy levels of comfort, service and quality well above that provided then, but — and it is a big but — so have our competitors' customers. Needs and expectations are far greater now than they were in 1980 and the industry must continue to improve services for all existing and prospective users.

In preparing for the 1990s what is British Rail preparing for? Is it just the ability to achieve a further set of objectives? I think not. British Rail in the year 2000 will bear little resemblance to B.R. now.

In my final few minutes let us look at the prospects for the next 10 years.

There are going to be enormous opportunities for B.R. to play its part in ensuring the U.K. profits from 1992 and from the opening of the Channel Tunnel a year later.

We have heard, and I know, how hard our French friends are working towards making Charles de Gaulle Airport the hub of Europe, connected by new high speed trains in every direction. Furthermore, the amalgamation of British Airways and Sabena will now make sure our Belgian friends will create a second European hub at Zaventim Airport, Brussels, equally well served with a network of high speed trains.

But, we could counter these threats, provided we expedite the British Parliamentary Bill procedures, make an early start to the rail link from Paddington to Heathrow, make sure money is found for the CrossRail projects of Paddington-Liverpool Street and Chelsea-Hackney, and find a way of financing the exclusive rail link from Kings Cross and Waterloo to the Channel Tunnel.

Without this extra capacity congestion on the roads and the railways will begin to strangle us all and make possible the French and Belgian vision. Government has already made it clear that B.R.'s investments can in certain circumstances be judged on the basis of cost benefit analysis. Let us hope they will use it to good effect in the next few years.

In the meantime the re-equipment of B.R. will proceed apace backed by the massive and increasing investment base I have already described.

I would be foolish to predict what the competitive environment for the railway will be in the year 2000. But it will be very different to 1990 and not what we now may expect.

So we must be flexible and able to respond quickly.

Looking back to 1980 I realise how ill-prepared we were for the changes in our fortunes. The down turn in the economy in the early 1980s, and then the miners'strike, knocked us badly. We recovered because the economy did. Now we have to see if the changes we have made enable us to do just as well in a period of much slower economic growth.

I think we shall. We understand that our long term future depends on our efficiency and our attractiveness to our customers. Our future depends on our ability to react quickly and positively to changing demand. The static language of the P.S.O. in 1974 'to provide a public service which is comparable generally with that provided by the Board at present' cannot be the guiding light for U.K. railways in the year 2000.

Whatever Government is in power, it will have to depend on its railway for the appropriate share in the transport market based on competitiveness, value for money and efficiency.

I am certain I shall hand over British Railways well prepared to meet that challenge.

15

1980
1990
2000?
158701
EXPRESS
471001
165001

APPENDIX III
TRAINING

People talk with respect of the training carried out by British Rail, particularly of the training centre called The Grove. Paul Watkinson tells the story, which he should know, as he ran personnel for a while.

Watkinson: The railways had quite a long tradition, I'm talking about the Big Four before the war, of training their own people to operate and engineer the railway. They offered major apprenticeship schemes for graduates and non-graduate engineers and something similar for operators. The training centre, The Grove, was an early example of a training centre on London Midland and Scottish.
: Post-war that tradition continued. The railway was a huge employer, well over half a million people.
: 1962, I joined the traffic apprentice scheme. It was open to graduates and non-graduates. In London Midland, which I joined, there were six of us. As the name implies, it didn't matter what you'd done before, you were now being trained to operate the railway. There was some initial training and then for three years you went round watching and doing jobs. It was overseen by a training committee consisting of one of the assistant general managers and some other people and you were directed and measured and at the end of the three years you were allocated to a job, which was usually a job in charge of a small operating unit. Three years was a long time, and it was later reduced to two.
: The thinking was that we had to train our own people because this was a specialised business.

(Frank Patterson, Gordon Pettit, Richard Goldson, people mentioned in this book, all trained as traffic apprentices.)

Watkinson: After a few years and after you had done your first job you might then be sent for training in management and leadership to the staff training college at Derby for about a month. It was not just for traffic people but also engineers, who before that had had their own pupilship schemes. I went there in 1967. Other regions had similar schemes.

: As you progressed through the ranks, if you were seen as being senior management material, you went to the Staff College at Woking. This was for three months. Twenty or twenty-five people. A rigorous programme: finance, balance sheets, statistics, management skills, leadership skills, all that sort of thing. People went there from all sections of the railway. There were outside speakers and something everyone look forward to, an overseas visit. It was run by an someone from the army, Colonel Beard. His wife had something to do with a port company, so there was a plentiful supply of that.

: I went there in 1974, I was on course number 34. John Edmonds was on that with me and one or two people from outside the railway, someone from Tate & Lyle, I remember, and someone from Nigeria.

: The idea of training both in the railway and in society generally began to change. The railway, being a huge employer, did rather lead the way in finding natural talent and bring it on. What we did served us pretty well. Most of the people who got into senior management, and there have been some very competent people, went through that process. It was not a discriminator. You did not have to have a degree, it was open to people from the railway to apply, and many did. That was the basic training philosophy.

: By the early 80s we were questioning whether the railway should be running this sort of thing. Three months away from the job was quite a long time and we started sending people to business schools instead – and on short courses at universities.

: This became the preferred method and Woking was closed down.

: In the late 80s, things changed again, and we started to ramp up our graduate training scheme. In earlier years, fewer people had gone to university but by then very many did. So, every year we selected graduates, being fairly flexible as to who we would consider, put them through a much-shortened period of formal training and sent them off into jobs. Much of the induction and early-stage training was centred at The Grove until about the mid-1990s and many of the people running the railway now went through that scheme.

: The engineers had their own scheme, because they required professional qualifications which other departments didn't. Much later, after privatisation, Gordon Pettitt and others set up the Institution of Railway Operators to develop professional standards and a qualification.

BIBLIOGRAPHY

Beeching, Dr Richard, The Reshaping of British Railways,1963.

Blumenau, Ralph, *A History of Malvern College 1865 to 1965* (Macmillan & Co Ltd, 1965)

Bonham-Carter, Victor, *Soldier True: The Life and Times of Field-Marshal Sir William Robertson 1860–1933* (London: Frederick Muller Ltd, 1963).

Childs, David, *Britain Since 1945* (Routledge, 2012).

Clough, David, *APT The Untold Story* (Ian Allan Publishing, 2016).

Elliot, Sir John, *On and Off the Rails* (George Allen & Unwin, 1982).

Erhard, Ludwig, *Prosperity through Competition* (Frederick A. Praeger, 1958).

Faulkner, Richard and Chris Austin, *Holding the Line: How Britain's Railways Were Saved* (Crecy Publishing, 2018)

Fiennes, Gerard, *I Tried to Run a Railway* (Ian Allan, 1973 and Crecy Publishing).

Ford, Roger and Brian Perren, *HSTs at Work* (Ian Allan, 1988)

Gourvish, Terry, *British Railways 1948–73* (Cambridge: Cambridge University Press, 1986)

Gourvish, Terry, *British Rail 1974–97* (Oxford: Oxford University Press, 2002).

Green, Chris and Mike Vincent, *The Network SouthEast Story* (Ian Allan Publishing)

Griffiths, Robert, *Driven by Ideals: A History of ASLEF* (Associated Society of Locomotive Engineers and Firemen, 2005)

Hamilton MC, Stuart, *Armoured Odyssey, 8th Royal Tank Regiment in the Western Desert* (London: Tom Donovan, 1955).

Hare, T. Bernard, *British Railway Operation* (Modern Transport Publishing Co. Ltd, 1927)

Hidden QC, Anthony, *Investigation into the Clapham Junction Railway Accident* (1989).

Leeds University, *European Railway Comparisons; Final Report*, March 1994.

Luger, Katrin, *Chinese Railways: Reform and Efficiency Improvement Opportunities*

Markovits, Andrei S., *The Politics of West German Trade Unions* (Cambridge University Press, 1986).

Marsh, Richard, *Off the Rails, an Autobiography* (Weidenfeld and Nicholson, 1978)

Moyer, Neil E. and Louis S. Thompson, *Options for Reshaping the Railway* (World Bank, 1992)

Nelson, John, Losing Track: *An Insider's Story of Britain's Railway Transformation from British Rail to the Present Day* (New Generation Publishing, 2019)

Newby, Eric, *Love and War in the Apennines* (Harper Press, 2010)

Nock, O.S., *British Locomotives of the 20th Century*, vol. 3 (Guild Publishing, 1985)

Parker, Peter, *For Starters: The Business of Life* (Jonathan Cape, 1989)

Reid, Sir Robert, *Years of Change in Bengal & Assam*, (Ernest Benn Limited, 1966)

Sloan, Alfred, *My Years with General Motors* (Sidgwick & Jackson, 1986)

von Stockl, Dr Fritz, *Eisenbahen in Deutschland* (Bohmann-Verlag, 1969)

Torp, Cornelius, Chapter 12 of *The Oxford Handbook of Modern German History* (Oxford University Press, 2011)

Weighell, Sidney, *A Hundred Years of Railway Weighells*, Robson Books, 1984

Williamson, David, *A Most Diplomatic General: The Life of General Lord Robertson of Oakridge* (Brassey's, 1996)

ENDNOTES

1 Source for the battle description: Hamilton MC, *Armoured Odyssey*
2 This and other quotations from conversations with Frank Paterson
3 Gourvish, 1948–73, p. 5
4 Gourvish, 1948-73, p. 3
5 Bonham-Carter, p. 5
6 Source for this description, Williamson, *A Most Diplomatic General*
7 Williamson, p. 148
8 Picture in the *British Railways Magazine*, held in the National Railway Museum
9 Elliot, p. 68 and Dr Bonavia in *Modern Railways*, July 1971
10 Dr Bonavia in *Modern Railways*, July 1971
11 Elliot, p. 84
12 Sloan, p. 53
13 Gourvish, 1948–73, p. 149
14 Gourvish, 1948–73, p. 148
15 Williamson, *A Most Diplomatic General*, p. 181
16 Gourvish, 1948–73, p. 162
17 Williamson, *A Most Diplomatic General,* p. 184
18 The website, Steamindex
19 Gourvish, 1948–73, p. 270
20 Gourvish, 1948–73, p. 287
21 Ibid, p. 287
22 Nock, p. 9
23 Gourvish, 1948–73, p. 286
24 Engel, *Eleven Minutes Late*, p. 202
25 Gourvish, 1948–73, p. 199
26 Gourvish, , 1948-73, p. 304
27 Quoted in Yorkshire Post, 7 June 1973
28 Quoted in *Yorkshire Evening Press*
29 von Stockl
30 Markovits, p. 97
31 Erhard, *Prosperity through Competition*, p. 257
32 Ibid. p. 233
33 Williamson, *A Most Diplomatic General*, p. 110
34 Source: Luger
35 *Daily Mail*, 5 October 1970
36 Gourvish, 1948–73, p. 325
37 Gourvish, 1948–73, p. 342
38 Gourvish, 1948–73, p. 343
39 Gourvish, 1948–73, p. 338
40 Beeching, *Reshaping of British Railways,* p. 65
41 Faulkner, pp. 248–50

42 Beeching, Reshaping of British Railways, p. 54
43 SNAP, 'The history of haulage and road transport in the UK', website
44 An archived BBC recording of an interview with him
45 Dr. M. R. Bonavia in *Modern Railways* magazine July 1971
46 Faulkner & Austin, *Holding the Line*, p. 100
47 Engel, *Eleven Minutes Late*, p.232
48 Gourvish, 1948–73, p. 349
49 Gourvish, 1948–73, p. 379
50 Jim Collins in conversation
51 Nelson, p. 13
52 Griffiths
53 His granddaughter's recollection
54 Griffiths, *Driven by Ideals*, p. 180
55 Griffiths, *Driven by Ideals*, p. 202
56 Childs, *Britain Since 1945*, p. 166
57 Source: Westlock Interlocking web site
58 Gourvish, 1974–97 p. 77
59 Quoted in Engel p. 232
60 Simon Jenkins in conversation
61 Parker's autobiography
62 *Railnews*, January 1979, p. 1
63 *The Times*, 16 February 1977
64 1977 Transport White Paper, para.178
65 1977 Transport White Paper, para 179
66 *The Times*, 16 February 1977
67 *Railnews*, January 1980, p. 3
68 *Railnews*, December 1979
69 Jim Collins in conversation.
70 *Railnews*, May 1980, p. 6
71 Conversation with Simon Jenkins
72 *Guardian*, 18 September 1980
73 Griffiths, *Driven by Ideals*
74 Griffiths, *Driven by Ideals*
75 *Evening Standard*, 15 March 1982
76 *The Times*, 21 April 1982
77 Quoted in Evening Standard, 1 July 1981
78 Griffiths, *Driven by Ideals*, p. 236
79 Faulkner & Austin, *Holding the Line*, p. 177
80 Gourvish, 1974-97, p.116.
81 Gourvish, 1974–97, p. 111
82 Nelson, *Losing Track*, p. 72
83 Address at Sir Robert Reid's Memorial Service
84 *Financial Times*, Sue Cameron, 19 July 1985
85 *Daily Telegraph*, Graham Turner, 19 August 1985
86 *Financial Times*, Sue Cameron, 29 August 1985

87 *Financial Times*, Sue Cameron, 29 August 1985
88 *Daily Telegraph*, Graham Turner, 19 August 1985
89 *Daily Telegraph*, Graham Turner, 19 August 1985
90 *Daily Telegraph*, Graham Turner, 19 August 1985
91 *Daily Telegraph*, Graham Turner, 19 August 1985
92 *Scotsman*, 22 June 1985
93 *Observer*, 1 September 1985
94 Daily Telegraph, Graham Turner, 19 August 1985
95 *Financial Times,* 2 September 1985
96 *Times*, 30 May 1985
97 *Times*, 30 May 1985
98 *Financial Times,* 18 July 1985
99 *Daily Telegraph*, Graham Turner, 19 August 1985
100 *Management Today*, February 1985
101 *Financial Times*, 2 September 1985
102 *Management Today*, February 1985
103 *Financial Times*, 2 September 1985
104 Faulkner & Austin, *Holding the Line*, p. 176
105 *Observer*, 18 August 1985.
106 Bob is looking down at David Lindesay-Bethune, the 15th Earl of Lindsay, the owner of the train. (Photo Jim Collins)
107 Moyer and Thompson, World Bank report, para 66
108 Moyer and Thompson, World Bank report, Summary para iii
109 Moyer and Thompson, World Bank report, synopsis
110 Moyer and Thompson, World Bank report, para 30
111 Leo Ploeger address at Memorial Service for Sir Robert Reid
112 *Hidden*, Appendix G, para 35
113 *Hidden*, para 8.16
114 *Times*, 12 May 1989
115 *Hidden*, para 13.40
116 *Hidden*, para 16.66
117 *Hidden*, para 16.77
118 *Hidden*, para 17.3
119 Obituary written by Peter Parker in the *Independent*
120 Quoted in Moyer and Thompson, para 29
121 Address at the Memorial Service for Sir Robert Reid
122 Obituary written by Sir Peter Parker in the *Independent*
123 Leeds University, para 7.2
124 Railtrack flotation prospectus, p. 46

INDEX – PEOPLE

For **SUBJECTS** see page 349

INDEX – SUBJECTS

WITH GRAPHS OR DIAGRAMS